Disko Id.
Harcourt, Brace Ice Cap
Nugsuak
Umanak Fiord
story)
Nugsuak
Sarkak (of Emanuels story.
There are no
houses there now)
pernivik
Mt. Jas. N. Rosenberg
Sound
Mt. Zigrosser
Point Steff
Igdlorssuit
Ingia
Ubekjendt Eiland
(Unknown Island) now
Kjendt Eiland
r d
DISCOVERIES
[see Chapter XXXVIII] of the Kent Greenland Sub Polar Expedition, 1931-2. Lest the backers of the expedition be disappointed with its results it must be explained that someone, unfortunately, had already given names – and what names! – to the larger bodies of land and water. We have, however, done our best with what remained. But: the expedition – continuing its work through 1934-5-6 – is faced with a deficit in cash and supplies. Should there be generous souls or corporate bodies desirous of furthering the aims of the expedition we should feel that it would be advancing the glory of America to write their names upon the map – even if we have to scratch out the old ones. Think of a "Liggett & Meyers tobacco co peninsular"! Or "——'s Applejack sea"!
Motor boat of the expedition.
"City of Ausable Forks"
(Essex County, N.Y.)

SALAMINA

This is Salamina — apparently hanging out nothing but a clothes pin. If I had given her wash it would have covered up her hands. She always tried to cover them, for they were working hands. This book permits of no concealment.

SALAMINA

ROCKWELL KENT

Foreword by Scott R. Ferris

Illustrated by the author

WESLEYAN UNIVERSITY PRESS

Middletown, Connecticut

Published by
WESLEYAN UNIVERSITY PRESS
Middletown, CT 06459

First paperback edition 2003 by Wesleyan University Press.
Reprinted by arrangement with the Rockwell Kent Legacies.

Library of Congress Control Number 2003106763
ISBN 0-8195-6677-2

Printed in the United States of America
5 4 3 2 1

Wesleyan University Press would like to acknowledge and thank the Plattsburgh State Art Museum, Rockwell Kent Gallery and Collection and the Plattsburgh College Foundation, Plattsburgh State University, Bequest of Sally Kent Gorton, for permission to publish this edition of *Salamina*.

ENDSHEET MAPS

Front: "Discoveries" map reproduced from pages viii and ix of the original edition.

Back: Detail of map of Greenland with travel annotations by Kent.

Courtesy of Gordon Kent. By permission of Plattsburgh State Art Museum, Rockwell Kent Gallery and Collection, Bequest of Sally Kent Gorton.

TO F., SOMEWHERE IN AMERICA:

HERE IS A GREAT SURPRISE

OUR GREENLAND BOOK AT LAST! BEING ABOUT *OUR* FRIENDS

—WITH JUST A SEASONING OF MY ENEMIES—

EXPRESSING MOSTLY HOW *WE* THINK OF THEM, MAKES IT HALF YOURS. THE OTHER HALF I DEDICATE TO YOU. IT IS IN LARGE DEGREE CONTRIVED FOR YOU TO LIKE. FOR SEE: IF I HAD TRIED TO BE SCIENTIFIC AND LEARNED YOU WOULD HAVE LAUGHED; IF I'D TRIED TO BE WISE YOU'D HAVE BEEN BORED; IF I HAD LIED—YOU WOULDN'T HAVE BEEN SURPRISED. ALSO, IF I HAD TOLD EVERYTHING YOU WOULDN'T HAVE LIKED IT. SO I HAVE TRIED TO TELL, WITH SOME DISCRETION, ABOUT THAT SMALL REGION OF GREENLAND, ITS PEOPLE AND ITS AVERAGE EVENTS, AS I, THEN YOU AND I, THEN I AGAIN, FOUND IT TO BE. AND, TOO—THAT HAD TO BE BROUGHT IN—

HOW YOU WERE MISSED.

CONTENTS

PART I

CONTENTS

CONTENTS

PART II

CONTENTS

LIST OF ILLUSTRATIONS

FOREWORD

IN THE PRESENCE OF LIGHT

> Speech at its highest art—its metaphors and symbols, its rhythms and harmonies, its moods, its forms, its being—is derived by man from his environment.
>
> —Rockwell Kent, *Salamina*

The manuscript for *Salamina—Rockwell Kent's Greenland Book,* as it is otherwise known—first arrived at the publishing offices of Harcourt, Brace and Company (New York City) in an odorous caribou skin parcel. Shipped from Igdlorssuit, Greenland, on March 14, 1935, the manuscript, along with eighty drawings, docked in New York on June 20. By October a limited author's and first trade editions were simultaneously released. Since 1961, the manuscripts (the first and final drafts), along with the typescript, have gathered dust in a cabinet within the Pushkin State Museum of Fine Arts (Moscow).

The October publications were wrapped in a dust jacket that displayed a tantalizing portrait of our Greenland heroine—Salamina—bathing in an icy fjord. Kent, an irredeemable humorist and no bluenose himself, undoubtedly intended to titillate the reader. Another edition followed within two years. This subsequent printing was cloaked in a jacket that portrays an eagle, defiantly poised, as if to safeguard Kent's Greenland paradise against a world rapidly turning on its head. A detail of Kent's painting *Seal Hunters: Greenland,* which covers the edition you hold in your hands, repre-

Caribou skin parcel in which the manuscript, *Salamina*, was shipped to New York. Courtesy of the author. By permission of Plattsburgh State Art Museum, Rockwell Kent Gallery and Collection, Bequest of Sally Kent Gorton.

sents two aspects of Kent's life and work, as abbreviated in this tome: his conveyance of his own spirituality through a modern interpretation of light and the life of the laborer who enriches himself by providing for the good of society.

While considering the appropriate contents for this foreword I re-read several of Kent's prefatory writings: many were solemn, some were witty, others prophetic. The "precarious, card-house nature of our social edifice" was the topic of his introduction to the early editions of *Salamina*. Kent's compassion for the human condition was a consistent act, felt (and documented) by the same man that proclaimed that he did not renounce his citizenship when he picked up the brush or pen. As you will read, the forthcoming chapters entitled "On Things" and "On Mutual Aid"—a direct reference to sociopolitical philosopher Peter Kropotkin's essay,

"Mutual Aid" (1889–1895)—tell much about Kent's belief in socialism as well as the failings of Progress and self-centeredness over personal betterment and mutual support for the welfare of the community.

Salamina is autobiographical in that it recounts a brief chapter in Kent's long life—his 1931 through 1932 stay in Igdlorssuit; it is ethnographical in that it documents 1930s west Greenland culture; and it's a treasure trove of art historical and philosophical squibs for the student of Kent. At the time of publication, *Salamina* was Kent's longest literary work and, according to a few critics, was considered to be his richest. In many respects it is the rightful forebearer—for its narrative styling, illustrations, and design—of his voluminous 1955 autobiography, *It's Me O Lord*.

Rockwell Kent's writings were never meant to be literary masterpieces. They were accounts of his adventurous life, penned on the spot, of which *Salamina* is literally and figuratively a classic example. Indeed, Kent spent much of his first several months during his 1934 through 1935 stay in Igdlorssuit close to the pages that would become *Salamina*. Unlike the story of *N by E*, which tells of Kent's journey and brief visit to Greenland for the first time, *Salamina* hits the turf running. The author immediately involves us in a local event: a story about a performance by the local *angakok* or "wizard" (the Danish trader and amateur magician, Trolleman). Kent encourages the reader to accompany him on an enjoyable though not frivolous, informative but not prosaic, account of his life among a now lost colony of primitive peoples.

At the time of *Salamina's* first publication, Lewis Gannett of the *New York Herald Tribune* wrote that *Salamina* "has in it a moving sense of the wonder of the virgin universe, the dignity of mountains and of sea, and a rarely intimate picture of Greenlanders at play." Kent's "style is abrupt, rhapsodic, hearty . . . it is good anthropology and even better adventure narrative," wrote a reviewer for *The New Yorker*. This is why Kent's sagas continue to be reissued.

Marie Ahnighito Peary, daughter of the North Pole explorer Robert Peary and a birth child of Greenland, commented on her

Dear Catherine :-

This – by the very first mail out of Greenland this year. And it can hardly reach America before some time in June. It will perhaps not be far ahead of me – for I shall have to return this summer. A decoration in the Washington Post Office has been offered me, and I shall have to go home to do it. And in the seven months that I've been here I've hardly had time to even look at Greenland. Work? In September I built a little 10 x 12 turf house — built it in 3 days; then I moved into it. And except to gobble my lunch and supper at the "big" house I haven't been out of it until just about now. Day and night I've worked. And now my book is written, the pictures for it are all done; and I've illustrated a saga, for publication. All that accomplished, and just ready to begin on the feast of Greenland, when I have to go home!

But I have loved working in this little house all winter. It is a tiny place – only 5'-4" high inside. I put a bay window in the thickness of the turf walls and on the broad sill of that I worked. Here it is:

What a rotten picture!

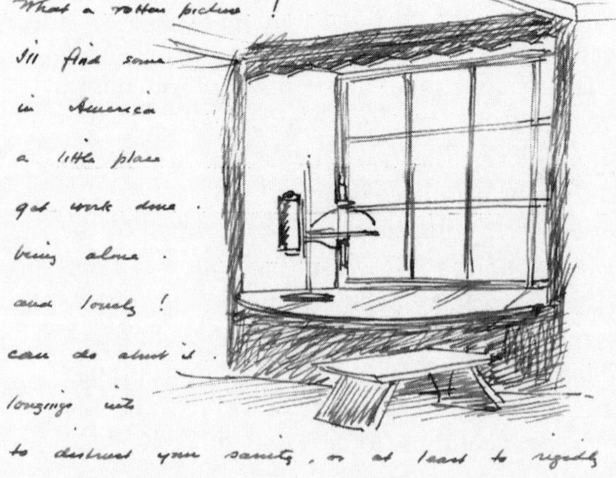

I have an idea that I'll find some remote but magnificent spot in America and build myself just such a little place to go off to and really get work done. Only I'm fed up with being alone. Gee! you get homesick and lonely! And there's nothing you can do about it. You can't even pour your longings into your work, for you get to destroy your sanity, or at least to rigidly suppress the emotionalism that loneliness engenders. Well – we'll see what it has done for me when my book appears. Maybe the book will be no good at all.

It has been a great experience for my little son. In seven months he has grown from a normal boy of 14 to man's size and man's character. He works all the time — hunting seal, just like the native hunters. Off all

Page one of letter to Catherine Mattison, from Kent, March 23, 1935.

enjoyment of the story in a critique she wrote for *The Saturday Review.* She approved of Kent's observations of the native peoples and the terrain they inhabited. Furthermore, unlike some of the haughty desk side reviewers of the time who considered Kent's writing "loquacious," Peary appreciated his "chatty and familiar style which has the advantage of presenting places and people in an unforgettably vivid manner." She recognized that Kent was an artist first, and that his viewpoint of this one group of Eskimos was as legitimate as any other's. Peary considered Kent's "word pictures" and illustrations a "revelation to all those who think of Greenland as a desolate, unimpressive island, peopled with uncouth savages." As she well knew the beauty and grandeur of the land were always present, but it took Kent to capture their majesty, to bring it all back home for the "less adventurous spirits to see and enjoy."

It is little wonder that Peary held this view of Kent's chronicle for the artist considered his arctic travels in grave detail. His pre-excursion readings included *A Description of Greenland* (1818) by Hans Egede and Ossian Elgstrom's *Moderna Eskimaer* (1916). In addition he acquired atlases—"Meddelelser om Grønland" (1921) and "Vestkysten af Grönland" (1888)—for use during his sojourn. Once in Igdlorssuit Kent carefully calculated his impact upon the villagers when planning the building site for his house. As he describes in *Salamina,* "I had hoped to be an observer in Greenland rather than one observed, and naturally preferred looking down on others to being looked down upon"—even to the extreme of choosing a rock littered site, nearer the base of a mountainous overhang, that resembled a "battlefield." Kent felt that by "lying uphill from the settlement, it was enough removed from the other house sites to promise privacy, and yet so reasonably situated as to offer no suggestion that seclusion had been sought for."

Once settled into his abode, Kent required a *kifak,* a "housekeeper": someone to keep his stove lit, his food from freezing, make his clothes—his *kamiks* (boots) and anoraks—and occasionally peel them off. Salamina, for whom this book is titled, became

Detail of map of Greenland with travel annotations by Kent.

Courtesy of Gordon Kent. By permission of Plattsburgh State Art Museum, Rockwell Kent Gallery and Collection, Bequest of Sally Kent Gorton.

his *kifak*. Along with Salamina came her two children, one of whom, her daughter Helena, stayed the duration.

The traditional Greenland home in 1935, we learn, was a single room turf structure, barely "ten feet square and scarcely man's height high," that would accommodate, or compact, a family of six or seven with an additional distant relative or three. As Kent in-

Inside Kent's hut; the artist (far right) seated with Salamina and (possibly) David. Used in a 1934 General Electric radio advertisement. Courtesy of the Plattsburgh State Art Museum, Rockwell Kent Gallery and Collection. Bequest of Sally Kent Gorton.

forms us, "they ate from one pot, and they slept all huddled close for warmth and happiness on one broad bed—the sleeping platform. There had the children been conceived and born; there would, at last, the parents die. Life was an open bed to Greenlanders."

These tiny dwellings, like the Greenlanders themselves, were indeed small in structure but generous by every other means. Into these cramped rooms passed a familiar parade of guests. Villagers hosted regular *kaffemiks*—coffee parties—to help while away endless winter nights. Baronial feasts were not uncommon. Traditional foods included boiled seal, fjord cod, halibut, and *matak*—

"that succulent hide of the white whale," Kent wrote—that was also used for whips and lines. The hunter who devoured a serving of newly beached whale during the initial carving process was thoroughly besmeared with blood.

Kent's knowledge of the local Eskimo language was limited to, as he wrote, "a few mispronunciations of the names of common things." Nevertheless he relates to us, the readers, an intimate understanding of Greenland life. While reading *Salamina* we discover that it was socially acceptable for the Greenland husband to offer his wife in exchange for cigarettes, schnapps, or Kent's pipe; we also learn of the perseverance of pagan ways two hundred years after the young Norwegian Lutheran priest, Hans Egede, reestablished Greenland as a Christian settlement. We discover that village elders were still able to resurrect the music and dramatic dances of their ancestors and recount tales from their "Ancient Testament"—stories of the spirits *Mitatdlussokune* (the helping spirit) and *Arnakune* (the female spirit)—much to the dismay of the local catechist who considered these activities to be "the outlawed past." We read that Kent learned how to maneuver a kayak and handle dogs to drive his sledge and how he came to appreciate the climate in its dangerously infinite variety—the balance of life and death in Greenland was weighed by one's knowledge of and respect for nature's cycles.

Regardless of the physical and emotional challenges Kent faced, he believed, as he wrote in *Salamina,* that "all solitudes, no matter how forlorn, are the only abiding-place on earth of liberty." Few other American artists, since Frederic Church and William Bradford, would expose themselves to such hardships in exchange for the exhilaration and inspiration nature offered. From Kent's window on Igdlorssuit he "came to feel—as though for the first time in [his] life—the beauty of the world!" Living, virtually outdoors, was "far profounder a devotion . . . than any Godward posturing of conscious worshippers! There," in Greenland, "was God's countenance itself, its light, its majesty of form, its power of life and death."

Kent was an insatiable doer of heroic adventures and multifarious tasks. Throughout his career, Kent's work often expressed a sense of boundless energy. As a young painter his brush strokes were barely contained as we see in many of his Monhegan canvases circa 1907. Take a close look at the strokes that define *Winter, Monhegan*—on the surface as well as the underpainting—they are slashed on the canvas as aggressively as the paint we see in Jackson Pollock's *Blue Poles.* The energy conveyed on Kent's canvases is emotionally or some would say spiritually charged, the manifestation of a unitary experience perhaps. It has been said that William Blake had a vision of a tree imbued with angels. Kent perceived "truth and beauty emanating as the light from Heaven, God's abode." That same force, now harnessed in his Greenland canvases as seamless swaths of limitless hues, is no less energized.

As a painter, printmaker, and designer Kent was a "modern" artist. During the "nineteen teens" his paintings visualized his oppressed emotional state by depicting modeled, representational symbols in the style of Franz Marc. However, by the 1930s several of his most successful paintings were devoid of symbolic elements, emphasizing instead vibrant light and stacked horizontal planes—a precursory view of what would come in the work of Mark Rothko. Kent matured in an era of rapidly evolving technology, though unlike many modernists of his time, he did not find the *machine*—its design, its sense of *progress,* its urban origins—deeply inspirational. Instead he found his muse in the remote, austere landscapes of Newfoundland, Alaska, Tierra del Fuego, Greenland, and closer to home in northern New York State and New England.

Kent's adventurous spirit has stirred the imagination of countless other artists and authors. It has been said that George Bellows, upon first seeing Kent's paintings of Monhegan Island, Maine, was envious of his friend's accomplishments and vowed to go to the island to paint better compositions. Early in his career Fairfield Porter was influenced by Kent's illustrative work and depictions of Monhegan. Harry Cimino's illustrations for *Seven Horizons,* and Edward Shenton's drawings for *This Is My Country* and *Northern*

Kent with his dog team and sledge, set up for painting, ca. 1932.
Rockwell Kent Papers [ca. 1840]–1993 (bulk 1935–1961), Archives of American Art, Smithsonian Institution. By permission of Plattsburgh State Art Museum, Rockwell Kent Gallery and Collection, Bequest of Sally Kent Gorton.

Lights paid homage to Kent's creativity—Shenton's illustrations for *Northern Lights* virtually duplicate many of Kent's images from *N by E.* Author Gretel Ehrlich took all three of Kent's Greenland books—*N by E, Salamina,* and *Greenland Journal*—with her on her trip to that largest of islands, and quotes generously from each in her own adventure story, *This Cold Heaven: Seven Seasons in Greenland.* And in Barry Lopez's book, *Arctic Dreams,* he discusses Kent's relationship with the wilderness and notes that Kent "argued in his art and heroic prose for the essential dignity of human beings and for the existence of man's Godlike qualities."

Kent's visual and literary creations continue to uplift the virtual adventurer and inspire the more expressive soul. Like his polar explorer/author friends Knud Rasmussen and Peter Freuchen, Kent has preserved a lost chapter in human history. In his introduction to *Greenland Journal*, published nearly thirty years after *Salamina*, Kent reflects that these books became a "record, intimate and authentic, of the past, of a way of life that has vanished beyond recall, and of a people the remains of whose ancient, cultural identity are fast being submerged by the tides of 'progress.'"

Let's partake in this little known world Rockwell Kent considered paradise. Slip on your anorak, step into your *kamiks,* and without further ado, we'll pull back the curtains and see what magic our friend Trolleman is up to.

SCOTT R. FERRIS

Franklin Springs, New York
March 2003

INTRODUCTION

IN THE WINTER OF 1932–33 *affairs in America seemed as desperate as could be short of a complete breakdown of our whole industrial machine, and the chaos consequent to that. The breakdown was averted, and we enjoy today what we have termed Recovery. Yet even if Recovery be made a fact, we'd be unwise to relapse again into that unreflecting acceptance of prosperity which was, before the crash, the way of most of us. We've had our scare, a glimpse of the precarious, card-house nature of our social edifice; we've done some hard, fast thinking, most of us. What we have thought should be remembered, and in these days of change and revolution make itself a factor in our reconstruction. It may be that we have, as individuals, no voice or choice in the directing of our national destiny; that in the aggregate we must pursue, as water flows, a course determined by the contours of necessity. Yet the doctrine of economic determinism is far from being as determinative as it sounds. What is necessity? What* do *we need? And if we adopted toward ourselves, as individuals, or heads, perhaps, of families, the attitude of the physician who determines what we need by what is good for us, we might find our necessities to be of quite a different order from those to which we are accustomed and for the production of which our social structure has been reared.*

Of life without the luxuries that we enjoy in America, without most of the gadgets that we have come to call necessities, of life in a barren country where even bare existence is precarious and the means of getting it a hazard, this book is a record. If I may claim for it a moral—and I'm not averse to morals in a book—it lies, through the betrayal of my own enjoyment there, in the implication that people don't need gadgets to be happy. That is a simple moral and need trouble no one.

What will, however, trouble readers is the Greenlandish words which I have had *to use, place names for the most part: they look difficult, and often are. Yet I have simplified them to the extent of discarding the approved orthography, which demands familiarity with somewhat arbitrary symbols, in favor of spelling which has at least the sanction of the charts. But even that helps little with some names. Take* Uvkusigsat*—a place name which means "Soapstone." The word is not pronounced as its spelling at once and clearly bids us say it. A nearer spelling would be* Oo-coo-see-sat. *But what if your author had sprung this upon you:* ekalugssuarniarfiliarniaruma-galuarpunga*—meaning, in a word, "I should certainly like to go to the place where sharks are caught"? Well—he would have gone there without the reader.*

One night, tenting, a young man, Lucas Upernangitok, told a long story for the entertainment of the assembled group. I have given that story, in its place, as in a very beautiful hand he wrote it out for me. That it is not an ancient Greenland tale will be apparent to everyone. It just displays a type of story that is current now. Emanuel's stories and songs were likewise written down. All were translated into Danish by an educated Greenlander, and into English by a cultivated Dane, Fru Estrid Bannister.

The frontier traveler goes deep in debt for such open-handed hospitality as it may never be his privilege to repay. He can at least acknowledge it: I do, with gratitude. I may particularly thank my friends Kaptajn H. F. V. Hansen, Ridder af Dannebroge, and Söminemester Janus Sörensen; and to Hr. J. Daugaard-Jensen, Kommandör af Dannebroge, Dannebrogsmand, p.p., Director of Greenland, say that living there among his wards I came to feel for him that same affectionate respect which is accorded him by all.

Carl Zigrosser, Vilhjalmur Stefansson, and A. Crooks Ripley made my departure multiply the blessed, single loose-leaf volumes of their friendship into shelves of well-bound friends; friends in the

General Electric Company ruined my health and fortified my spirits with cigarettes; a prince of Schenectady soothed me with China tea; the G.E. gave me a swell radio set (Perpendicular Gothic cabinet), which I ruined; and the Pan American Airways Corporation saw to it with what looked like tons *of paté de foie gras "with truffles," and so on, and so on, that I would be well sustained in the doing of their field work, and with six dozen quarts of emasculated fruit juice that I'd keep my head about it. All this in* 1934! *I lose my head in gratitude.*

Maxine S. Lowenthal, now known to the people of Igdlorssuit as "the good American lady," by putting coffee in their stomachs stormed their hearts; while innumerable good Americans have by the concord of sweet jazz—I must have handed out some hundreds of records—delighted their ears, softened their rude natures, and attuned their hearts to gratitude.

And now what is *this book about? Let Samuel Möller, Greenlander, catechist in the settlement of Igdlorssuit, North Greenland, and close observer—he had no more to do—of all that went on there, tell us in the very words of his leading article in* Avangnamiok, *the monthly of North Greenland, December* 1932:

Amerikamiup Rockwel Kent-ip Igdlorssuarne ukînera uk. 1931—32.

Ukiok 1931 Juli autdlartítok Landsraadit atautsimīneráne ilaujartordlunga Umánamut pigama, akaguane uvdlãnguak „Disko" íkivigssarput Umánamut nunalípok, tusarparalo Amerikamiok ilaussok Igdlorssuarnigôk ukîniartok, takunagule únúkâ Umánamit autdlarpugut Upernivíkôrdluta Kekertarssuarmut.

et cetera, for several pages, from which I give in translation (Oh, Pastor Hoegh and Helge Rördam, thanks!) the following informative passages. Samuel was absent from Igdlorssuit when I arrived there but—: When I came back [now Samuel speaks] I met with him; he shook hands with me very kindly, but I was not able to understand him because he spoke another language. And I saw a cement foundation for his house, and it was told that he would build his house himself with only very little help from others. As he was *a very able carpenter* [italics mine] he made his house very beautiful. The size was 6x3½ meters. He settled among us, and though he was a foreigner he very soon grew to be our good friend because he was so good to us.

When we played football he fell very often because in spite of his great strength he did not know how to "fure." [And since I don't know what "fureing" is I'll probably keep on falling.]

His handiness is to be seen in his paintings. He very often paints the landscape across from our settlement.—At sunset, with reddish colors, he paints it *very handsomely*. [Italics mine again. They always are.] *He is undoubtedly one of the best artists.*

When he was here he often visited the various houses, and when he was invited he always came. And when there was a birthday one always invited him, as it was said that he brought presents every time. When coffee was offered him he always said yes, but nobody knows whether he really likes the Greenland coffee. . . . It is said, too, that he is *very rich*. . . . He had a widow from Umanak as *kifak* [housekeeper], and when she had her birthday in the fall many people were invited. I was there too, in the first batch. A very large cake was served with her name on it. He told us to look out, something was to be found in the cake; and imagine! some found 50 öre, others found 25 or 5 öre, my wife found 2 öre, but I found nothing. . . . Toward Christmas he mentioned that he was going to give a treat, and it was soon to be seen that he was making preparations. Sometimes he came out to where we stood, all sweating from the preparations.

In the beginning of '32 he went to Nugatsiak with his sledge man; they were the first over the ice that year. Through them we heard how the people in the other places were getting on.

When he was away [I went on a long and perilous journey

overcoming innumerable obstacles and hardships with bull-dog pluck and determination; but I don't want to tell the *whole* story in the introduction]—when he was away his friends longed much for him; he had promised them something good.

But maybe I've already told too much. At any rate that's what the story is about—that, and much more: Adventure, Romance, brave men and beautiful unmoral women (Good Lord, this is the twentieth century and I must lure on the gentle reader). In short, great stuff. And since it does add glamour to Pilgrim's Progress *and* Fanny Hill *to know that they were written in prison, I am pleased to say that* Salamina *was written in a* 10′ x 12′ x 5′4″ *turf house which I hastily constructed, fled to, and barricaded, that by escaping the ardent solicitude of my heroine I might in peace pay her the tribute of a book. I took to cover on the twentieth of September,* 1934, *and, except for furtive sallies under the protection of darkness, I have been there until now. Today, March 4, the text, the pictures, and this introduction done, I by the grace of this line's final word am free. Thank God!*

IGDLORSSUIT, 1935 R. K.

ACKNOWLEDGMENT: *In this book all the mistakes in grammar and punctuation are to be attributed to the perverseness of the author who, unexpectedly returning from Greenland, put back some of those errors that his friends Louis Untermeyer and Carl Zigrosser had carefully eliminated from the proofs.*

ARIZONA, AUGUST, 1935. R. K.

PART I

I. THE CONJURER

IT IS a tranquil cloudless evening in July. The shadow of the hills of Umanak lies on the settlement: brown rocks, brown soil, brown native houses built of turf, and Danish houses bright with paint. And all around, seawards and landwards, on the blue bay islanded with ice, on mountainous islands, on the snow-tipped ranges of the mainland, on the near hill crests and on the towering flanks of Umanak's peak, the golden light of the Greenland summer's never setting sun.

Then, presently, like gophers from a warren, come the people. They stream out from the houses, come running down the stony hillside paths from everywhere; and they all meet in front of the carpenter shop to form, at last, a great multitude, brimming with good humor and restless with excitement. Something is about to happen.

The wide doorway of the carpenter shop is three steps from the ground; square in that doorway stands a table. The table is laid with a bright cloth and set with an array of bottles, tumblers, little boxes, and a nickel-plated urn. Behind the table moves a little restless man arranging things. All eyes are upon him.

A little white man, florid and ruddy-beaked, a rosebud mouth; the people watch his movements. Boys, crowding close, peer underneath the table at his crooked, wishbone legs. And now, all set, apparently, he rests his palms on the table, leans out, and turns a livid popeyed stare upon the crowd. A sea of upturned faces gapes at him.

What masks! Broad-boned and dark; the strong jaws and placid brows of men and women in their prime; the seared and weather-beaten faces of the old; young faces smooth as polished bronze and plump-cheeked as though formed by laughter; babies in arms, and smear-faced brats on boxes, roofs, and barrel tops—all gaping open-lipped at that hypnotic stare. It holds them, breathless. And when at last the white man slowly lifts a gruesome, maimed, three-fingered hand, holds it impressively aloft, stands there with elevated beak poised to begin—there is a silence as might be at Doomsday for the voice of God.

He speaks. In native jargon almost unintelligible he tells them what he is about to do, what wonder he'll perform. Into a little box he stuffs a dirty handkerchief; closes the box; holds it aloft tight-closed. They stare at it. Daintily he brings the box to his lips and loudly blows on it. Again aloft, to wave it round three times. He puts it on the table, taps it solemnly. He lifts again that gruesome hand—now look! Opening the box, he shows it to the people. It is empty. A buzz of charmed amazement from the crowd.

He swallows a butcher's knife; he lays an egg; he mixes the ingredients of soup in the empty urn and brings out—soup? Not soup: a Danish flag! He turns water into wine, and wine to water. In utter quiet, spellbound by each miracle, the people watch. The sound of the magician's voice has huge significance in the deep silence of the Greenland world.

There is a Danish freighter in the harbor; men have come ashore. A drunken stoker watching on the border of the crowd comes lurching over to me, takes my arm. *He* is no fool, he wants to have me know. "It's nothing but a God-damned bunch of tricks," he whispers. But no one hears, or no one understands.

At last, too soon, the show will end; one last great miracle. The magician, after moving the table aside and coming to the very front, takes a coin from his pocket and hands it to a boy; it is passed round for everyone to see: a Greenland kroner. They return it. With awe-inspiring earnestness the magician now prepares himself. He takes a sip of water, gargles it; he unbuttons his celluloid collar, his waistcoat, his waistband. All ready now? Good! Holding the coin aloft, opening his mouth he puts—in plain sight of everyone—the coin into the open mouth, closes the mouth, and swallows. One almost sees the brass piece passing down the throat. It clearly hurts a bit. It's down; he pats his belly. But suddenly, even as he stands there smiling, he is griped by pain. The agony of his contorted features is reflected in the faces of the enraptured, sympathetic onlookers. They gasp with pity. Now, suddenly, he stoops; the posture brings relief. A look of high expectancy illuminates that countenance: hope, faith, and will to do. Quickly he puts a hand to his backside; all hear a rending sound. The coin, reborn, is held on high. Roar of delight. He gives the coin to a near-by spectator, who takes it gingerly. It is the white man's gift to Greenland.

The crowd lingered to discuss the wonders it had seen. They called the wizard *angakok*, after the ancient miracle-workers of their race; and it appeared in no way to diminish their delight in what he had done to know, as they did, that there was one of their own people farther north who performed the same miracles better, and that, just as the stoker had guessed, they were all tricks.

II. UNKNOWN ISLAND

SEAWARD from Umanak—fully fifty miles away—is a large, mountainous island, christened by Dutch whalers Ubekjendt, or Unknown. Both by the suggestion of its name and by its position and character—its seagirt isolation, the simple grandeur of its stark, snow-covered tableland and higher peaks, the dark cliff barrier that forms its eastern shore—there is the glamour of imponderable mystery about the island which dignifies it even at the gateway of a region of stupendous grandeur. Its cliffs, proclaiming inaccessibility, preclude the thought of human settlements. When, therefore, on approaching its more mountainous northeastern end where, just ahead, steep mountain walls rise sheer from water's edge, the barrier ends, the shore sweeps inward in a mile-wide crescent of smooth strand and, cupped by mountains, there appears a low and gently sloping verdant foreland jeweled with painted buildings and dotted over with those little mounds of earth which are the houses of men, one's spirit, in sudden awakening to a need, exults in grateful consciousness of its fulfillment. Smooth shore, green meadow land with little footpaths crossing it, houses where people live, smoke from their hearths ascending in the breathless sunlit air: there is no beauty nearer to the heart than this. And the encircling wilderness, the appalling nearness of black mountain walls, enforce its poignancy.

And now a cry goes up, and from all the houses come the people to welcome us. Bright-colored figures in their native costume;

they keep abreast of us and line the shore to meet us as we land. Men wade in ankle-deep and beach our skiff. Our goods are lifted out and borne along in our wake as we all march—men, boys, and half the women—up to the trader's house that stands near by. The goods are put inside the doorway; the bearers go. "Sit down, speak nothing, make yourself at home," orders my host, my traveling companion, the outpost trader of Igdlorssuit, the angakok of Umanak. Queer bird, this fellow Trolleman; I ought to know him.

Throughout the nine interminable hours of our trip from Umanak he raved, poured over me imprisoned on the boat the turgid, ever branching, endless torrent of his reminiscences, the stored imaginings of soul-starved vanity. Lies—pointless, unresolved. Lies?—yes: he boasted of them. "I am," he'd cry, "the world's third biggest liar.—If I could only write!" he said. "I'd tell the story of my life. It would be *awful*." Boy runaway; hard years at sea; sailor and lugger hand; mate?—one questions it; turnkey and dairy hand; and trapper on the east coast of Greenland. And now, at last, by that indomitable will to power of the man not made for it, he was the trader at the outpost of Igdlorssuit, and the lord of a native wife. From cabin boy to king.

He liked command. His style was patterned on that authority from which in his past years he'd suffered most; he was at last the master of a ship, his home. His wife was mate, her sisters were the crew. And the spirit in which the young wife was admitted to the honors of the cabin table was consistent with that hard-boiled snobbishness which is the rule at sea. She knew her place.

There was something infinitely pathetic in her timid, half terror-stricken observance of her master's wants and ways—her anxious regard for trivial details in the setting of the table, her watchful imitation of his every move with knife and fork. Worry was there. And it had marked itself in lines about her eyes, between her brows. She had the look of a little child forever asking of itself bewilderingly, "What does he mean? What is it all about?" She was not quite a child. Sometimes, it seemed, she hated him—my genial, boisterous host, her lord.

"Regina! Come," he'd say. She'd go to him. He'd seat her on his knee and lend his head for her caresses. "Whom do you love?" he'd ask. And, never failingly, she'd answer like a child taught winsome ways, "*Min lille Trolleman.*" She knew her tricks. And her naturally affectionate and endearing nature gave itself to the improvement of such feminine arts as could serve her interests; she'd learned to wheedle. It was her one defense against the master's tyranny.

But on the whole, perhaps, she was content. Life had its sorrows but *her* life, its glory. And the contempt and hatred which sometimes smoldered impotently in her eyes was doubtless more than once dispelled by proud reflections on the social position that her marriage had brought her, and enraptured anticipation of that visit to Denmark toward which all that irksome training in the ways of white men was directed. Six years of it: how much had happened in six years!

III. REGINA

REGINA was a stranger, a newcomer to Igdlorssuit, having moved there but the year before at her husband's transfer from her birthplace, Agto. Both by her pride and by her husband's will she stayed a stranger. She maintained the prestige of her rank by the display of innumerable little vanities of dress and manner, which in the measure that they excited envy lost her the affection of the people. Her very position laid her open to the suspicion of being—what she may, in fact, to some extent quite thoughtlessly have been—a purveyor to the trader's ears of that secret ridicule and discontent with which the native may, for cause or none, view white officialdom. They neither loved nor trusted her, poor child!

Spring, summer, fall, and winter she watched from her closed windows all that life of her people—its work and play, and love and happy idleness—which had from childhood till six years ago been hers. She heard the laughter of the strolling groups on promenade, their songs on summer nights. She could detect the whispering of lovers pressed for concealment in a sheltering angle of her mansion house. Hunters returned; she joined the populace that welcomed them, shared in their pride in what their men had done, thrilled to her race's manhood. There stirred in her her sex's passionate response to youth, strength, hardihood. She paid within herself her woman's tribute to heroic man. All that from childhood on she'd learned to love and want, she wanted now.

Seated at a window that like an eye looks out all-seeingly on all the settlement is a little, crooked, white-haired man. He is writing. Long hours every day, painstakingly, with pride and pleasure in the Spencerian flourishes of his penmanship, he lists the day's events. Of all those feats of hardihood and skill, of all that has so moved the populace and made its life this day, he writes: "*x* kilos fat, *y* skins; value in kroner *z*." He is the recording angel of civilization. Regina, returned to her kitchen, sees while at her work that aged back, her man's. Unhappy child! God only knows her thoughts.

There had been some excitement among the girls of Agto at the arrival there of the new trader, Trolleman, a bachelor. And although no thought of marriage entered their heads, the girls did count upon him for such occasional favors as men liked to bestow; and, anticipating the privileges, notoriety, and honor incident to his special regard, vied with each other in that bashful hide and seek which was their way in courtship. Regina must at that time have been rarely beautiful, the full young oval face unmarked by care, its look as free and guileless as her life and thoughts. She had abundant beauty: long braids of raven hair coiled heavily about her head, an olive skin, red lips, and teeth as white as sun-bleached ivory. No wonder that the trader's eyes soon fell on her, and that he picked her out to be his servant.

Trolleman as a resident in settled Greenland was a newcomer; and those occasional adventures in the stalking of wild human game which had fallen to him on his Greenland voyages were of no help to him in the new sex problem of this new experience—domestic life. It may be that a sailor's one-night stands in love don't yield the knowledge of the ways of women that some claim for them, and that the Magdalenes of the back alleys of St. Pauli and Front Street are quite unlike the Marthas of that better place, the home. At any rate, hearth, home, domestic life, were strange to him; and whatever contempt for women he may have carried from his foremast days, the new environment imposed its holy hand, cloaking with circumspection the unholy lust that gnawed his vitals.

The girl's goodness—which may have been no more than the aspect of her native unsophistication—fitting as it did so touchingly his fancies of the home, was of itself potent at once to shame and to stimulate desire. It added to the confusion of his own mind as to what—how bold, how crafty, cautious, circumspect—the course of his pursuit should be. And knowing, as he did, that every secret act of his would be the gossip of the settlement, fearing, despite his white man's pride, the people's ridicule, he found himself encumbered by a self-consciousness that no amount of pompous posturing could hide. Regina knew his game: who wouldn't? She played her hand with an instinctive art. She was instructed in the ways of men: love was no mystery, and never had been. She had observed the procreation of her brothers and sisters, seen their birth; she had lived in the presence of all the phenomena of human life. Love was not talked about: it was an act performed. Its happening to her marked her maturity.

Regina was not innocent, but she was young; she was impressed by Trolleman, and scared. He was so boisterous. He'd strut about her in the kitchen, watching her with those protruding eyes. It troubled her. She did her best, too conscious of her ignorance of Danish housekeeping. Was what she did not right, that he should watch her so? He'd speak: it startled her, it was so loud. And he would laugh, and rub his hands, and clap her on the back, then quickly walk away. If this uproarious thing was mirth it was quite different from the mirth of Greenlanders. She understood, of course, no word of it. Why *did* he speak so suddenly and loud, touch her and jump away as though he'd burned himself? He'd pinch her waist, her thighs, then leave her quickly, always. It bothered her—such restlessness. If he had taken hold as though he wanted her she would have understood. Maybe he didn't want her.

When at night, her day's work done, she would leave for home, he'd follow to the door and watch her, lingeringly, until she'd turned the corner. She knit her brows; what was it he expected? Should she have stayed? He could have kept her, surely, if he had wanted her. She was herself conscious of an unfulfillment; not that she desired his embrace, she just expected it. And one night all was changed.

He had stood watching her as she put the kitchen in order. Finished, she started for the door. "Tomorrow—seven o'clock?" she asked. "Yes," he answered thickly. And as she moved away she heard him following. He was close upon her in the entry; he shut the inner door behind them, and it was almost dark there where the summer twilight hardly entered through a little window. He thrust his hands under her arms and covered her breasts; he drew her violently close and pressed his six-day beard against her cheek. Not in revulsion, not in fear, instinctively she struggled. Her hand was on the outer door; she pushed it open—wide. Daylight poured in, and laughter sounded from the rocks below. Then she was free. Turning as she ran away, she saw him standing, wild-eyed and disheveled, in the doorway. And from that moment she knew that Trolleman was hers.

Regina profited by Trolleman's ardor. She was not mercenary but she loved fine things. It made her happy to adorn herself, to hang bright necklaces about her throat, wear sparkling earrings, gaudy clothes; it fed her vanity to walk abroad in them and know herself to be the envy of her friends. Her finery was the badge of her preferment, and in the honor and rewards of that her family shared. It was a considerable family: a widowed mother and innumerable children. And as they came at last to throng the kitchen, to devour there the substantial leavings of the trader's table and spend as though by right what time they liked, they added a substantial hindrance to the courtship of one who shrank from the exposure in public of intentions that by his own romantic lights were far from honorable.

The pursuit of Regina—it was still a chase—yielded the sailor all those hopes, thrills, heart-aches, and despairs which first love claims. He was encumbered—and he knew it—by his years, his pompousness, and by the distressing consciousness that neither made him more a man. Love made him impotent to strike; and the

This is Regina — and she will
maybe never get used to her
fine things.

restraint that a romantic code imposed on him, the whole behaviorism of romantic love that might have proved so devastating to a Danish heart, was lost on his wild quarry. She knew reality, and only that; the one reality of what even she called love was passion. He could have taken her. She would have struggled—unconvincingly, have yielded—thrilled. Not thrilled by a responsive passion, but passively as the parched earth takes to itself the rain. To kindle man, to be possessed, devoured as by flame: that was her part in love. What tenderness that would evoke from her!

A pagan girl. How little had two hundred years of Christ affected what ten thousand unregenerate years, or ten times that, had made her! Say what we will of truth and beauty emanating as the light from Heaven, God's abode: she trod a pagan earth. Her roots were there; its moisture oozed about her feet and nourished her. Her race's ancient ways lived on in her. "Beauty is strength," its poets might have said, "strength beauty." Men wooed by force; rape was the ritual that crowned a courtship. She could as little fall for words, or *give* herself, as a young tree could bend toward the wind.

That first abortive violence of Trolleman's had disconcerted him; he'd spent himself. Her struggle, the sudden daylight flooding in, laughter, her escape: had people seen them? Had she told them all? When he appeared next day in public he was more loudly convivial than ever; he'd clap men on the back and laugh—so heartily. He'd pinch the babies' cheeks and pat the mothers. He broadcast handfuls of figs and sugar for people to scramble for in the dirt. He beamed—and watched for signs of ridicule. With Regina herself he resorted to his most pompous manner of authority. Master and servant: stern but not unkind. He ate, as usual, alone, but now sat quite immersed, it seemed, in last year's newspaper. She did her kitchen work demurely, smiled to herself, and waited on him faultlessly. She merely brushed his shoulder as she set his coffee down, passed back into the kitchen, forgot to shut the door; and, turning for that, saw that he was staring at her.

Regina, now that she knew her master's mind, enjoyed herself.

She understood just why he needed to be waited on, why he so often summoned her, why on the barest pretext or on none he hovered round her as she worked. She read his eagerness in every tentative advance, and could embarrass him each time so deftly. Why, he could even lay his hands on her—and by a look be made to drop them. They two alone there in that house! One night when she had worked late he called her to his bedroom. He stood there half undressed, striped flannel shirt-tails hanging about his uncouth, pallid legs. No thrill went through her at the sight of him, no urge to yield herself; and no disgust. Suddenly embarrassed, he contrived to hide his legs behind a chair, gave her some trivial order with what dignity he could, and so dismissed her.

It was as though in his pursuit of Regina he had entered upon a path that, however near to her it kept him, promised more and more never to coincide with hers. Their codes of love were incommensurate; and, adhering to his own by what to him amounted to compulsion, he found himself so deeply committed to a definite rôle in their relationship that, however hopeless it at last appeared, he couldn't—such is man—discard it. It is possible that under other circumstances—without a public hovering about, a dignified old mother squatting in the kitchen, staring youngsters—he might have abandoned chivalry for passion. But public, mother, and the kids were there; and in the face of them a gentleman could no more hazard an assault than Regina, by her lights, could yield without one. A stalemate at Platonic love confronted him, and every passing day committed him more deeply.

It happened, however, that in the course of his managerial duties he was called upon to make a tour of inspection of the several outpost settlements that were dependencies of his trading-post. Since this required a stay of several days' duration and involved the maintenance of some degree of domestic comfort on the boat that would be his home, Trolleman, quite in accordance with Greenland custom, decided to be accompanied by his servant, Regina. The ample cabin of the motorboat held bunks for both. She should prepare his meals, wash up, and generally minister to his comfort. Regina was of course delighted. She liked to travel, and she had innumerable friends and relatives in the outpost settlements to whom, in her elevation, it would be a pleasure to display herself. She dressed most charmingly to go: white boots with ornamented tops to just below the knees; above them, to mid-thigh, white cotton "stocking" covers embroidered with cross-stitched roses and bordered with lace, the "stocking" top itself a band of jet-black sealskin; then sealskin breeches tight about her thighs, each leg ornamented with a broad band of alternating stripes of vermilion leather, fine white dog fur, and embroidered leather. Her shirtwaist, or *anorak*, fitted her body closely; it was of claret-colored plush with a sash or border of gaudy, Roman-striped silk. She wore cuffs and a wide-necked standing collar of black sealskin; above the cuffs a two-inch band of bead lace, and, attached to the collar and hanging about her almost to her elbows, a heavy, ornate cape of beads. About her throat was a close-fitting collar of white cotton embroidered with flowers and pinned with a great brooch of sparkling emerald glass. Her lustrous black hair was parted over her low brow and coiled in braids on either side; bright ear pendants peeked from underneath the coils. Her black eyes sparkled, her white teeth gleamed, her sweet young face showed innocent delight in her bright plumage.

No doubt her loveliness on that fair day of their departure filled Trolleman with pride. He was, if possible, more aggressively pompous than ever, strutting about on his queer bandy legs and ordering that embarkation like a little admiral. At last they sailed, and to the dirty, tattered, friendly crowd that waved farewell it must have seemed Regina's day. It was.

Never truly used to the lordly rôle that he had played as master of his house, Trolleman on shipboard yielded to old environment, and by the force of long-established habit, worked. Soon, busied with the motor, he was as grimy as his crew; unthinkingly he came to wait upon his lovely passenger and thus sustain her in the idleness which her fine clothes enforced. This was so in keeping with her own mood that she accepted it unthinkingly; they were at one, that day, in honoring her clothes. And if the inciting of love is the motive of adornment, it had now so far outrun its purpose as to circumvent it: the man's desire had been transmuted to reverence, and hers to tremulous regard for perishable plush and fragile beads. Embarked upon what should by every circumstance have been their honeymoon, they were more hopelessly apart than ever. And when near midnight they dropped anchor in a quiet cove, when the deck had been put in order and the crew had turned in on the lockers of the motor cockpit, a thoughtful, solitary man sat puffing at his bedtime pipe; while in her cabin below, his sweetheart slept.

It was a summer encampment that was visited next day. Long before the tents were visible the travelers could discern innumerable figures sharp against the sky line, scurrying along the ridges of the hills to greet them. The figures gained a promontory, waited there; then, as the boat drew near, came running down the hill to follow scramblingly along the rocky shore in gleeful welcome. The encampment consisted of three or four tents and two turf houses; as much as anything that now survives of west-coast Greenland's past it could recall pre-Christian times: skin tents, two great skin "women's boats" drawn up on shore and overturned to serve as sleeping-shelters; the scene itself as it had always been: low, treeless, rolling hills, dwarfed underbrush and grass, scant soil, outcropping ledges everywhere; dreary, monotonous, and grand. "Back to the soil"—even in Greenland, there even more, the people feel that urge, the need to cast off and revert, to live and be like animals. And die like them. For while the crowd has gone across the hills to see the boat, while now they stand along the shore to greet the visitors, an old woman, ailing for days, has glided quietly from life, a solitary traveler.

Meanwhile Regina is embarking for the shore. They have brought the skiff alongside, wiped its seat dry, and with great consideration are helping the rather awkward, clothes-conscious girl into it. Trolleman, washed up and cleanly dressed, stands proudly at her side. They are rowed ashore. Men wade in, beach the skiff; the two alight. And while Regina is surrounded by her dirty compatriots, staring and clamoring for news, the hearty trader is conducted to a house.

Trolleman stoops low, and enters creepingly a pitchdark passageway. Feeling continuously before him, his hand encounters the rough and greasy surface of what must be a door. Finding no latch, he pushes it; it falls away as though it had come to pieces, and discloses a low and dimly lit interior, a sort of square walled cave of earth, dirt floor, dirt walls, a roof of sod supported on sagging poles. What light there is comes in through bladder panes. Two women stand up as he enters; a box is offered him to sit upon. Half of the little room is taken up by the sleeping platform. The platform is disorderly with dirty feather-bedding. There, pillowed in the midst of it, appear the head and shoulders of an old woman. The yellow skin is drawn tight over the broad bones of her face; her eyes are closed. She is lifeless as though dead.

Many people had followed Trolleman into the house; they filled it now. They all stood watching him expectantly. Being graced with great assurance, being stimulated rather than abashed by the attentions of others, Trolleman arose and approached the deathbed. He drew the covers down, drew out an arm. He held the lifeless hand in his. Raising the sleeve a little, he felt for the pulse. Long moments he stood there, and there was not a sound in the house but the people's coughing. He laid the arm down and it sank heavily into the feather-bedding. And, turning toward the people, he most solemnly and slowly shook his head.

Everyone had by now entered the house; they made a dense crowd in that little place. In the doorway stood one of the boat's crew. Trolleman by signs, and what he knew of native speech, addressed this man. His language was grotesque, absurd; yet no one laughed. Apparently it was a box on board the boat that he was sending for, and in his attempts to describe it he used the word *kivitok*, of no application whatever and denoting one possessed with a certain supernatural madness. The man departed on his errand, and Trolleman, turning toward the lifeless woman, fixed on her a prolonged, unwavering stare.

At the messenger's return the crowd parted to admit him. Trolleman took the box from him and set it on the platform, at the same time undoing the strap which bound it shut. That done, he faced the corpse, while everyone in a continued silence watched him. Slowly he raised his arms and brought them forward till the hands, palms down, were poised above the dead one's countenance. He moved his hands; they seemed to stroke an unseen emanation. His staring eyes now bulged enormously; their pupils were but spots in glistening hemispheres. What if the woman now had opened her eyes? What could that aged heart have borne?

Slowly, still stroking with his hands her emanation, Trolleman withdrew toward the box. He stooped and opened it. Quickly he took a bottle and uncorked it. He moved to the woman's side and held the uncorked bottle to her nose.

Some seconds passed—a breathless interval. Then every eye there saw the dead lids flutter, saw them open. She turned her head a little, looked listlessly around. She moved her skinny hand to draw the covers up. She was awake, alive!

The event made a profound impression on the bystanders. That miracles *could* be performed, and had been, they all knew, for the people's present familiarity with the impotent priesthood of the Christian Church had only fortified their memories of their race's pagan past, and deepened their respect for the remembered supernatural powers of the ancient priests. Here, then, was one again who could wake up the dead, an angakok: they called him that. Like the rings from a thrown pebble traveling over the still surface of a pond, his fame spread out at last to reach the farthest settled shores of Greenland.

Fear had gripped Regina's heart at the display of such weird powers by one to whom she was so closely bound. Those ways of his that had seemed strange and almost humorous to her were now recalled, and vested by her imagination with terrifying significance as the expression of a superhuman personality. She dreaded him, and yet took pride in being in a measure his. Her little spirit crowed with rapture at the attention which her nearness to him brought herself. That the people stood in awe of Trolleman and feared approaching him, brought them the more eagerly about her, clamoring for such gossip as only she could know and tell.

And so it was that only late that night, when Trolleman, tired of waiting for her, had turned in, when the light of a new morning had crept into the sky and everyone was moved to sleep, that Regina was sculled out over the still water, set on board, and whisperingly told good night. Stealthily, so as not to awaken her sleeping master, she descended to the cabin, and stealthily proceeded to undress. She drew off her white boots, thrust her arm into each in turn and straightened out the toe. She carefully took off her beads and her plush anorak, folded them tenderly, and laid them by. Usually she kept her breeches on, but these were new. She took them off, and stood there now barelegged in her shift. She mounted the locker to climb into her berth and, turning, glanced at Trolleman. She clutched the bunk, she almost fell with fright: his eyes were open, looking at her.

Powerless to move and to avert her terror-stricken eyes from that unearthly stare, she hung there: then he spoke.

"Look out, Regina, I saw a *kivitok* there in your sleeping-bag."

Regina leapt, then whipped about and stared back at the haunted bed. For a long time she watched that bed, to gasp at last:

"No, no. There's nothing there." Timidly she ventured nearer, reached out and made as though to try the bed again.

"Look out," said Trolleman—and she recoiled.

Time passed. There was no sound but the liquid lapping of the tide, and not a movement. Regina stood with staring eyes while Trolleman watched her.

"Trolleman," said Regina in a tiny voice, her eyes still on the bed, "maybe I can come and sleep with you?"

Not many weeks before Regina's child was born, Trolleman, with proper pride and an honorable defiance of the efforts that his countrymen had made to stop the misalliance, led Regina to the altar and there married her. It was, of course, to her, the crowning point of her young life and of an ambition to whose timid whisperings she had at first but lent an ear—at last to take it to her breast and nourish it. Not only had she dared to hope; she'd willed. And with all the resources of her nature—wit and simple wisdom, tears and smiles, her beauty, grace, and charm—employing all she had and knew with an instinctive art, she had kept her lover hot with desire and desperate with fear of losing her. She won—if we should call it that. That was six years ago.

Six years: Regina wife of the Danish trader at the flourishing outpost of Igdlorssuit, mistress of the mansion house, is dressed in "Danish clothes." She wears a knee-length calico dress loose as a bag around her waist and hips and scant about her legs. A flannel petticoat hangs down two inches low behind. Her bowlegs are clad in checked cotton stockings that wrinkle over cheap high-topped laced boots. "She *shall* be Danish," said my host, explaining her. Timidly she interrupts her lord to say that dinner is ready. "Sit down!" cries Trolleman, and beats my back. "Sit down, speak nothing, make yourself at home." Whew, what a boisterous and hearty chap! "Come, eat," he cries, "take more. Oh, yes, you shall." He heaps my plate with more. "Beer?" "Thank you, yes." He fills my glass. "No sugar, thank you." "But you *shall.*" He dumps a tablespoonful in. Eat, eat! Drink up. "That's that!" he roars; and hurls the empty bottle clattering along the floor to crash against the kitchen door. Ox-eyed and apple-cheeked Helena, young sister to Regina, the household's kitchen maid, comes in demurely with more beer. "She shall, you shall, it shall, they shall!"—if Trolleman had ever known more than the imperative he had forgotten it. "They shall obey!"

Two sisters of Regina's lived as servants there. They slept together in a narrow trundle bed upstairs; a few square feet of floor space in the littered junk hole of the open attic was their room. Of the two, while Helena had obviously more vivacity and, in a way, more charm, Lea, the younger—she was only fifteen—promised to become even more beautiful than her married sister in her prime had been. Lea was shy and taciturn no doubt by nature; added to this she was dispirited to a degree that could only suggest prevailing unhappiness in the environment in which she now was living. One might have wondered at unhappiness where such free-handed hospitality prevailed.

It was one of Lea's duties every morning to awaken her master and mistress. However late the sunlit summer nights might keep her up, however she might love her midnight freedom after sixteen hours of household drudgery, use and prolong it till the sun was high, and want to dream about it afterwards, the tin alarm clock by her bed recalled her to her work at 7 A.M. That was her rising-time. She'd dress and hurry down and, passing through my room, wake Trolleman.

One morning of the days I stayed at Trolleman's I waked up early; so, at least, it seemed. The house was still, all out of doors was breathless. I lay there on that couch in the living-room which was my bed and looked out through the window across from me into the new day luminous with sunlight. Daytime—and all the world asleep. Then, suddenly, I heard the sound of feet alighting on the floor above me. Lea, I thought. And in a moment she was hurrying overhead and down the ladder of the loft. The door opened; Lea crossed my room to Trolleman's and entered there. She spoke; I heard a questioning answer in his voice. Lea came hurrying back. I heard her climb the ladder to the loft, run quickly overhead. Again the steps above—over the attic floor and down the ladder; again my door is opened. Lea comes through; she carries the alarm clock in her hand. And as she enters Trolleman's room she shuts the door behind her. It is quiet in the house, I can hear Lea speaking. Then like a lion's roar the voice of Trolleman. I hear him, roaring, leap upon the floor; the sound of heavy blows; then silence. The door opens and little Lea, head hung down and face averted, crosses to the kitchen. I hear her stifled sobs as I get dressed. Lea had lied.

IV. FOUNDATIONS

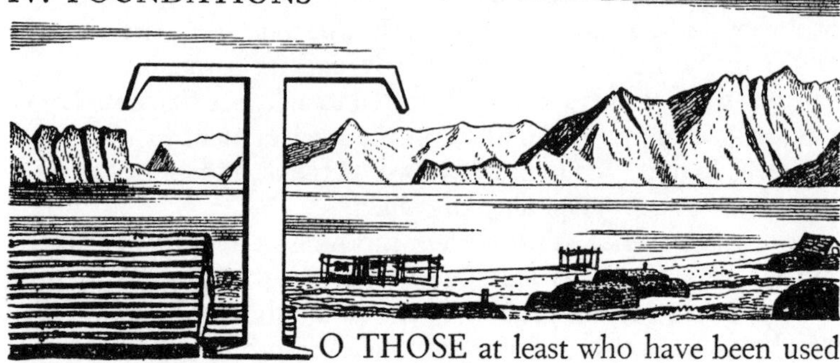

TO THOSE at least who have been used to living where every foot of land is some man's property, the unowned wilderness invites possession. Unpeopled hills and valleys, virgin meadow land, sites that command a world, and sheltered glades that promise refuge from it: each in its way suggests the thought of living there, and kindles the imagination to what each different environment and man would make of one another. It is not Satan but God who, taking man by the hand, leads him to a mountain top that overlooks the wilderness. "All this," God says, "is yours. Make of it what you will." And God might add, "You *will* bow down and worship Me."

Strangely, the realization that the scene, the land, may be—and is for wanting it—your own, endears it. Let all your dreams have been of warmth and tropical luxuriance; let what at last is given you be bare, bleak, cold, in every way unlike your thoughts of earthly paradise, your chameleon soul cries out, "By God, I *love* this barrenness!" Why otherwise have men gone out from comfort, from the pleasures of city life, from all the cultivated beauty of a developed countryside, and in hardship and poverty, in unremitting labor, in all the hard conditions of some frontier life, found happiness? Why do men love the wilderness? For its mountains?—there may be none. For its forests, lakes, and rivers?—it might be a desert; men would love it still. Desert, the monotonous ocean, the unbroken snow-fields of the North, all solitudes, no matter how forlorn, are the only abiding-place on earth of liberty.

The free land around the little settlement of Igdlorssuit had little but its freedom and the view to favor it. A steep-pitched, grass-grown slope of shale backed by the crumbling mountains that had made it, a low-lying level area that appeared to have been avoided by house-builders, the gentle eastern slope of the Igdlorssuit bowl, and a level, gravelly foreland to the west—these were available to who might want to build. But the level foreland showed clear signs of being the stream bed of spring torrents, the eastern slope and the avoided areas were bog, and the dry land at the mountain's base, to judge it by the rocks that littered it, would be no safer than a battlefield. These rocks, pried from the mountain face by frost, released in spring, were a perennial menace to the rearward houses of the settlement. Some houses had been struck, and one, not long before, almost demolished; even within the built-up area, rocks to almost a cubic yard in size lay where they had come to rest, a continual reminder of how destruction might come without warning upon a sleeping household.

I might, in looking for a building site, have found a vacant spot within the settlement but that I feared to encroach upon the privacy and rights to view of others as, by the placing of the native houses, such rights appeared to have been recognized. Moreover, I had hoped to be an observer in Greenland rather than one observed, and naturally preferred looking down on others to being looked down upon. I chose the elevated battlefield; and with what judgment I possessed picked out a site at best less in the path of hurtling rocks than others. It proved to be a fortunate if not a safe location. But aside from its exposure to bombardment the place was perfectly suited to my needs. Lying uphill from the settlement, it was enough removed from other house sites to promise privacy, and yet so reasonably situated as to offer no suggestion that seclusion had been sought for. My window, like all windows of the settlement, would face the view; yet in the foreground of *my* view would be the settlement itself with all the action of its daily outdoor life enlivening its stage. Outdoors!—I was to learn what that could be to man.

How, living there, partaking of the conditions of that Northern life, watching it from my window, I came to feel—as though for the first time in my life—the beauty of the world! How much to those reared there that scene, that segment of the world's horizon which appeared between the inclosing headlands of the crescent bay, that stretch of sea, those mountains—how much of all the people's lives, of all life's incidents and moods, hung on the changeful aspects of that changeless world! There in the North they watched the seasons, the going and the coming of the day and night, the rising and the setting of the summer sun and of the winter moon, the tides, the weather, rain and snow, and ice; they read in these the order of the day's activities—each day of all the years and lifetimes of the generations of Igdlorssuit. How far profounder a devotion was that constant northward looking than any Godward posturings of conscious worshipers! There was God's countenance itself, its light, its majesty of form, its power of life and death; His countenance so beautiful that people made the open strand their playground, meeting-place, the place to loiter or to stroll, the courting-ground for lovers. We pride ourselves on loving nature: what is our love of nature to that love of those who are its children? Summer—and winter, as I was to learn—in sun, cloud, rain, snow, storm, or bitter cold, all hours of the day and long at night they thronged the shore. And as they breathed the air so they partook, unconsciously, of all that beauty. Is air less wholesome that we breathe it thoughtlessly?

Goethe writes of an environment so perfectly contrived of beauty that youth reared there attained a loveliness of soul that one could never meet with in the outside world. What of the beauty of the Greenland world? Not palaces, parks, statuary, wallpaper, rugs, hangings, music, and pictures, all that rehash of man's experience which he terms art, but the eternal fountainhead of all that is beautiful in art and man, the virgin universe. How must that presence day and night have worked upon the souls of those poor people!

It is summer, as I stand there on my house site, and the broad water of the sound lies blue and calm. Icebergs float here and there; they have the bulk of mountains and a livid translucence far more tender than the most lovely of pale flowers. Eight miles across the sound—much nearer to the unaccustomed eye—is the mountainous island of Upernivik, its steep wall cleft by glaciated valleys. The glaciers are like curving highways of pale jade leading from summer at the water's edge to the eternal winter of the lofty inland ice. Beyond the northern promontory of Upernivik opens a far receding vista of blue ranges rising from the sea to snow-tipped summits. That is the glamorous region of Umiamako; its waters are a wilderness of ice throughout the year, its land the haunt of evil beings. Against this distant mountain vista stands the Gothic mass of Karrat Island; and, terminating it, the large island of Kakertarssuak with its Fujiyama of five thousand feet. Past Kakertarssuak the land again recedes beyond a maze of mountain-rimmed fiords; then with the foreshortened coast of Svartenhuk Peninsula it draws swiftly near again, to lose itself to view beyond the northern headland of Igdlorssuit Bay. The sky is golden where the mountains meet it, and on the mountains, sea, and ice the golden sunset light of the midsummer sun that never sets.

Of the events which brought me into contact with the people and helped to level the barrier to mutual understanding which does exist wherever there are rich and poor, white men and colored, a privileged class and others, the building of my house with my own hands, the working at it with native helpers at my side, was, coming at the very outset of my residence at Igdlorssuit, the most fortunate. The mere building of the house was an event in the prevailing uneventfulness of local life; to many it was a source of employment, and to the rest a spectacle. It drew them all—men, women, children, from the very old to the very young—to throng my hillside, to recline there, smoking, chatting, watching through the many idle hours of the day and evening that pleasant sight to comfortably idle ones—the spectacle of other men at work. Even the days of waiting for materials to come, my own impatience at that first prolonged delay, came to be shared by everyone. The house site found, the building staked—what now? Days passed. The schooner that should bring the lumber, nails, cement, my household goods, the whole astounding paraphernalia for keeping alive which the Greenlanders had learned to associate with the coming of a European, that wealth of new and often strange material things—what held the schooner up? Almost no hour of the day or night but someone watched for it, stood on the harbor hill and scanned the fifty miles of calm blue water toward where, behind the solitary, heart-shaped mountain of Umanak, the schooner lay. From the harbor hill they looked off eastwards for the schooner; and southwards, beyond the receding promontories of the island's shore, for the coming of my motorboat. That too was overdue. Meanwhile, what could be done I did.

The Greenland outpost stores should be, are *meant* to be, supplied with whatever necessities and simple luxuries of European life the local natives in their progress toward enlightenment have learned to want. Guns and ammunition, knives, pots and kettles, dishes, dress goods, coffee, tobacco, sugar, biscuit, flour, oatmeal, rice, dried peas and beans, figs, prunes, molasses, chocolate, rope, fishing lines and hooks, lumber and nails, beads, pictures, souvenirs and toys, and useless knickknacks of various kinds. With what kinds of articles and in what quantity an outpost store is stocked depends on to what extent experience has taught the trader to estimate the people's wants, on his judgment, on the intelligence and goodwill of the colony manager and his assistants in Umanak, on their moods and whims and memories—on things, at any rate, beyond all reckoning. The Igdlorssuit store received the season's stock whenever, from midsummer until fall, those Umanak authorities would find it not too troublesome to send it. And it was remarkable with what patience the people continued through the months of spring and early summer trading-in the little brass tokens of exchange, which they had received for their produce in skins and fat, for those unwanted left-over European commodities with which alone the now almost depleted store could furnish them. "We have no biscuit, no hardbread—but we have candles; no oatmeal—but we have dried beans. We have coffee—but no sugar. Molasses?—Why, you finished it last fall." There were no beads for the girls' adornment, but there was an assortment of old tarnished and corroded finger rings just short of large enough to fit a Greenland woman's wrist. There were no dress materials, but shop-soiled remnants of drab patterns. The outposts, it is held, don't need good clothes. Of cigarettes the trader didn't approve—for others; but how about a nickel-plated cigarette case with a pretty picture on it of a French girl in her drawers? There was, of course, no butter; but margarine, perhaps? No, none. But lumber? Yes, the most expensive kind; the people can't afford it. Cement? Two barrels. No one uses it. Nails? Sorry, not a nail in stock for months.

Lumber for concrete forms, cement: work can begin. Word of my need of nails went round the settlement; men brought their bent and rusty savings. A boy was put to work to straighten them. Trolleman produced odd lengths of wire saved from crates; I had a pocket level, hammer, hand ax, in my bag. A Greenlander lent me an old saw. And now a dozen men start carrying lumber, sand, and gravel to the job.

It was a steep walk up the hill, yet no one minded it. Their mood was festive; the loads they chose to carry matched it. It was a holiday to work; they kept it one. Sometimes, by way of sport, someone would take a staggering load and stagger with it while the others laughed. He'd make the grade and drop the load on its allotted spot; then he and all the rest would sprawl out on the grass to take, as it would seem, a well-earned rest. They came at seven and they stayed till five. They were faithful to the hours of their employment, and delightful company throughout them; it was their *hours* that they'd sold to me for hire, not, it appeared, their labor. Thus every day was a prolonged social event that brought me the acquaintance of many charming people and, incidentally, somewhat advanced the work in hand.

I was too grateful for the numbers who put themselves at my service to mind about the daily changes in their personnel. If, after working for a day or two, a man chose to lay off and go fishing, or, tired of the monotony of his employment, preferred to merely lie on my hillside and watch the others work, it was little to be concerned about. A people who had never known compulsion did, naturally, as they pleased; and not having learned to like material luxuries as much as they disliked the drudgery of earning them, having of food sufficient for the day, what fools they would have been to choose to work.

It is told that a certain Danish contractor who had the erecting of a wireless station in Greenland thought to overcome the people's sloth by offering a two days' wage for one day's labor. The people responded with enthusiasm; they worked a day, were paid. And next day not a soul showed up. Having earned two days' pay in one, why work the second day? Well—why?

When at last enough sand and gravel had been carried up the hill, I set the crowd at collecting stones of various sizes from the steeper slope above the house. This didn't go so well; and if I hadn't hit upon getting boys to do it the house might still today have been in process of construction. They made a game of it, and sent such an avalanche of stones rolling and tumbling about us that we had to run for safety. By the time that the stevedoring was finished I knew who of the workmen earned his salt. I kept four men, and let the others go. Let me present the four:

Janus Sivert Jens Nicolaj Upernangitok was, by his name, a violator of the law which limits Greenland Christian names to three. In other respects he was a peaceful, dull, law-abiding, reputable citizen suffering somewhat in public esteem through no greater fault than having come to Igdlorssuit with Trolleman. He was the darkest of the Eskimos. He was nicknamed Dukajak.

Ludwig—oh, why give all the names?—Ludwig Wille was remarkable for his diminutive stature, and for his pitifully sore eyes. He was a clever worker with his hands, and he worked hard. He was no hunter, and he owned no kayak, sledge, or dogs. He was a cheerful, good young man who would probably never amount to much.

Thomas Lövstrom was to be thought of as an old man—though he was only fifty-six. It is possible that his relinquishment of the activities of the hunter, enforced by the visitation of the dreaded kayak dizziness, had brought him such reflections upon his uselessness as to impose on him the gentle manner of resigned old age. He counted himself among the old whose hunting days, whose lives, were finished. I think that I have never seen such mellow sweetness in another human countenance.

Karl Tobias Paulus Street, called Olabi, was a phenomenon in Greenland. He had never been in a kayak, he never went hunting; he owned no dogs, and knew nothing about driving them. The entire world of what were exclusively men's activities was beyond his experience. Yet Olabi was a hard worker. He went fuel-gathering with the women, coming back laden with heavier loads than most of them could bear. He carried water, cooked, and did the household chores. Along with the boys of the settlement and an occasional woman he fished for shark; that was his chief means of livelihood. He sewed exquisitely, and in the designing and making of his own clothes showed an originality of taste that marked him out among a people who conformed undeviatingly to long-established rules of fashion. He embroidered linen, crocheted lace, knitted caps and mufflers to order; he worked with beads. Olabi was a well-built, robust man of average height; he walked with a mincing gait as though affectedly; he swayed his hips. He had had no more experience of European manners than the least-cultured men and women of the settlement, yet in his manners—in general, and in my house at table—he was noticeably dainty. Olabi lived with his vivacious, aged, and decrepit widowed mother—alone with her. Once, years ago, when Olabi had lived as one of the household of the Greenlander Hans Nielsen, and slept—so crowded was that house—on the floor with Hans's sons, he had one night attempted a familiarity which was immediately repulsed. That is, I believe, the only known overt act of Olabi's life; it is remembered. Olabi's hair hangs in long ringlets to his shoulders. His face is prematurely wrinkled—he is only thirty-nine. One might remark its sadness in repose but that so many Greenland faces are sad. His smile perhaps dispels the sadness less. Olabi is spoken of as being like a woman, yet no one taunts him. It is as though the people felt for him in what must be his loneliness.

These were the men who mixed and poured the concrete of my cellar walls. And when, the forms half filled, the two barrels of cement exhausted, we *had* to stop our work, we did, and from that time on throughout a good part of the long remainder of the days until the schooner came, we betook ourselves to the harbor hill to scan, along with many more, those tranquil fifty miles of sea toward Umanak. So I, the latest comer to the island, had become like all the rest of them, a watcher for the next. Let me then, sitting on that hilltop there with nothing in the world to do, retell the story of my coming—not as *I* knew it, but as it looked from land, particularly to the eyes of one young girl the course of whose whole life should, curiously, by that stray event be changed. It is right that I begin her story here; having begun it I must tell it through—even though it lead us far ahead of our main narrative. So, with the day I came there, we begin:

V. CINDERELLA

IGDLORSSUIT, July—and not a soul was doing anything.

The women were not at their housework—they had none.

The men were not hunting—there was nothing to hunt.

The children were not at school—it was vacation time.

And everyone was out of doors.

It was a breathless sunlit afternoon. "God, what a day!" we'd cry. And they cried nothing. Only breathed its beauty, drank it in as people would, or do, in Paradise; as people *have* in countless centuries of summers in the North where nothing happens. Then suddenly a far-off, high-pitched cry:

"*U-mi-at-si-ar-tor-pok!*"

And as a hundred voices roar it back the peace is shattered.

People are running toward the harbor hill, all, old and young, a straggling crowd. A long way there, a long and steep ascent to reach the top. They scramble up. There where their eyes command a Greenland world of sea and far-off mountain range, they stand and stare. And on that calm and sunlit waterway they see—still far away, minute and faint—a speck. A boat! It's worth while living in the North where such things happen.

What boat? Who's coming here? Good news, of course, but what? What drama of suspense! How slowly the small craft draws near, with not a mark to judge its progress by! How imperceptibly it grows: from nothing into—being! How, finally, the even chug, chug, chug, chug of the motor comes to be!—as though, like the ticking of a timepiece in a silent room, it always had been. Then with what suddenness, with rustling bow wave it bears down on them, and past. All turn and follow it down hill, along the shore: the mob its escort. And as the little boat drops anchor abreast of the settlement, there at the land's edge stands the populace to stare its welcome.

The coming of a stranger, of a white man, and particularly, let us believe, of *any* American (How reluctantly we underline the word!) to take up residence in a remote Greenland settlement is, of course, an event of the most terrific local importance. It would, for some reason, cause the bedridden to get up, the cripples to run, the blind to see, the deaf to hear, and girls to prink and wash their faces. Yet the personal satisfaction, the pure deep pleasure, with which, upon appearing on deck, I observed the delight in my looks and bearing of the people in general and, in particular, of the many gaily dressed and fairly ravishing young girls, is not to be, by me, forgotten. O Prince of Wales, we too have our great moments.

How fortune favored me that day! No place to sit down in the overladen skiff. *Standing*, I'm rowed to land. They draw the skiff up high and dry. Dry-shod I step ashore. And with an air of majesty tempered by covert glances right and left I stride through those awe-stricken ranks to make the trader's house and, for a fortnight, home. What follows now I only learned about months later.

In one of the smallest, most dilapidated, and most filthy of the turf houses of the settlement lived the great hunter, honorable man, and leading citizen, Abraham; lived Abraham, his wife, four children, a foster son, and a poor relative—a niece—named Justina. There in that one-room house not more than ten feet square and scarcely man's height high lived all of them! They ate from one pot, and they slept all huddled close for warmth and happiness on one broad bed—the sleeping-platform. There had the children been conceived and born; there would, at last, the parents die. Life is an open bed to Greenlanders.

There were few duties to perform in that untidy household: the floor was rarely scrubbed, few clothes were ever washed. They lived there in the carefree neglect of housekeeping which necessity in earlier times had made their race's habit. Nevertheless, what with carrying her pails from the distant muddy trickle that supplied the settlement with washing water, with carrying up ice chunks from the shore to melt and drink, or sea water to boil the seal ribs in, and above all with tending the latest baby—wiping up its puddles, spreading in the sun the feather bed the babe had wet—with toting the children around and amusing them when they wanted to cry, Justina who—it was her job—must do it all was to all appearance just such a household drudge as Cinderella, just as imposed upon and dirty and, as events turned out, as fortunate. Justina's was a modest, self-effacing nature, and she was so faithful to her duties as to be rarely met with on the promenade. At least one *saw* her rarely, for despite the childlike sweetness of her face, her finely drawn oriental features, her white and faultless teeth, her light did not so shine as to transcend the squalor she was clothed in. She was *protectively* attired, toned down by dirt to match the soil it came from. Soiled.

Yet at sixteen she was innocent, incredible as it may appear, of even the comprehension in theory of those facts of life which were the practice of the normal boys and girls of her own age. She was a child, in mind, and shed corruption from her by sheer inability to retain it. Her lack of wit appeared as virtue and, combined with her precocious mother-love, lent her, contrasted to her ribald playmates, an air of unaffected saintliness and flowerlike purity of soul. And if her thoughts and her emotions, springing as they did from no true comprehension of reality, were not profound, they were dignified by the very efforts that her small mind made as one could read them in the plaintive puckering of her brow.

She wanted love—God knows what she imagined it to be! She wanted *love*—men frightened her. "Tassa!" she'd say, "not that!" —and push them off and run, reminded by such show of what love wasn't, to dream of—storks, if she had known them; of babies; of a hero mate; of a snug home, her own. No one can ever know Justina's thoughts but by the sweetness that they lend to her.

To virgin Elsa of Brabant there came when she most needed him the champion of her dreams. Beauty and chivalry and strength: he was as a garland woven of the flowers of Asgaard. So to Justina at Igdlorssuit there came—in the very hour, perhaps, of some assault upon her frightened innocence—the swan boat of her champion; and when one July afternoon there reached her ears the cry, "A boat!" she with the rest leaped up and ran to see. The swan boat neared; she heard with pounding heart the chug-chug of its motor. She followed it and saw it anchor. Stood with the rest on shore, and stared. And from that swan's inside stepped *I*.

What *of* what all the others in that crowd there thought! What of them all—those gay girls in vermilion boots and gaudy chintz! Unspeakable Justina—drab, soiled, tattered, filthy girl—looked once. And it came over her that never—not in all her life and all its dreams—had she beheld such beauty. Justina looked and loved. Life, for Justina, has begun.

It was, as I have said, months later that I learned of this. And in looking back upon that July day of my arrival, I became curious to account for my devastating effect upon Justina. She was, of course—I realize it—just a little simple. That would account for much. Then, too, all Greenlanders are at sea in judging white men's age by how they look. We're different. Baldness, for example—what do those thick-maned people think of it? And Justina seeing my head could only have associated its appearance with such comparable heads as she'd observed upon the very, very young. I'd *like* to know why fair Justina loved me!

She did—and made no bones of it. She told them all. Told it, and showed it in her looks. Broadcast it to the settlement. And how they laughed! How cruelly they twitted her! What chance had *she* against the rest of them? And what chance *had* she! All day on promenade, all day and night on that broad strand, the Boulevard, bright figures strolled: bright clothes, bright looks, alluring glances, laughter, song. Youth on parade.—And drab Justina plodding by from time to time with laden pails: poor drudge!

And now I've set about the building of my house, my one-room palace made of wood. *That's* an event, a show for all the settlement. All idle people throng the spot; sit there to watch, to bask in the warm sun, to smoke, to gossip, laugh, to help. I get to know them, all. All but Justina.

There is in the settlement a man of most substance, named Rudolf. He is the cooper; he works by the year at a salary of thirty-seven cents a day. And his wife, Marghreta, keeps, as she should, a neat, clean house and wears fine clothes. So to Marghreta's door one day comes poor Justina, comes in and shuts the door, and with her head hung down, embarrassed, stands.

"Well, Justina?" says Marghreta.

Justina's chin is strangling her. She murmurs unintelligibly.

"Come! speak up," says Marghreta.

Justina tries. She raises up a blushing face and says, quite clearly now, "May I borrow your earrings?"

Marghreta laughs. "Are you in love?" she says.

Justina smiles as though from deep within.

"Who is it?"

Justina, with a sigh like one awakening, answers: "Kinte."

When Justina a few minutes later hurries home she holds clasped tight in her hand not, of course a *pair* of earrings (Who'd lend her that!) but one odd earring made of glass: her own, to keep.

There's nothing much in the way of a looking-glass in Justina's house, just a broken bit of one. She props the fragment on the window muntin and, locating a fraction of her face in it, begins to beautify herself. Dirt!—with a dirty rag she rubs off some of it. She puts back straggling hair, tightens the knot. The pink lobes of her ears just show; they must.

Now Justina takes the earring in her hand, holds it, and hesitates. She thinks—decides. The *left*. She fixes it in place. Then taking up two empty water pails she leaves the house.

The path from where Justina lived came not near me. My house was up the hill, the path led down. But Justina's life has, as we've said, begun. The paths of others are no longer hers. Uphill she comes, up toward my house, and, nearing it, she turns and walks across my view, right in the foreground of it, my house near to her on—who guesses it?—her left.

Justina stubs her toes on that rough hillside. Eyes to the front! There, stupid kid! She stubs her toe again. Oh, if he'd only look! she prays. And the glass pendant twinkles in the sun.

And all the time right there in sight of her I'm working. I'm spiking rafters to the plate. And every time I drive a twenty-penny home, I pause to drink the view, to feast my eyes on God expressed in mountains, glaciers, sea, and ice; to gaze upon God's countenance, to be enriched, ennobled by familiarity with Him. God doesn't give a damn for me.

So, unobserved, Justina passes by.

Justina at the water hole sets down her pails. Kneeling, she bails up water with a cup; she fills the pails. That's done. Now she takes the jewel from her left ear, looks at it lovingly a moment as it lies glittering in her palm. Enough. She returns the jewel to her ear, fixes it there. No, not the left this time, the *right*. The pool is still again, the child leans over it, looks down. From the dark surface of the pool her own face golden with reflected sunlight looks up at her. God, if He sees at all, sees her.

But only God. And merely by the trodden pathway that appeared, in time, below my house did I come to know that it was the custom, strangely, of some people to employ that devious way.

When at last my house was finished I began to live: to know people, to entertain them as my guests, to visit them. I now made friends. So it happened that one day not long before Christmas I was sitting with my dear housekeeper, Salamina (she for whom this book is named), in the house of our friends Rudolf and Marghreta. What pleasant evenings those were! Rudolf would play the harmonica and I would play the flute, and, for those who liked it, that was sweet to hear. And Salamina and Marghreta gossiped.

"Who," said I, lowering my flute, "is this Justina that you're talking about?"

his is Justina — as she might
ome day have appeared if amauts
nd loving your babies that much
ad not gone out of fashion.

"What!" cried both of them. "You don't know her? Why, she's in love with you." And they burst into laughter.

Thereupon they told me, pretty much as I've retold it, the story of Justina.

"And now we'll have her over!" And they laughed again, while Rudolf went to fetch her.

Whew! she was dirty as she stood there in that spick and span clean house. What filthy rags of clothes! Poor thing!—And how she took it. Took ridicule and laughter. She was used to it. Embarrassed?—Yes. But strangely self-possessed as though even among others she maintained connection with an inner world that was exclusively her own. We laughed, and she smiled back. Only remotely could she sense that we laughed *at* her.

They put her through her stunts.

"Whom do you love?" they asked.

She murmured, "Kinte."

"Now count for us."

Justina's education had been limited; in mathematics she had never gone beyond twenty. "One, two, three, four, five"—on one hand, (so they count), "six, seven, eight, nine, ten"—on the other. Justina stopped.

"Go on!" they urged—for here the fun began.

"*Nagga*," murmured Justina, shaking her head. "No, no."

"Go on, go on!"

She sighs—and yields. She treads hard on the heel of her right boot, draws her right leg out; she treads on the heel of her left boot and draws her left leg out. Barelegged to her thighs she stands there, and on her ten bare toes counts up to twenty.

Justina, it appeared, had half a crown; roughly, a dime. And she told us how for Christmas she was going to buy herself a kilo of coffee, a kilo of sugar, a kilo of hardbread, a kilo of chocolate, a kilo of figs, a kilo of rice, a kilo of this and that and everything, and—a cigar! Poor child, I thought—for I'd been thinking quick—you're going to get the whole of it on Christmas day if it costs me all of two dollars.

Salamina, surprisingly, entered right into the spirit of "A Merry Christmas for Justina." When we had bought all the things that Justina had thought of, we bought more. And when there was no more to buy we turned to those stores of treasures which a devoted wife had bought for me, and packed, and labeled "Girl Lure." What a store! Beads, brooches, bracelets, earrings, necklaces; ribbons and calicoes: the pick of all the best that 5 & 10's afford. We chose the smartest for Justina. More—I have a piece of silk. Salamina makes for Justina a chemise. (Can you beat *that?* —a silk chemise upon an Eskimo?) Still more: we commission the best bootmaker of the settlement to make Justina boots—and keep it secret. Chemise, an anorak of gaudy calico with silken sash, boots, earrings, necklaces, et cetera. What more? Oh yes!—the pants. Well, Salamina made them. All's ready now; it's Christmas Eve.

At ten o'clock at night, when most people have gone to bed—for it is, of course, the dark time then in Greenland—Salamina fetches Justina. Come in, Justina, shut the door. It's warm inside the house, and cozy with drawn curtains. On the stove are big kettles of steaming water. On the floor is the washtub.

"Now, Justina, strip."

Justina knew no more about life than she did about mathematics. Not so much, in fact; in life she'd only reached sixteen. Not half a minute, and her clothes are off. And in that time we'd filled the tub. With Justina in the tub Salamina and I, each with a floor brush, get to work. We start at the top and we work down. And when we get to the water we decide that it has all of Justina in it that it can stand: a saturate solution of Justina. Step out, Justina—there, behind the stove. And we stagger out with the big tub, and empty it.

With clean water in the tub—Justina this time sitting down—I give her a shampoo. That's fun!—the long, thick, black hair all lathered up with shaving cream. Keep your eyes shut, Justina. There! I pour a pailful over her. Now—stand up. Again we scrub her off from head to foot.

You know—she came out fine!

We wrapped her in Turkish towels and sat her down close to the stove to dry her hair. We fed her hot coffee and rich cake. And then, and *then!*—we gave her her new clothes.

Justina's triumph at the church on Christmas morning was but a prelude to her triumph later, later at dinner time. We fed the settlement that day, twelve at a time, men, women, kids, all afternoon by shifts. We'd brewed and baked and boiled for this for ten days past. Pea soup with vegetables, with seal and whale meat in it, and little cubes of *matak*, that succulent hide of the white whale! We had a barrel of it. Pea soup, and bread with butter on it, jam and cake, and beer to wet it down. And piled up at the place of every guest were Christmas presents neatly wrapped. Gee, we had fun.

At Justina's table were gathered the very cream of the aristocracy of Igdlorssuit. Rudolf and Marghreta, and Abraham and his wife, Louisa, and Rudolf's brother Hendrik, and his Sophia, and —well, all the best and most important people of the place. And at the table's head, Justina.

And while at the places of all these important people and dear friends were piles of handsome presents, at Justina's place were at least as many as all the rest put together, so many, in fact, that we'd put chairs around to hold the overflow.

The guests came promptly to that sitting, for all knew of the surprise that awaited Justina. She, the heroine of all of it, came last. How sweet she looked! We led her to her place: here, these are yours, Justina.

She gave a little gasp, a swift and audible intake of breath. Then she was calm. Again she became as though of a world somewhat removed from ours, a world to which my coming and this Christmas were not unexpected happenings. She opened up her presents one by one, so carefully! Each one she then rewrapped to lay it carefully aside. And it seemed that by this act each separate thing was taken to herself to be a part of her.

So might end the story of Justina. Yet it goes on. She is a living child, and all that happened on that Christmas now lives on in her. More surely than before she goes her own complacent, quiet way. Be clean!—we'd said. There in the dirty house she lived in she would wash herself: that had become her way. And when we'd have a party she'd be asked.

"Come in, Justina. Have you washed yourself?" She'd nod her head.

"All over?"

"Yes."

"Come, show me."

And she'd come close and pull up her shirt to show her clean-washed belly.

"Good girl."

And Justina would smile with such complacent pride!

A clean, hard-working, faithfully industrious girl. And when in June the head nurse of the children's sanitarium in Umanak came to Igdlorssuit I told her of Justina, of how clean she was, of how she loved all children and toted them about.

"Let's see her," said the nurse.

Justina came. She stood in the doorway dressed in all her best, so bright, so clean, so glittering with earrings, brooches, necklaces, and things. And how her teeth gleamed when she smiled!

The head nurse laughed. "I'll take her."

And now—I write in '34—Justina is at work in the great sanitarium at Umanak. She lives well, works well, earns her pay. With money she can buy fine clothes. And in fine clothes she, not too often, goes on promenade. And at last, grown skillful in the arts of housekeeping and the care of children, she'll marry a fine hunter, live in her own house, have a lot of children of her own, and—God bless her—live happily for ever after.

VI. AT HOME!

A YEAR has passed; I mean that we have told about a year and prophesied for years ahead. *Now* has the schooner come? Yes, two weeks late—that's two weeks later than they said it would—it came. It had my goods on board, my boxes, bags, crates, bales; a marvel for the crowd to see. I stored them in an empty house whose owner was away in summer camp. The lumber came, a huge amount, it seemed; cement, stove, stovepipe, roofing paper, doors and windows, concrete chimney blocks, a raft of stuff. They'd sent the makings of the house, complete, from Denmark. Now all had come, I guessed. And when the schooner had discharged, it sailed away. Now work.

Again my motley crew of men and women stevedores is swarming on the hill; it's like a carnival. The work has livened up the settlement, as though the people had needed to be given boards to play with, as we give children blocks. They played, but somehow got some work done too. So that by the time I had finished pouring the foundation forms, the lumber lay at hand all sorted out and piled. Now for the frame!

Square, saw and hammer, lumber—nails? Where are they? We search through everything, open every box, go through the whole of my effects: no nails. They had forgotten them in Umanak.

It would be hardly fair to write of Greenland, of its noble fiords and mountains, of its unending summer days, of its calm seas, blue skies, and flowering meadows, of the aurora and the stars, of the beauty of its winter-spring, of the goodness of its people, of the warmth of the hospitality of the Greenland Danes, of the benevolence of the whole Danish enterprise, and not say—if it's true—that winter days are dark, and storms at sea severe, and cold intense, and flowery meadows often bogs, and summer days infested by mosquitoes, and people dirty—often lice-ridden, and not always good—and Danes, however kind, too often lazy and incompetent. As I may hope to write exultantly of stirring things, so let me vent my spleen at badness and stupidity. That they exist in Greenland is an open secret to the Danes themselves; that they annoy one let me be a witness. And to those who may respond, quite properly, to my peevish whining about nails, "Who are you, that the authorities should put themselves out for *your* needs?"—I can only say, "Nobody in particular"—for therein lies the point. It wasn't personal, they had no ill intentions; it wasn't only *my* nails they forgot, but everyone's. Not only nails, but oatmeal, bread, molasses, chocolate, lumber, hardware, matches; some one year, some the next. For people hired, put there, to remember things and get them done they're dismally incompetent.

Yet in fairness to the whole colonial management let us remember that I had experience only of Umanak, and that just as prevailing rain may be confined to one locality, so may bad management.

With lumber and no nails there was, nevertheless, enough to keep me busy for some days. The house as planned, I must explain, was Danish in construction. I'd made a sketch of it and, lacking knowledge of Danish timber sizes, had sent it to a talented young Danish architect—may he at last get his reward in fame—who had thereupon drawn up plans and the most minute specifications, in strict accordance with which the Greenland Department in Copenhagen had faithfully shipped out—as I was to find—every last stick and bolt and nut and nail, together with, of course, the specifications. These last were held in Umanak. I'd had one glimpse of them while there and asked to have them. "We'll send them," I was told. I often wrote and spoke of them again. I never saw them any more.

So here was a great lot of unfamiliarly dimensioned lumber;

and what to do with what, that was the problem. And if the house as it now appears isn't just as it was meant to be, it is, nevertheless, a good, strong, tight, substantial little edifice, put there to stay, until some spring the mountain side—it will—rolls over it. The nails? In course of days my chartered motorboat arrived. I went to Umanak and got them. They were expensive nails that came to hold that house together.

The building of the house, that was exciting, stimulating work; house-building is, particularly one's own house. I worked, I'd say, from daylight until dark—if we were writing of the temperate zone. With no such thing as dark to limit me I worked, intemperately, all I could. There was no limit to the working day, just constant hindrance—and of that none but the most exasperating of all hindrances, unwanted help. Two hands God wisely gave us; it is all we need. *More* than we need most times; hence pockets. And to be gifted all at once with a dozen hands, over but two of which you have control, ten extra hands that won't stay put in pockets, is about as disconcerting as anything can be. Reach one hand for a board; have ten more seize it simultaneously. Pick up your saw; and find it weighted with unwanted hands. It's worse than that: the hands have arms attached to bodies on slow-moving legs. You're hemmed in by a crowd; you bump your elbows into them, you stumble on them when you move; you have to wade through them. It's worse than that: they stare. Shall I ever forget the hanging of my inner door! There at the outer doorway, four feet off, massed, filling the entire frame and shutting out the day, were faces. From the faces of little ones peering over the threshold they were ranged in tiers as masks might be displayed upon a wall. The people mounted boxes to see in. Without a word, just looking, watching every little move I made, they stayed and stared. I could have screamed at last from frenzy of annoyance. My best times were at night—daylight, of course, but after suppertime. The people then, as though their union had restricted them to a nine-hour staring day, knocked off and went on promenade. Then I could really work, speed up the job, see progress, get things done.

To finish it, move in: that had become a desperate need. To get away from Trolleman.

My host—I was the guest of Trolleman—was generous to a degree. His hail—"Sit down, speak nothing, make yourself at home"—he meant. Food, drink, a comfortable place to sleep: as host he spread himself. He talked incessantly—the talk became a trial. Let's, for example, stage a bedtime scene:

Midnight. The living-room of Trolleman; couch in corner made up with a feather bed (my sleeping-place). The sun is pouring in and straight across the room, a shaft of golden light.

Kent (*yawning*, *stretching*, *sighing pointedly with weariness*, *says for the third time*): Well, Mr. Trolleman, it's late. I think I'll go to bed. I must be up on time.

Trolleman: Yes, Mr. Kent, me too. Be up on time: that's it. Things shall be done on time, that's my way. Yes, Mr. Kent, on time. They *shall* be. I will wait for nobody. Once, Mr. Kent, I was going to get married. Well, no—I wouldn't say that we were properly engaged—engaged? Is that what you call it? You see, it was this way: There was a party one night in Copenhagen—well, certainly, you might call it a party. There were maybe half a dozen people there. No! now I'm lying, Mr. Kent. There were only five. There was one girl—well, properly speaking you wouldn't exactly call her a girl; she was a grown woman sure enough. She worked in—now what was that street? Do you know the old part of Copenhagen? Well, no matter. And there was this friend of mine. Well, Mr. Kent, I wouldn't say he was my friend as much as my brother's, but we were together a lot. You see that was in—now let's see: I'd come back from Greenland, the East Coast—that trip, you know; the one I told you about; the time I had that picture taken with the whiskers; when the *Teddy* was sunk. Well, yes, you might say she was properly sunk. They had a lot of trouble about . . .

Stop! reader. Don't go out. We'll make this short—if any *want* to hear the end. It's curious. Trolleman, you see, liked this girl, so they planned an evening together. "You shall meet me," said Trolleman, "in the center of the railroad station concourse at eight o'clock." The evening came, the hour neared. At two minutes before eight Trolleman stood in the center of the concourse, his eyes upon the clock. No girl was there. He waited while the minute hand moved up. Just as the hand touched eight he saw the girl come running toward him from the train exit. He turned upon his heel and walked away. He walked fast, out of the station and across the square. He hurried on and on. He heard, at last, the breathless girl draw up behind; he still strode on. She caught up, clutched his arm. "What is the matter?" she cried. "I was there." "Were you," demanded Trolleman, "in the center of the concourse at eight o'clock?" "No, not exactly, but—" "Then I am through with you," said he. He left her, and has never seen her since.

It *is* a curious story. It was more curious as he told it. . . . I came to yearn to finish up my house, move in. Eight days from when I'd laid the sills, I did. It was near midnight when I finished up, swept up, and put the place in order. Then I went down to the little house where all my goods were stored and fetched my bedding. I spread my blankets, shut the door, sat down. I was at home in Greenland.

It was the fourteenth day of August.

VII. ENTER SALAMINA

THE pleasures, pastimes, and dissipations of Greenland life are, as will appear, of the most simple nature. The coming of a boat is an event, a coffee party—a *kaffemik*, as one is called—a festival. And in summer time the mere making and drinking of coffee out of doors is, for the pleasure it affords, a common practice of the people on fair days. They'd always rather be outdoors than in. No wonder! one exclaims who knows their houses.

Now one day during my nail-awaiting period, having been invited to such a kaffemik, I arrived at the appointed place, a lovely hillside stretch of meadow land that faced the Sound, to find the dozen guests already met, and the blue smoke of their little fire of brush ascending peacefully to nowhere. There were Rudolf and Marghreta, Hendrik and Sophia—oh, a lot of people all of whom we'll know well later on—and Anna, who was destined to play a fleeting part in the small domestic drama of my earlier months in Greenland. Anna was neither young—no sweet young thing, I mean—nor beautiful. Not beautiful to Greenland eyes that like blond skin and hair, nor to my own that aren't accustomed to slant eyes, small noses, and big mouths. She was, in looks, pure Eskimo. There is distinction to that type; there is to every type that's cleanly and precisely drawn, defined, that shows a clear intention and achieves it. That quality her features had, perhaps no more. Her narrow eyes were as though drawn by a master hand with firm, strong, delicate precision; her nose—we'll leave that out; her Maker nearly did. Her mouth was, we'd say, huge, no doubt of that. But it was meant to be—as though that Maker had proposed a generous mouth and good strong jaws as all the better, seal, to eat you with. It was a modeled, sculptured mouth with sharp-lined, clearly tinctured lips. And teeth! Anna's were beautiful—quite even, shining white, and small. Yet I have made no case out for her looks: exotic certainly, but disproportioned to our eyes. So I met Anna, and from that moment I'd as lief the rest had been most anywhere but there. She was the day. Yet who she was and where she lived stayed mysteries to me.

As though fair weather had held on for weeks that I might finish building, it began to rain the day that followed on my moving in. It poured. Despite the rain I moved my goods from storage and unpacked them; despite the rain a great crowd stood outdoors and watched me through the open doorway. And there, happening at last to look up and out, my eyes encountered Anna with the rain just running over her in streams. "Anna, come in!" I cried, and in she came. I made her take her wet things off and put on something dry of mine. I stoked the stove and warmed the house. "Now help me work," I said. The way that Anna worked, the quick, deft, noiseless, pleasant way she got things done, the sense of order she displayed, that—if she'd won my heart—now won my hand. "Anna," I said, "will you be my *kifak?*"

A young American lying ill upon what was to prove his deathbed, in winter, in a shack on unpopulated Wrangel Island in the Arctic, lamented in his diary what They, his friends and family at home, might think of the presence there alone with him, nursing him and fending for him, of an Eskimo woman. Strange reason for lament. The friends of men might better feel for those unfortunates for any cause or anywhere left womanless. There's nothing brave in living by yourself—unless one wants to make heroic virtue out of housework. I don't. Who—it had troubled me—would keep my stove alight, my food from freezing up? Who'd have my dinner ready when I came from work? Wash up, trim, fill my stinking blubber lamp? Make my skin clothes and keep them in repair? Work up my boots—those temperamental Greenland kamiks? Friend Olabi? (I've told of him.) He'd been suggested. Bah! If women minced like Olabi they'd drive one mad. Who?—And along came Anna.

"I will," said Anna, "if my husband will let me." For *kifak*, it should be explained, means neither wife nor concubine. Nor does it mean servant in that menial sense that servant has to us. *Employee* is its honorable equivalent.

So Anna came next day with her Johan in tow, a stalwart and well-favored man.

"She may work for you," said Johan pleasantly, "until you can get yourself a permanent kifak. And in return for that I want a glass of schnapps."

"Done!"—And I led Johan indoors. I put two glasses on the table, poured the drinks—first his, then mine. While I was pouring mine, Johan drank his; and while I was corking and setting down the bottle, he drank mine.

"A cigarette?" said I, proffering an open box of fifty.

"Thank you," said Johan. And he put the box into his pocket.

That's valuing your wife.

It is not my intention in this story of which Anna is extremely far from being the heroine to do more than adorn her for that sacrifice, for which most sadly she was destined, by giving her such form and substance as may make the final rout of her and all her forces of allurement to some degree as real and poignant to those who may now read of it as it was then to me. How detail the innumerable moments of deep felicity that we achieved together when, in faithful modest response to, for instance, my explicit directions for the making of baking-powder biscuit, she would serve them up to me hot from the oven, tender, light—how good! How quietly she moved about, mouselike on soft-shod feet; how of the very texture of her were her quiet ways! Her coming, silent as a shaft of sunlight; her last act of the day's routine, the opening of my bed—how by her touch she blessed it for repose!

Often the three of us would dine together; for Johan, reluctant

And this —
is Anna.

though he had at first shown himself to be about even *approaching* those premises to which by bargain he had assigned his wife, was at last led into occasionally consuming in our company that food which otherwise he must have eaten cold and by himself as Anna sneaked it home to him. And it came to be that we all stared mournfully ahead with growing sadness at the inevitable and already appointed day of separation on which, with my departure in search of a permanent housekeeper, this sweet interlude in life would end. So that when I had slept on the last bed that Anna should make for me, and eaten my last breakfast she should maybe ever cook, when she had packed the food for my journey, and tied up for me a little change of clothing in a bandanna from her own head, then we three descended sadly to the shore. And with earnest assurances from me—who knew so little about life—that things on my return would go on virtually as before, and palpably forlorn, straw-clutching words of hope from them—who knew, it proved, so much—we shook hands, and I sailed away. They knew, for Greenland is a little world, of Salamina.

Of all the women of North Greenland, it had been told to me, the most faithful, noble, and most beautiful, most altogether captivating, was she named Salamina. Too much? Ah, no! Not for a housekeeper in a one-room house. And *if* my parting from the gentle Anna and her good Johan allowed one mitigating thought, it may have been of her. We steam away. Smaller and smaller grow the little figures on the harbor hill, their waving handkerchiefs but dots of white. They're gone—and Umanak lies straight ahead.

The Danes of Umanak took an immediate and active interest in my domestic problem. A housekeeper? Of course. You've got to have one. There's Karen—but she's old and feeble; and Martha—well, *I* wouldn't have her. Yes, Dorthe is a beauty, but she's spoiled. And Antoinette's an "*aftenblad*"; you know—an evening paper, spreads the news, *your* news. Oh, Salamina? Yes, she's here. No use; she'd never go. There's . . . "I'll look at Salamina," I broke in.

I used to know a young fellow—a good fellow—of such low-down principles as to employ the telephone to make dates with girls he didn't know; and who would then at the rendezvous hide behind a pillar to first look them over. He played safe; a low-down, wise, abominable practice. I pursued it.

"Take me," I asked, "to see her. Not a word of why."

As I now look back upon that first meeting with Salamina, my thought is of light, of light so bright that I am dazzled by it. I know that the sunlight streamed in through the window, that its shaft cut sharp across a shadowy background and laid a gleaming patch on a scrubbed floor. I know that red geraniums stood on the window ledge and glowed against the sunlight like vermilion fire. I see a room suffused with light, its shadows, even, golden with it. A golden light, and in it, of it, source of it—who knows!—a woman.

"But I have three children," said Salamina, for of course I blurted out my errand, "and I won't leave them." Of course she shouldn't! They must come.

It became very quiet in the kitchen. Salamina thought. "Well," she said, "then I will come. I'll stay with you a while and try it. And if I like it I'll stay always."

Whew! it was storming hard next day. The land ran torrents, and every gulley was a watercourse; and wind! A half-gale swept the fiords. It stormed all morning, and all afternoon till four. Then in a lull—it looked like clearing up—we sailed. We were a boatful: three men, two women, several children, seven dogs. We were a grateful boatful when some hours later we made a halfway port—just made it, with the ravening, white-toothed gale in full cry at our heels. Yet throughout those turbulent hours battened down below, Salamina, wading in a running mess of seasick kids, displayed her quality. She tended them; she cheered a moaning woman, held her head; she mopped and cleaned and put the place at last to rights. Great woman.

Our arrival at Igdlorssuit was no less an event than every other boat arrival. Someone, as always, climbing about on the hills descried the boat a long way off. Up went the shout to be reëchoed by the settlement. The houses all, at that, disgorged their inmates; and long before the boat drew near, the harbor hill was thronged with people. For maybe the first such time in all her life Anna, on the day of our arrival, was neither on the harbor hill nor on the shore. Smoke from my chimney told the tale.

It was a great procession that climbed the hill to my house: I with a child in hand, my family, my dogs; the populace with all our goods shared out so that as many as possible might have a reason for coming. We all marched up together and we all, or all that could, marched in. Here, children, Salamina, here is home! And here is—Anna.

There Anna stood. She was dressed in her best clothes and wore a spotless apron, that I had given her, to protect her costume's spotlessness. She stood demurely there and from a lowered face looked up at us and shyly smiled. Then Anna came to Salamina, came up close, sweetly reached out her arms and moved to kiss her. That kiss was never given; it never will be. What harm, what lasting enmity one swift, hard, calculated look can start! Anna took her apron off, dropped it on a bench, went out. She was the first to go.

VIII. O LIBERTY!

THE house that we have come to, with the family, is small: one room. There is a sleeping-platform in an alcove, and over it a trap door to a low and narrow loft. There's a low cellar underneath; there had to be, on that side hill. It proved as cold in winter time as all outdoors. I hadn't planned that house for family life, and when I'd signed on Salamina and her brood in Umanak, I'd thought to add a room, and told her so.

But one night, soon after we had all returned, as I was sitting there drawing, and Salamina sewing, and the children—there were only two, she'd left one child behind—the two children asleep in bed, Salamina, lowering her work, looked up and said, "Why do you build another room? One room is quite enough." And I, thrilled at escaping all that work—I had a shed and storehouse still to build—said, "Good! we'll go on as we are." So far one thing alone had troubled her: my sleeping on the floor. She was in all respects, I was to learn, a stickler for propriety; she cared what people said. The master's sleeping on the floor reflected, she contended, on her credit. She wept at my insistence. I told her that in America men always gave their seats to women—and offered them their beds.

So lived we four, for weeks; until Frederick, the elder child, aged maybe eight, was taken to the sanitarium in Umanak: incipient t.b. That left us three. Two, I might almost say: that little mouselike, silent, five-year-old Helena, one rarely heard a whisper from her lips, never a cry. She answered yes by arching up her brows, and no by wrinkling her small nose. That is the Greenland way. She'd sit an hour on the platform edge without a movement or a sound. A sweet, round, healthy little child, her playground was outdoors. She kept what hours she pleased, did as she pleased —except when, rarely, given an order. Then she obeyed, at once, implicitly. She was never punished; Greenlanders don't punish children. Is it in consequence of this that Greenland children are so good?

To Salamina I relinquished all the cares of housekeeping, except—this brought contention—instruction in the art of cooking. She knew a little that she'd picked up here and there; that little made the trouble. She was glad to be shown things that she knew nothing about—such as how to make baked beans or cook spaghetti with tomato sauce—but she didn't like my criticism of her bread nor being told her sauce had lumps. When she would listen she was quick to learn, but having learned she didn't like man's meddling in affairs that were, she held, exclusively a woman's. And over bread-making we had unbelievable scenes. I'd show her how: I'd mix the yeast, the sour dough, and ripen it. She'd never worked with sour dough before. I'd mix and knead the bread. I'd fix it for the night, tuck it up warm against all drafts. I'd work it into loaves and stand the loaves to rise. She'd watch me scornfully. And the minute I'd be out of sight she'd pop the half-risen bread into a half-ready oven, and ruin all. Again I'd make the bread—to have it again ruined by her defiant disobedience. Once, having set the loaves to rise and strictly ordered her to lay no hand on them, I flew into such a fury at her putting them ten minutes later into the oven that I pulled them out again and hurled the lot outdoors. That tamed her for the moment; she left the house in tears. I made and baked new bread. It turned out—God be praised!—perfection. That settled things. And now Salamina, using old-time sour dough—she swears by it—makes the only first-class A-1 white bread that I've tasted in North Greenland. If you're going to do a thing you'd better do it well.

That might, in fact, be Salamina's motto. She did things well and took great pride in it. If my kamiks were not well cut and made, my anoraks—the hooded cotton shirts that all men wear in

Greenland—not exactly right in cut and fit, and *clean*, if the house was not always in order and the floor and benches scrubbed, she held it to be a reflection upon *her*. "What will people think of *me?*" she'd say. She was of incorruptible integrity in her craftsmanship. She was a kifak, to be sure, an employee; but not to be employed except to do things well.

And she was more than that, took more than mere employment on herself. She made herself the mistress of the house. In the absence of another woman there, that was, to her, her right, responsibility, and privilege. Her immediate and ruthless disposal of Anna was but the first act of cleaning out *her* house. No interlopers should be there; she'd have no carrying over of old debts or old encumbrances. Or did she sense that I *liked* Anna?

That too was her concern. The house, the home, and me: the lot, as one, the woman's chattel—hers. Liberty in the choice of friends and guests, in choice of whom I'd greet on promenade, or promenade with, liberty in general which I had so taken for granted as not even to have thought of it, was suddenly made something to aspire to, to scheme toward, assert. It was, to put it mildly, disconcerting for one who liked in general the conducting of himself to find himself a chattel of the house, pursued, dogged, watched and spied upon, whenever he was pleased to stroll abroad. That we should attend each other when invited out to kaffemiks, or on evening calls upon our mutual friends, was natural enough; and I was as punctilious in the observance of established social conduct as she, my social sponsor, was herself. Then, too, we strolled together—sometimes; *always*, was what got me. The inevitability of her dear company on *every* stroll, of her constraining company. For let me but address myself—address? smile, *look*—at any human creature but a male or a babe in arms or a woman over sixty, and at a look from Her they'd flee. She had strong character; all knew that, felt its force. They visited their fear of her on me; my friends avoided me.

Escape! There was one loophole to a week of freedom: a plan I'd made with Anna and Johan.

IX. SALMON FISHING

JOHAN and Anna, Johan's brother Martin, their cousins Niels and Peter, I; we are the salmon-fishing crowd. The motor-man and crew make altogether nine on board. We sail at seven in the golden afterglow of day, sail on through darkness to the dawn; at dawn, gray early dawn, we're there. And before we can even move our scant camping-outfit up from the slippery rocks on to the shore above, the boat has left us to steam home again. Five men, one woman, on a point of land, marooned.

The land is sodden after the September rains, a bog. Laden with our camp gear and my heavy canvases we wallow inland to a stony ridge, and there on good dry soil make camp. Within ten minutes we are roasting coffee over a crackling fire of green creepers: good! How good it smells—the burning evergreen, the coffee smoke, the earth. The coffee roasted, Martin mashes it by pounding it with a stone. We brew the coffee, pour, and drink. How good that steaming coffee tastes—and feels! At last what sensual delight to sprawl there on the ground and spread our arms and legs to the delicious warmth of the new-risen sun.

The secret of contentment seems to lie in never *having* to do anything. And in always being privileged—if you should want to do—to do exactly what you want. Accordingly, after an hour or so, the four men gathered up a little gear and set off in the skiff that had been left with us, to row across the bay to the salmon stream: they want to fish. I take my paints and a canvas and go off along the shore: I want to paint. And Anna just stays sitting by the tent: she doesn't want to do anything.

It is possible—one seeks an alibi for every failure, and for that morning's work I needed one—it is quite possible that if Anna had not chosen to sit there so alluringly idle, that if she had not immediately upon arrival at camp brightened her looks in the cold water of a near-by trickle and ordered them by a little pocket mirror, if she had not for "roughing it" gotten herself up in her best clothes, that if she had not been Anna or not been there at all, I would have loved the scenery undividedly, and painted better. At any rate very little of the splendor of that day came to be reflected upon my canvas; so that, after the mildest and most perfunctory effort to make something of the picture, I quit, packed up my gear, and walked back home to camp. There, sitting as I'd left her, by the tent, was Anna. Oh, how much more worth while, I thought, than sea and sky and ice and russet mountain sides is Anna, sitting there!

And how much that all gained as, sitting there beside her, I faced out upon the same scene I'd been painting; how it contented me. We sat there silently and looked. One had no need to cry, "Look! see!" to tell the other what was there. Each drank of it as he desired: that was good. If life could always be like that we'd have no need of art. It was therefore of little consequence that my knowledge of Eskimo was limited to a few mispronunciations of the names of common things, and to the understanding of still less. We couldn't talk. Who cared! And although there were times during those camping days when participation in the general conversation would have been a bit enlivening to me, speech with Anna, now, could only have served to give conventional substance to such thoughts as substance doesn't make more real. Some things don't gain by being talked about.

Not mountains, certainly, nor space, nor ice, nor the sea. Nor day and night. "Still as the night, deep as the sea"; "as cold as ice"; "as vast as space": these things as elements of man's environment are elements of thought, emotion, speech. Speech at its highest, art—its metaphors and symbols, its rhythms and harmonies, its moods, its forms, its being—is derived by man from his environment. To Anna sitting there what *could* be said? Did my exotic culture fit me to point out to her new beauties in that world which was her own from birth? What could I feel that was at most not part of her experience? What did I know, what *can* one know of all-essential things, that all men don't? We couldn't talk; and that contented us. And it was with reluctance that we at last heeded the murmurings of empty stomachs, and cooked dinner.

Boiled seal! We sat with the pot between us and fished out the chunks with our fingers. Then we'd each grip a mouthful with our teeth and, hanging on to the chunk with one hand, slice the mouthful off. I cut my nose, and Anna looked distressed; I laughed, then so did Anna. And when we had eaten all we wanted we put the cover on the pot and wiped our knives on the grass; with that, the housework done, we stretched out in the sun like well-fed dogs. We peered off into the purple zenith and thought how deep is space. We closed our eyes against the sunlight, and the red translucence reinvoked the deep security and peace of the prenatal world. We slept.

I woke up with a start, sat up, sat blinking at a colorless gray world. What! lying round like this, and no work done! Still drunk with sleep I staggered to my feet, picked up my painting gear. Anna moved slightly. She looked at me through half-closed lids, and smiled. She recomposed herself and in an instant was asleep again. I strode away. Damned working conscience!

At least, I thought, as three hours later I regarded my picture from a distance and realized that I had made a sky that looked almost like space, a mountain that looked almost like rock, a sea that was almost water—had made, in short, two dimensions look almost like three, and pigment to suggest, remotely, light—at least I've painted a fine picture. So, this time packing up my conscience with my paints and brushes, I ran off to join Anna, whom I had observed for the past hour far up on the hillside busily making blueberries into flesh and blood. She smiled a purple smile and showed me hands dyed purple with the berries' gore; showed me her hands and what her hands had done: a gallon pail half full. So we browsed about together, Anna steadily progressing from bush to bush and I, as though in competition, dashing off for more spectacular finds. And when I'd get a handful of particularly big ones I'd give them to Anna to eat; and when Anna would pick a handful of big ones she'd eat them herself. Maybe she thought I didn't like the big ones—that I gave them all away.

It was different that evening as we sat at supper, again fishing out boiled seal meat with our fingers. Then Anna, seeing that I left the better parts for her, assumed, quite rightly, that I didn't know which parts were best. She chose and handed me the choicest morsels—that, tasting them, I so might learn to help myself.

Darkness had come, a raw east wind, a splash of rain.

"Where are the men?" I asked.

"Why, they're not coming back tonight," said Anna, fishing out another chunk of meat.

She must have read my thoughts or heard my heart. She looked across and laughed.

Anna was some time finishing the contents of the pot. No hurry, Anna; all the night is ours. And stuffing into the fireplace what remained of the creepers that we had gathered, blowing them into a blaze, I ran off in the light of that to pull up more. We'll celebrate, I thought, and having deposited a great bale of fuel near at hand and fed the flames with more, I turned toward Anna with eyes that in the lurid firelight must have blazed and sparkled with my thoughts. I looked at Anna. God!

"Anna," I cried, "what's wrong?" I leaped, and knelt beside her. "Anna! Look up!"

She hung her head, she clasped her belly, groaned. "Oh! O——h." She rocked with agony, and turned a haggard, pain-distorted face my way. Good God! Poor child! a bellyache.

With extraordinary tenderness I got her up and led her groaning into the tent. I lit a candle there and laid her bed. I covered her and tucked her in. And there she lay all huddled up with pain, groaning and softly whimpering. I blew the candle out and lay down next to her. Pitch-darkness; the gentle sound of rain on the canvas of the tent, and Anna's whimpering. O night of love: come dawn!

Sometime before daylight Anna's pain grew worse. Now what to do! I got up, lit the candle. We had a cooking-pot, a coffeepot, a berry pail, and a quart bottle. The berry pail had holes in it: that was useless. The bottle had petroleum in it: I'd deal with that in time. Taking the cooking-pot, I groped my way down to the shore and filled the pot with sea water. Returned, I lit the primus stove and put the pot to boil. I poured the petroleum into the coffeepot. Then when the water was hot I poured it by means of a paper funnel into the bottle. I corked the bottle and wrapped a shirt around it. And I placed it carefully on Anna's aching belly. And inasmuch as the next I knew it was broad daylight, the bottle must have done the trick.

Anna *was* ill; she looked it the next day. She was not of a robust type, being even more femininely fashioned than most Greenland women, and her pain had left her wan and pale and spiritless. She lacked, too, the moral fiber to resist displaying that she suffered —or the will to. And after a morning spent in coddling her and humoring her plaintive mood, it was more with the thought of *making* her pull herself together than out of real impatience that I at last reproached her, picked up my painting things, and left.

After some hours of work I returned to find Anna sitting up in bed, considerably refreshed, and looking over illustrated Danish reviews which she had brought with her. She greeted me with a sad smile, at the same time stowing away behind her with an air of rather blatant secrecy that copy at which she had apparently been looking as I entered. So, entering into the spirit of her little game, whatever it might be, I sat down and with the hidden review as my objective took up the others one by one and studied them. There were pictures of Copenhagen and pictures of the King and Queen and Greta Garbo; of motorcars and airplanes; of soldiers and big guns and tanks (God knows what Anna made of *them!*), pictures of things and people of the world outside. I looked at them—too long, perhaps. For presently Anna drew out as though covertly the hidden copy, opened it just a trifle, and peeked in. I become all attention.

"Anna, let me see."

She claps it shut and holds it tight against her breast.

"Come, let me see," I urge, and gently force it from her.

I open it. Not Greta Garbo this time, not the King. It's *me!*—a snapshot that I'd given her, tucked in those pages, brought along by her.

Anna has hung her head again; she's crying. And she's laughing too.

Far off across the bay appeared a dark speck on the water; it was the boat of the returning fishermen. Slowly throughout an hour it drew nearer, at last near land to disappear behind the shore. And when the four heavy-laden men came tramping up across the bog I had the home fire roaring out our greeting. The men came tramping up each with a heavy sack. Four in a row they halted, dropped their loads; they drew themselves up straight, relieved, and grinned. And then, as one, stooped down, and lifting up the sacks by their bottom corners spilled out the gleaming fish. Johan went straightway in to Anna, and while that loving couple billed and cooed, we started dinner. With the whole fish cut in chunks to fit the pot, the pot stuffed full and filled to brimming over with sea water, the fire stoked, the pot set on to boil, we fell to eating sliced raw fish—hors d'œuvre. Then suddenly the pot is boiling and the fish is done. Out come Johan and Anna hand in hand; now serve the meal.

Two flat stones have been brought and planted near the fire. A selection of the choice parts of the fish is taken from the pot and laid on one stone; the remainder is poured out in a big heap on the other. I am to eat, it seems, alone. I came to thank my stars for that. For no sooner has the common mess been served than the natives fall upon it like a pack of ravenous dogs. And after about one minute of the most terrific gulping and sucking and spitting out of bones their stone is clean. And they sit licking off their well-smeared hands and chops and watching me toil on. After a second pot has been disposed of, and a third, we call ourselves well fed. The men are tired; it is dark and cold. We go to bed.

The flimsy, crazy, flour-sacking tent had been pitched by its owners with incredible disregard of what terrain it covered. The spot was fairly level, but since the dry elevation on which our camp stood was essentially a glacial stone dump, there were not only rocks sticking up all over it but rocks of every size not inches deep below its spongy top soil. What cleaning up and filling in I'd done for the comfort of Anna and me was of little use now in the disposal of six bodies in that crowded space. I had the half-delirious thought through half the night that I was a being of gigantic proportions—and gigantic sensibilities—reclining with my head and shoulders on the Rocky Mountains, my rump on the High Sierras, my calves on the Coast Range, and my feet—it rained—in the Pacific Ocean. No wonder then that in that subconscious adjustment toward comfort which sleepers practice I managed to crowd over into Anna's feather bed; nor that Anna sleepily impelled to reach for room should shove Johan off under the drip of the tent eaves; nor that Johan, being very tired, should sleep on undisturbed. Nor that on the other side of me, Martin, Peter, and Niels should for warmth's sake crowd me close. Good God! we *had* to crowd. For had these fellows brought a thing to sleep on or to cover up with? Scarcely. A child's size feather bed for Anna; and gunny sacks for them. So that the fortunately wide guanaco robe which I had brought—for *me*—became the cover for us all. They were a very tired lot, those fishermen; they must have been. For what their lice—they had a few, it proved, not many—what they could do to wake their hosts, they did. And failed. The sleeper's snores proved that, and how! I'd never known how hoglike man could be, I'd never guessed that men could strangle in their sleep and live. Whew! what a night of noise. The rain, the wind, the flapping tent, the swash of waves along the shore, the periodic thunderous reports of splitting icebergs as the storm herded them against the shoals, the itch-maddened scratching of fingernails on cloth—like claws on wrinkled walrus hide; the belchings of glutted guts; the snores like the death agonies of strangling men! They'd start at nasal pitch and descending gutturally increase in fervor to a choking orgasm that would burst in spasms of coughing. All this in darkness in that crowded tent, by darkness magnified, made horrible.

We two lay there together, side by side, awake; and like children of a fairy tale lost in a storm at night in an enchanted forest we drew as close as possible and put our arms around each other. Somehow I must, at last, have slept.

For when next day I said to Anna, "Do all Greenland men snore so disgustingly at night?" she answered, "Perhaps; but you slept too."

Five men, a woman, forty fish: the fish would last two days. In two days we'd be traveling home again: why trouble to catch more? That was apparently the reasoning of the Greenlanders; it was certainly their mood. And so, although the whole enterprise had been embarked upon in order to catch fish for winter use, the fishermen now abandoned themselves to eating up what had been caught, to desultory berry-picking, and to sleep. I plied my trade, ate fish and berries, slept. Except for a couple of hours of general conviviality in the tent preceding bedtime the repetitions of this sequence constituted life. The evening was the day's event.

It was as much for warmth as from the crowding of the little tent that we sprawled there in the close, familiar contact of a family of dogs. The tent was damp, the nights were cold; and while in bringing along my primus stove I had yielded to the men's last-minute request for that luxury, I had defeated them by bringing very little petroleum. I meant to live those days in Greenland style. So like true Greenlanders we communized our body heat, and by the most familiar rubbing of elbows kept approximately comfortable. All the men showed Anna great consideration; yet in the seating arrangements of our evenings at home she can only be said to have occupied a place *between* the two best seats. Those places were by courtesy Johan's and mine. And if it so happened that there was room at but one side of Anna, and that Johan occupied it, he invariably yielded it to me for some small fee in cigarettes. Johan was not a man to miss one chance at profit. And in offering me his wife for my pipe, as he eventually did, he only showed how little Christianity had done toward altering his race's ancient concepts. He liked my pipe. "For that," he said, "you may take Anna off into the hills and live with her as long as you want to."

A reasonable offer, one would say; and my declining it upon the ground of special sentiment toward that pipe was understood. For Anna? Pipes by the dozen if I had them—but not that one. And although we failed to come to terms—I offered my aluminum pot or a carton of cigarettes, and refused my movie camera—the negotiations did establish this: Since Anna could be reasonably bought, one might not steal her.

At any rate I might sit next to Anna. So tendering Johan an empty milk tin for the privilege, we exchanged places, adjusted ourselves to the topography of the floor, lit pipes and cigarettes, and sang. If in the eyes of God wife-trading is a sin, the ears of God forgave us. How sweetly, with what rhythm and true harmony, those people sang! Add to your thought of gems in dark unfathomed ocean caves, of unseen flowers, violets by mossy stones, that music in the wilderness that night. Look down, O God, upon the Northern world, look searchingly and close; let Your celestial eyes grow used to that pitch-darkness, to the wind and rain. Pitch-black? No, look again where Greenland lies. That endless, tortuously winding, quivering thread of lesser darkness: see it? The surf? That marks a shore. Inside the line, inside its loops and circles, there, if You like, *is* darkness: that's the land. Do people live there? Is there life at all? Look close again—there in the blackness of what seems to be a great peninsula; look hard. We've had to look—we men, to strain our eyes and powers of faith—for God. *We've* peered off heavenward on starless nights to find one solitary little gleam of hope, one star. *You* look. Ah, have You found it? Yes, it's faint; only a tallow candle shining in a tent. It is a wild night, and the candle gutters in the wind. What sound!—the gale, the roar of surf along a thousand miles of shore. Your uproar, God. Incline Your ear as we've inclined ours—

sometimes—to Your still, small voice. Lean toward the tent and listen. Hear it?—a song? It's sweet. The words are strange to Your trained European ears; the melody You know. You love it, God. It's sweeter to You in this wilderness than the choirs of St. Peter's and St. Paul's. What! weeping, God? Because they're really "Nearer" than they know "to Thee?"

That night the tent went down. Something got under it—the wind, I guess—and lifted it, and hurled it clear; it left us lying in the rain. While the rest still lay there laughing at so quaint a happening, I jumped up in a rage at everything to fix it back. That got the men on to their feet; otherwise, rather than trouble themselves, they would have merely huddled closer and endured it.

Nights passed, and days. We sat up late, the fourth, all packed; the boat was due. We lay down, slept; then daylight came, no boat. No boat that day. The little coffee we had brought was gone; we lived on fish. The salmon gone, they took to fishing near the shore for fiord cod. Boiled fish was every meal. It rained: the tent, our clothes and boots, got wet, and stayed. The nights were best: we huddled closest then and slept.

It came to be the seventh night; what time?—who knows? Dark, calm, a fine rain rustling on the tent, waves lapping on the shore, the snores of sleeping men, two throbbing hearts. "Thud, thud, thud, thud," they went; they had been pounding so through hours of near-consciousness. "Thud, thud," they pounded on. "Thud, thud, chug, chug, *chug*, *chug*, CHUG, CHUG." Anna sat up. Sh! Listen! Clear to our ears through every sound came that: the motorboat.

A Greenland doctor's periodic visits to the outlying settlements of his district rarely coincide with times of imminent need: how could they? He can at most inspect the general health, leave a fresh supply of medicines with the native midwife, give the people his best wishes, and pass on. Quite unexpectedly, so late in so tempestuous a fall, the doctor visited Igdlorssuit. "It is good that you come now," said the people to the doctor, "for five human beings and Kinte are at Umivik. Their boat is in the harbor quite disabled, and they are without means of returning." It was the doctor's boat that fetched us home.

It was the doctor's food most generously sent along that we consumed: hot coffee, bread, and meat. And when at last even Johan had ate and drunk his fill, I sent them all except Johan and Anna aft to the motor cockpit, to huddle there and get what shelter from the rain they could. It was the doctor's boat, hard luck! I knew the rules. But it was not too comfortable in the cabin, for our clothes were wet. Anna lay down on one locker and I covered her with my guanaco robe; I lay uncovered on the other, and Johan sat up at Anna's feet. Brrrr—it was cold! I thought so; it seemed Johan soon thought so too. For presently, pushing Anna over to make room for him, he lay down there beside her, and tucked the guanaco robe about them both. My robe! My—no, I had kept the pipe—*his* wife; his deft appropriation of them both exasperated me. He snored: that settled it.

On the cabin shelf lay two cigars, the doctor's. I got up, took them in my hand, crossed to that snoring boor, and woke him. "If," said I in the clearest language of word and sign, "you'll get up, go on deck, shut the hatch, and stay away from here until we get to Igdlorssuit, I'll give you these." He did.

Salamina was not one to whom explanations were ever in order. If at such a crisis as that homecoming she lowered herself to even listen to my eulogy of my own conduct, it was with so disconcertingly skeptical a smile as to shake one's faith in one's own alibi. "*Imaka*,"—"perhaps"—she would say when I had faltered to an end. That settled it. This day she met me at the shore and led me home.

"I have things on me that bite," I said. "A few."

She made short work of them. "That," she said as she finished, "is what you get for associating with such people."

And when that night, not long after her two children had been put to bed, she had tucked me into my bed on the floor, and had put out the light, she came and knelt down beside me. "What . . ." I started to say, when my questioning mouth was stopped by a cold wet washcloth. She wiped my mouth with it, knelt over me, and kissed good night.

X. BELUGA

SEPTEMBER, late September; cold. The Northern sky is luminous under a heavy canopy of low, dark clouds. A north wind penetrates your clothes, your flesh; it nips your bones.

Hands in his pockets, shivering, the sluggish-witted son of Tukajak stands by bewildered by my whirlwind speed. Come! step on it, you Lucas! Here, rip this plank. You priceless Tukajak, slap on that paint. What! cold? Well—toddle home and get your mittens on. But hurry; work. We'll finish up today. I make and hang two storeroom doors, fit in a cellar window frame, calk it and board it tight. Now up with all the perishable foods. Pack this—and that—in straw. Good! Now the yard. Clean off that ice-caked lumber with a spade. Stack it, with strips between. Sweep up the chips. Whew, how they blow about! A whirlwind, north-wind finish. Done!—and it's six o'clock, the thirtieth. Come, winter.

And it occurred to many who had watched the work all day that fixing up one's house for winter was a sound idea, that they would do it for themselves some day. Some day? Forever will the sod lie blooming on the meadow lands, the winter's turf uncut, the house walls crumbling. Spurred by necessity at last, each year too late, half-frozen men will pry a few clods from the frozen ground to plug their eaves where winter whistles in—and let it go, this year, at that.

Yet there is enough desultory tinkering going on in the settlement to complete with sound of saw and hammer and with show of work the season's drama of impending change. Men *are* at work, some men, and compensate for the neglect of their houses by overhauling and repairing such gear as work of a day or week ahead requires. Down on the level strand they're spreading out and mending nets, big nets with eight-inch mesh of heavy twine. October promises, it seems, some monstrous harvest.

It is curious how little our imaginations concern themselves with the world beneath the surface of the sea, strange that imagination soars, and never swims. We project ourselves in thought so readily into an element which in its lower strata supports no mammal life, and in its upper, and beyond, prohibits life in any form, and rarely even dream ourselves into that subsea universe which is a habitat of our own kin. So while poets rhapsodize about the feathered lower vertebrates and dress the angels in their wings, such real kindred of ours in flesh and blood as, for instance, *Delphinapterus leucas*—as sweet, as sleek, and (if we may judge him by his silly countenance) as pleasant an enormous relative as man may have—is born, aspires, swims his life out, dies. And no one cares.

Yet if we did, if we but followed him in thought into the fluid element which is his world, in thought looked upward from those depths, saw the blue sky, the sun, the moon, the northern lights, the stars, the day and night through varying depths of that translucence, soared in thought surfaceward through an inverted wilderness of ice—inverted bergs eight times the height of ours, stalactite mountains pendant from the sky—burst foaming out into the blinding day to feel the sun's hot rays an instant, breathe the air, if we could comprehend *that* gamut of experience and realize in thought one day of what is life to the insensate whale, it might, in fact, prove more than mind could bear. No wonder whales look stupid.

Just as the pupil of the eye contracts when looking at the light, so may whales' brains have shrunk, their bulk increased, to fit them to endure the daily spectacle. To fit them to endure the *hazards* of existence there; they too must be of monstrous nature. Imagine the autumnal overclouding of the arctic depths as ice forms over them; that sudden imposition of a deathlike stillness there; the threat of that to every swimming thing that breathes our air. Seals make their breathing-holes and keep them clear; whales can't. Thick ice, to them, means death. And the occasional desperate crowding of the monsters to a lead in ice of wide extent, their persistence at that lead, heads out for air, despite the gathering of hunters to a slaughter, proves last necessity.

The southerly migrations of *Delphinapterus leucas*, or Beluga, or, as he's really called (but not to be confused with the gigantic Moby Dick), White Whale, are of such perennial regularity as to time, and follow so undeviatingly one course, that what befalls him isn't to be wondered at. His fat is plenteous and rich, his meat is good, his hide is succulent. Men know his ways: God help the whale!

The nets of Igdlorssuit were set on October 2: promptly on October 3 the cry goes up, "*Katakak!*" The whales have come: one's caught.

Out come the people from the houses, all of them. They run far down along the shore to where a few rods out some men are laboring in a boat. It is a dull gray morning, bitter cold. It's cold enough to watch that work—let alone plunging your hands into that icy water as the men are doing. Slowly, fathom after fathom, the heavy net is drawn from the water, passed along. The men are straining now, and their weight bears down the gunwale so that the choppy sea slops in. White flukes emerge; a rope is passed around the tail, secured. They clear the net and let it go. Time out to chafe numbed fingers. Now to the oars. They pull along the shore down to abreast of Trolleman's, there beach their prow. The crowd takes hold; they draw the boat on land. Then all, men, women, children, putting their shoulders to the whale's towline, draw him out—across the beach, across the flat, to—snap! The line has parted and the people sprawl. There is a roar of laughter—but there lies the whale.

And now from bed and house emerges Trolleman, struts Trolleman, all puffed out with his furs and feathers and his pride. "Well, well, well, well!" he cries. "What's this? What's this?— See how I do it, Mr. Kent?"

"See how *you* do it?" I say, innocently enough, for the smallest child seems to have had more to do with it than his nibs.

"Why yes, Mr. Kent; my net, my whale."

"I see: your crew."

He stopped in his tracks, for he had all this time been strutting about with a superb air of command. "Crew!" he cried in excited astonishment. "There is no crew. I do it. I always do it. No, Mr. Kent, no crew. You see, Mr. Kent," he went on confidentially, "when you have a crew you divide with them. That doesn't do. No, no. I do the work myself. Oh, well"—a little deprecatingly— "I let them go and help. They like that. Oh, no, Mr. Kent, no, no, no, no; no crew."

Meanwhile the whale was being expertly dissected, the fat and meat being carried off and deposited in the owner's store shed, and the hide—*matak*, as it is called—being as rapidly devoured as half a hundred human jaws could do it. And although the scene was one of carnage in which everyone got thoroughly besmeared with blood, I must at once dispel the thought that white-whale hide, either raw or cooked, is anything less than one of the most palatable delicacies of the world. Yet how describe it as a thing to eat? Tough? As rawhide it is used for whips and lines. Fresh, in the teeth, it has almost rawhide toughness and the resilience of rubber bands. Chew rubber bands to know how eating matak feels. Imagine rubber yielding, as you chew it, the flavor—hardly that, the sweetness, the degree of sweetness—of a watermelon. It isn't that, of course, but let that do: sweetish, with flavor undefined. Cooked it's quite different. Cut into little dice, in soup, it is not unlike green turtle. Cut into strips of little-finger size and fried, it curls up prettily, comes to have the consistency of rather tough fried scallops and a flavor less like them but equally delicate. In rich brown gravy stews, plain boiled, or, better, boiled and served with rice and curry sauce, young matak is too tender for a knife and good enough to make a French chef's everlasting fame. But eaten icy cold; gripped with the teeth and hand-sliced nose-wards, bolted down: that is the best, they say who know. And until Trolleman put a stop to the feast by carrying away what slabs of hide remained, just that was going on magnificently.

When all that was of interest to man had been removed, the dog pack that at whip-lash radius had all the while been held at bay was let come in. There was a rush, a hundred-throated snarl. Two deep they seethed above the whale's remains. Dogs weltering in blood and guts: exit Beluga.

My net—I had, of course, to set a net, get matak, meat for man and dog, get fat, get rich (great plans I had!)—was late in getting finished. The season was upon us before I grasped its full importance in our local life, and realized that I too might catch whales. Now I was not, like Trolleman, going into this thing alone. One thinks of whale-catching as being a communal sport; as such I welcomed it. I was primarily—the student of mankind must be—a fisherman of men. So, with my men, the crew I netted, we'll begin the tale.

A stranger entering a busy community to take his place in it in enterprise may not expect to find its best men at his service, unemployed. I was therefore surprised and pleased at finding at Igdlorssuit, at the very moment when I needed men and least could hope to find them, a man of such striking superiority as my near neighbor, Abraham Abrahamsen. He was a decent, upright, and industrious man, a fair hunter, and one who in general pursued his own way and minded his own business. I trusted him at sight, and made the enterprise ours jointly. And whom he picked to be his crew, and whether they'd be one or two, or what share of his half he'd pay to them, that was his own affair; the cost of net and gear I bore. Quite simple, so it seemed. Nevertheless I was a bit disturbed at learning that his crew when picked was neither one, nor two, but three, and that they were of such character that their aggregate, like that of minus quantities, diminished, not increased, their single worth. Lucas, my trusty's son, might in good company have shown some class—Lucas and Abraham. But what, assuming that they had it, was their mild willingness to work when opposed by the inbred, inborn, cultivated, and cherished professional laziness of Jörn and Joas, by the inertia in the one of a congenital imbecile, and in the other, of a constitutional bum. Not Abraham, I'll bet, picked Jörn and Joas; they picked him. They'd sensed snug berths; they got to bed in them. And the crew's proposal that they set the net at five-mile-distant Ingia, which they proceeded to lay before me, much as it gratified me at the time by its great show of energy was no more, as far as that precious pair was concerned, than a shrewd plan to camp where no one could disturb their holiday. But not even that interest could sustain them against the threat of Isaak's wrath. Who, then, is Isaak?

Closely allied by marriage with the numerous and powerful Nielsen clan of Igdlorssuit was the family of Isaak Zeeb. Isaak himself, though now through age retired from the more active pursuits of Greenland life, enjoyed a reputation for prowess that his diminutive stature made the more remarkable, and for character and wisdom to which the solid qualities of his sons and their respect for him bore witness. His grown sons were Abraham, Johan, and Martin; and of these the eldest, Abraham, was by election, by the universal respect which had won it for him, and by that most substantial ability and integrity upon which the respect was founded, the headman of the settlement. The Zeebs, operating together under the leadership of Isaak, had for many years made the northeasterly point of Ubekjendt Ejland, known as Ingia, their base for the prosecution of the whale fishery, and established themselves there by the erection of two rude turf houses to serve them during the season. This far-sighted provision for themselves, coupled with Ingia's distance from Igdlorssuit and the impossibility of traveling there by land except at lowest tide, put them in the exclusive enjoyment of one of the strategic spots for intercepting the white whale, and encouraged them in that sense of proprietorship of the whole north shore which I and my whale-catching crowd were to run afoul of. Isaak forbade us Ingia.

At any rate that's what I made of what my hoodlum crew were telling me when, in apparent consternation and, I thought, some fright, they flocked to my house. "Why not?" I asked. "How can he keep you out?" Then Abraham explained.

"He says," said Abraham, "that you, being an American, have no right to fish in Greenland."

And Isaak Zeeb, I guessed, was right.

That his point was purely academic, that it was not directed against a threatened extirpation of the white whales by my net, that it was not against myself but us—as fishermen invading Ingia—that it was just old Isaak keeping for himself the whole north shore, that his whole cause was leaky, and Isaak himself a selfish old devil and as shrewd in his defense of vested interests as a hard-boiled corporation lawyer—all this was clear enough. It looked like checkmate in one move.

"Abraham," said I, "if the net were yours, if it belonged to you, would you set it at Ingia?"

"Yes," said Abraham.

"The net is yours," said I. "All you have to do is pay me for it at the rate of half your catch."

Everyone looked at Abraham, and Abraham stood thinking.

"No," he said, "I am a newcomer at Igdlorssuit, and I don't like to make trouble."

I had had no intention of going to Ingia, but now nothing could have stopped me. "Come on," I said, "let's go. The net is yours. I'll take the blame for what we do." And having actually roused a sort of fighting enthusiasm in that half-dead crowd, I packed them off to get their gear together.

And now, damn mad, farewell to common sense. For when an hour later, that October the fifteenth, we embarked, there was loaded into that filthy leaky old rowing tub that we were traveling in as fair and virginal an equipment of sporting goods as ever graced a show window. O tent, so virgin white, O shining pots, O golden primus! God, what desecration was to be! And coffee, sugar, hardbread, pemmican in tins, rice—food: I'd treat them right, my fighting boys! Push off!

This is Jörn — dressed in the pants of a white whale or a Greenland Colony Manager.

It isn't fun to row a Greenland boat. A homemade hybrid, begotten of the dory and the *umiak* by men not sailors and not carpenters; unstable, clumsy, water-logged. Oar fittings?—here one rotten tholepin, there a piece of string, and there again an old bent rowlock flopping in immensity. Oars?—sapling pines with Mississippi steamboat paddles fastened on. Not fun, not work. You *can't* pull hard; I tried. "Now pull, boys, pull!" I cried—and tumbled backwards as my sapling broke. We laughed, and patched it up. It looked, they all did, like some pants one sees: all patches and no pants.

It was a pleasant early winter's day, not cold to one who worked, but bitter if you idled. There were three oars: we froze by turns. And at last after two and a half hours of desultory rowing we turned the point of Ingia and emerged from shadow into the sunlight of late afternoon. There, close behind a rocky promontory, stood the stronghold of the Zeebs. There was their umiak drawn high on shore, there were the two turf houses, and from two stovepipes came the smoke of home fires not for us. We paddled on, and no more greeted the women and children who came out to stare than they did us.

For an hour and more we followed that north shore, a many-mile-long stretch of sand or pebble beach. We passed the Zeebs' three nets, still rowing on. And at last, not far from where the strand was ended by a headland, we took soundings, found four fathom right, and came to land. Meanwhile a strong north wind and all the swell of Baffin Bay had risen against us; we got a thorough wetting in the surf.

The crowd did work that day: we had to; we were cold. We spread the net out on the sand, secured five seal-hide floats along its reach and a whole seal-hide buoy at the corner. We picked two heavy rocks for anchors, and furnished them with wire lashings. We gathered fist-sized stones for leads, tied loops to them, and strung them on. All ready? Set the net.

Both wind and surf had risen steadily; it was a rising tide. Try as we would we couldn't hold the boat bow-on to load it; loaded, we couldn't launch it. In half an hour we had snarled up everything. At last, undoing all we'd done, taking the anchor stones out one by one, planting them there and buoying them, fastening the weights on as we set the net, we got the job done—well. Then having carried the unwieldy boat high up against the gravel bluff that backed the strand, set it upon a rock pile, lashed it down, we slung our camping gear upon our backs and set off to make camp. Yet I don't know how we should have carried all our stuff but for the timely arrival of two youngsters from the "enemy" citadel at Ingia, one of whom, Josef, out of exuberance and to show us what a man he was, picked up a big man's load and came along with it. Nor, but for the leadership of Jörn, who, picking up almost nothing at all, had run ahead quite out of earshot, would we have traveled all the way to Ingia without stopping. He knows a camp site, I had thought, and leads us there. He did: the snug, tight post house there that stood all fuel-stocked to let, to travelers—two kroner a day. There, anyhow, he stood awaiting us. And when I refused to sanction using it, the crowd looked heartbroken.

The whole adventure was beginning to lose its warlike glamour. Not only were we now about to establish our camp in the very dooryard of the enemy, but the enemy himself seemed undisposed to fight. Hear this: Halfway to Ingia, when the weight and clumsiness of our loads was becoming unbearable, we saw through eyes half blinded by the driving snow and sand five men, five Zeebs, approaching us. Here trouble starts, thought I. And as they neared I glowered savagely ahead and passed without a word or look. What then do those men do but turn and overtake me, greet me most pleasantly, and take, insist on it, my load. The situation was bewildering. And fearing lest the Zeebs completely ruin matters by inviting us to come and live with them, I got us all to setting up our tent. Which, with the Zeeb clan lending hand, was quickly and abominably done.

Abraham Zeeb was a stocky man, broad-shouldered, barrel-chested. He was swarthy, black-browed, shaggy-maned; and heavy-featured with Igdlorssuit's Nielsen-Bourbon lip. His was a dour countenance. He came in, tied the tent flap, turned, and smiled in greeting. Dour? His face just shone with warmth and friendliness. Abraham sat down and partook with us of what we had to offer—hardbread with butter on it, coffee; he found it as we all did, good. He stayed a while for courtesy, then left. An hour later he returned and brought as gift to all of us a generous slab of matak. From that time on the greatest friendship prevailed between the rival crowds. Our tent flap was being continually opened for the bursting in upon us on the gale of friendly visitors. Burn, little primus, as you would, the tent stayed cold. And at last after getting warm from inside out—and full—on pemmican and matak stew with rice, we made our several beds as one, and stretched our lengths for sleep.

It was a bitter night, and wild; and the fury of our flapping tent had as its background the continuous thundering of the sea that was now pounding in heavy breakers along the whole north shore. As we had disposed ourselves, I lay with Abraham—not Zeeb—and Jörn on either side of me, while Lucas and the mournful Joas had the wings. Abraham had brought a sort of large pillow measuring two feet by four; Lucas had a proper dogskin sleeping-bag; I had a half-completed reindeer bag, a guanaco robe to compensate for what that lacked, and a woolen poncho to lie on. The other two had nothing. I gave that pair the poncho; they rolled up in it and each other's arms. I spread the fur robe over Abraham and me. And so we slept those nights at Ingia. I've spoken of the sounds: the wind, the flapping of the tent, the thundering of the sea. They didn't drown the gruesome chattering and whimpering of Jörn. What a forlorn and tortured soul that was, to whimper to itself in sleep! Then he was cold, no doubt; still sleeping on he'd kick and jerk his limbs about so that at last in self-defense I took to pounding him. Yet Abraham slept on. And by the light of the still burning candle he looked, with his worsted cap drawn down to just above his eyes and the hood of his anorak across his chin, like a bronze figure of a good and noble knight, his soul at peace. And when the gray light of the dawn came filtering through the tent it found not Abraham. The net—he'd stolen out to visit it.

All the nets were found to be in trouble. The gale kept up; the work we had to save the nets from damage by the ice showed me the risk of such investment. But by the rising-time of Jörn and Joas we had finished.

The wind blew unabated all that second day and night. Except for an occasional trip down the shore there was nothing whatever for us to do but sit indoors; sit there, drink coffee now and then, or cook and eat a meal; sit there and smoke and entertain our guests by welcoming them in to stand and stare and smoke our cigarettes. Sit there—or tumble out to rig more guys against the gale, or pile on rocks to hold the tent to earth. The tent by day was a bleak and cheerless refuge; at night, by candlelight, it was as the warm and glowing heart of the universe. It invited idleness and composed us to the enjoyment of our pipes and of each other's company. So, sitting there that second night, with all our *friends* the Zeebs, and Anna—she was there—all in the tent, all huddled comfortably close, the tent flap tied, young Lucas starts a tale:

"This," says Lucas, "is a story about Dalage."

XI. DALAGE

ONCE upon a time a king's daughter had disappeared, and although the king had sent people to search for her no one had found her. Then the son of another king went out into the world to look for her. He walked and walked. At last one day he saw a castle with three towers. He drew nearer and nearer to the castle and, finally reaching it, could see no people there. He went inside, and there he saw a woman so pale and thin as he had never seen the like of before. She asked him what he wanted. He answered, "I am looking for you." Whereupon she began to relate her story.

"When I disappeared it was Dalage who kidnapped me. There is his picture." And she pointed to a picture hanging on the wall which resembled a big imitation bird, with a tail.

"One can call him," she continued, "by touching his picture. If one touches it carefully he will come and be ever so kind; but if one touches it roughly, he will come and be very angry."

"Oh," said the king's son, "I will call him."

"No!" cried the king's daughter. "Let him come of his own accord if he wants to." And as the king's son reached to touch the picture she strove to stop him.

When, however, he had done it she said to the king's son, "Now hide yourself."

He had just hidden himself under the bed when Dalage appeared. He was furiously angry, and he said: "Why do you summon me so suddenly? It is frightening when one is far away."

Thereupon he took her and let her fall upon the floor, so that a lot of blood flowed from her.

When the king's son saw that, he said to Dalage, "It was not she who called you; it was I."

"Nothing," said Dalage, "is impossible." Whereupon he picked up the blood and breathed on it.

As soon as Dalage had breathed on the blood the king's daughter came to life; yet she was now much paler than before. It was in this manner that she had become so pale. Dalage now took the king's son out of doors with him and, with him, flew away.

After they had been flying for a long time they came to a mountain so high that it could not be passed. Whereupon Dalage said, "Now you shall become a real monkey." And with that he flew away. The king's son looked around and discovered that he had indeed become a monkey.

He now walked around the mountain and observed that below him it was encircled by cliffs, and that a stream led down to a fiord. And he discovered, far below him, a crevice into which he could leap. Down there were trees which seemed to bear fruit.

So he thought to himself: "Now I am a big monkey, so that it doesn't matter if I die. I may, therefore, just as well try the leap." Upon which conclusion he jumped.

Catching hold of the edge of the cliff he crawled along until he reached the very edge of the crevice. He could not possibly, he thought, risk jumping into that abyss. "But," he continued, "what does it matter if I die?" And so he jumped. And he landed at the bottom on his stomach, but in such a way as not to hurt himself at all. So, going to the stream, he drank and drank. And then, going into the forest, he ate of the fruits until he felt satisfied. And he came finally to settle in that wood, to there continue eating of the fruit and drinking of the stream.

Now one day he saw the masts of a ship at the mouth of the fiord. He watched it drawing nearer until at last it entered the fiord and, sailing up, dropped anchor off the mouth of the stream. While the sailors were fetching water from the stream, the monkey cut branches from the trees and put some of them in the water and some on the beach. Then when the tide rose he got on to the branches and sailed out as the wind carried him.

Now the sailors, having fetched the water, wanted to set sail. Whereupon the captain, seeing the monkey, told the crew to take him on board, for a monkey's presence would insure them a fair wind. This having been done, and the skipper having taken the monkey to live with him, a fair wind arose and the ship sailed off. They had a fair wind all their way; and the monkey, being a monkey, copied everyone on board.

One day they came to a kingdom where the king's secretary had just died. The king requested samples of handwriting from everyone on board the ship, from boy to skipper. For if anyone could write as well as the secretary who had died, the king would take him for that place.

Now when the skipper started to write, down in his cabin, the monkey, who was there, copied him. And the skipper, hearing the scratching of a pen, looked around and saw the writing. He found it to be so beautiful that no one could possibly equal it.

The skipper, having finished his letter, took the letters from all the crew, and also the monkey's letter. He went with them to the king and displayed them—all, from the boy's to his own. The king had the letter of his deceased secretary at his side. He looked at all the letters, and compared them. Then he threw them all away.

"Now," the skipper said to the king, "try to look at my monkey's letter."

At this the king grew very angry, and said, "Don't try to make a fool of me by showing me your monkey's letter."

But the skipper said again, "Try to look at it."

And the king said, "Let me see it."

The king compared it with the writing of his deceased secretary and found that it was exactly the same.

Then the king smiled. And he said: "Let me buy that monkey."

When the monkey had become his secretary, the king examined it and discovered that it was not a real monkey.

Here one of the circle interrupted the story-teller. "How can you tell whether they are real or not?" he asked.

"It might be done by looking at the hair," suggested another. "A real monkey would have proper fur and not hair."

"No," said Jörn, "you can tell by the genitals. A monkey's are like a dog's. Aren't they?" he asked, turning to me.

I didn't know. There was considerable serious discussion of the point, for it was one of interest. But only I, of those present, having seen a real monkey, and no one having seen an imitation one, it was not decided. "Anyhow, that's how it was," said Lucas; and to a circle breathless with attention, he continued his narrative.

The king now called his daughter, and said to her, "Will you examine my monkey?"

Jörn looked around as though he had scored a point, but no one heeded him.

When she had examined him she said to her father: "This is not a monkey; it is a king's son."

Then the king asked his daughter if it were possible to make him back into a human being.

"It could be done," said the daughter, "but if we do do it, we make the one who made him into a monkey want to fight." But the king insisting upon having his way, the daughter yielded, and said, "Let us then go outside."

When they were come to the garden and had all seated themselves facing each other, a cock appeared from behind a tree. When it breathed, a little sword came out of its mouth; it twinkled and flashed at every breath.

Suddenly the king's daughter got up and started fighting the cock. While they were fighting they disappeared together behind a tree. Then suddenly the king and the king's son heard someone sigh, "Ai, ja," and discovered that the king's daughter had returned to her chair. She said, "I won over him, but he's going to come back."

A little later a large male snake came down the side of a slope. And every time it breathed, fire came out of its mouth. And the fire twinkled and flashed. All of a sudden the king's daughter got up and started fighting with the snake.

While fighting they disappeared down the slope, and a little later the king and the king's son heard someone sigh, "Ai, ja!" and discovered that she had returned to her chair.

Sitting down, she said: "I have won over them in a way, because they cannot fight any more. But as I was leaving, the snake breathed on me; so I have gotten fire inside of me." No sooner had she said this than she collapsed like ashes.

Then the king put her into a matchbox; and it wasn't even filled. They buried her in the corner of the garden where they had been sitting. Then the king tore out the king's son's eyes, and the one eye of his driver, and the one eye of his horse. And he let them go so that they should die of hunger.

"That is the story," said Lucas.

For some moments no one spoke. The fluency and earnest eloquence with which the story had been told, the reiterated cadence of the language, the rapt expression of the young man's face, had made a deep impression. What must have been the power of the ancient scalds!

XII. WHALES AND ROMANCE

THERE WERE other things to be done besides sit around in a cold tent at Ingia and wait for whales to strangle in a net; so on the third day I rolled up my bed, slung it upon my back, and accompanied by Jörn who wanted to fetch more to eat, and Abraham who wanted to visit his wife, and Lucas who wanted tobacco, and Joas who didn't want to be left alone, set off at the hour of low tide for the settlement. And after considerable slipping around on icy boulders, and a few rods of thigh-deep wading around a cliff, in due time got there. After all, I reflected, I only went to Ingia because of the war: and there was no war. And now my boys, my crew, should see it through. So, Abraham having found that his wife was quite well and happy with a young buck who had all but moved in to take care of her, Lucas having been supplied—by me, of course—with tobacco, Jörn—by me—with food, Joas with more food, all of them with tobacco, coffee, fuel, food—with everything—by me, they all at next low tide returned. And except the frequent times that one or all came back to me for more, I'd seen the last of them until in three weeks' time the white-whale season ended. I'd stuck it out, though patience, pride, and pocket-book were nearly bankrupt.

So one day there appeared the Zeeb clan's freighted umiak, and in its wake the water-logged old tub of ours by contrast fairly dancing in its buoyancy. A grateful sight to me, that homecoming. I ran along the shore to greet them as they came. "What ho!" I cried. "What luck?"

"Two whales," called back my Abraham. (The Zeebs had twelve.)

No matter; whales are big. "Bring up the meat," I call, and hurry home to clear room in my storehouse. It takes a lot of room for whales.

And presently there, sure enough, comes Abraham. And in one hand he carries something. "*Ak*," says Abraham. *Ak* means: I give it to you, take it, it is yours. And, taking it, I found inclosed in a piece of matak one foot square a gem of ruby red, a piece of meat. A special tidbit, was my thought, saved out for me. Good Abraham! good man! Come in. Have coffee, schnapps, cigars. No, take them all, the handful. Good—he did. Now fetch the meat along.

"That," says Abraham, indicating the morsel which now lay glistening on a plate, "that is the meat."

"No, no, good Abraham, you miss my thought. I must explain myself. I mean the meat, the whales. You caught two whales; one's mine. Come, trot it out." And dismissing a somewhat bewildered Abraham upon that errand, I waited.

Life is not drama. To reflect a little upon the innumerable causes which have no observed effect, the first and second acts that don't go on, intentions petered out, hopes unfulfilled, makes one wonder how drama ever came to be thought of. Here from my Greenland window I look out upon that panorama of sea and distant land and sky which is the setting of this book's events. There in that scene, in nature's face, I like to think, is drama immanent. And when like yesterday an almost breathless calm prevails, a glassy sea, a sullen, leaden, *brooding* sky, I know that prelude; I can prophesy: tomorrow, storm. Tomorrow dawns—today: by God! how sunlit, peaceful, calm, secure, how beautiful. So it happens that to this story of my white-whale crew there's no last act—no whale. Those whales, the two of them, their flesh and blood from head to tail, their guts, their hide, the marrow of their bones, their brains—were Lucas, Joas, Jörn, and Abraham.

The tent? The sporting goods? I got some back. The tent was

black, deep black, the deep, rich, velvet black of undiluted soot. Uncurable. The primus stove was ruined. The pots were stinking. One could clean them up; one did. I think that's all.

Meanwhile, beneath the surface of events and curiously related to the whole white-whale adventure, more truly maybe at the core of what had looked to be a little feud than I shall ever know, was romance. Anna?—well, yes; she was at Ingia; its sun, its glory, let us say. But that's just nonsense; this I'm speaking of was real.

On the day following my own return from Ingia, several of the Zeebs, among them Anna, came to Igdlorssuit for supplies. Anna, Salamina informed me, had hurt her hand, and she suggested, to my great astonishment, that she bring Anna to the house that I might look at her injury and treat it. The thoughtfulness of the suggestion and the continued kindness, even affection, with which she treated Anna upon her arrival were so at variance with her usual hard-boiled ruthless handling of a suspected rival as to fill me with wonder at the change, and pleasure at the thought of peaceful days to come. Why, there they sat, that mutually hateful pair, laughing and chatting over coffee like dear friends. "See," said I to Salamina afterwards, "how cheerful Anna is when you are good to her?" For it had been Salamina's pleasure to ridicule the girl for a mournful taciturnity of which Salamina was herself the cause.

"Yes," answered Salamina, but so absently that, wondering at her mood, I looked inquiringly. And thereupon she told:

There had been brought to her that day a letter; it was from Martin. "Here it is," she said. And opening her needlework box she took the letter out and gave it to me.

It was neatly written in lead pencil and began: "*Asassara Salamina*" (dear Salamina); but it entered at once into such Greenlandish as without my dictionary I could not begin to comprehend. Of course she had not meant that I should understand it; for when, using the dictionary, I appeared to be making some progress, she took the letter back, and promptly burned it. This much I had however read:

"*Dear Salamina: At last, little apple of my eye*" (for so the book absurdly rendered it) "*I can tell you what I feel. The time has come when you shall come to me at Ingia. . .*"

She burnt the letter up.

"So *that* is it!" said Salamina in the voice of one who has at last discerned some plotted villainy. "That's why they've asked me to their house for coffee, and sent me gifts of matak. That's it; I see it all." And weeping, she strode to her clothes chest, that treasure chest of all she owned, took out of it a little bottle of perfume, and flung it contemptuously on the table. "He sent me *that!*"

Yes, that was maybe it; their move to hinder us, that law trumped up to keep us out. How, with the bride approved, the nuptials planned in family conference, the coast—their north shore—clear for the elopement, how thwarting to the plot our Ingia move had been! They threaten us—and fail; they wait, they bide their time. And as my back turns, at my very heels, they light the match. Well—she extinguished it. She blew it out, and drowned it in her tears.

For she was really weeping now, quite uncontrollably; but why? "I'll send it back to him," she cried, and picked the bottle up to go with it—all streaming-eyed. Stop, Salamina; wait.

Now Martin was a good man, a substantial citizen; I told her that. She only wept the more, and looked at me reproachfully. "And if you take him—now or ever," I went on, "you'll get this house and everything that's in it."

"No!"

And as for the perfume which, she told me, he had bought and sent to her that day, she *couldn't*, I explained, now send it back. The silliness of such a thing! How like a fool he'd feel with perfume and no girl. And I persuaded her at last to make it less a gift than an exchange by sending him a hundred cigarettes. "Here, send him these." She did; and having settled the proposal by means of a long letter already written, so she told me, and dispatched, she now drove home the last transaction by a note. She spiked love's coffin lid.

The conduct of the Zeebs at Ingia toward my crew was not, I learned, *exactly* that of friends. Socially everything was all right; my coffee helped toward that. But professionally, as whale fishermen, the Kents were circumvented without scruple; and Martin, in retaliation for our having set our net a mile from his, moved his to blanket ours: whaleward from us, not fifty yards away, he caught our whales. And the one remaining move that my crowd could have made, and by it won the game, they didn't. It meant work.

Martin had won at war: that was his right. And yet his love remained. Because of that, I came to know him well. So that at last through Martin's magnanimity we got to be close friends.

XIII. EXIT ANNA

OF ANNA, in these days, I was seldom permitted even a furtive distant glimpse, for Salamina's eyes were not less keen than mine to spot her rival. Her kindness was a flare; and however craftily I might now manoeuvre to contrive a meeting, it proved invariably a rendezvous for three.

It was the nightly custom of the people of Igdlorssuit, even when with summer gone the nights were dark, to stroll the shore, their boulevard, their Promenade. It was my custom too—and Salamina's. And if I was often less happy in patrolling up and down alone—with Salamina at my heels—than I might have been in the unattended enjoyment of some carefree, rollicking young crowd, I'd gotten used to it. Though my steps wander, narrow their path shall be; just single file. Now one night, one merely starlit night as I patrolled, as said, the shore, who should come by me all alone but Anna! She passed; we neither turned our heads nor spoke; afraid. And I strode on. I strode and kept the rhythm of my tread; its *measure* changed. Beat, beat, beat, beat—so even, slow, that she my nemesis who followed in the darkness might discern no change of pace. And every stride I stretched to double length. I sped along. Soon quite secure of having lengthened out the gap, I dared look back: blank darkness. I stopped; no sound. Alone! With silent steps I ran ahead to where quite near the path some oil casks stood. I crouched behind them, hid, and waited. Then Salamina came. I could hear her quick soft footfalls, see her dark form approach—and pass, and vanish in the darkness. Now!

Keeping somewhat back from the shore to avoid other promenaders, making, I thought, no sound—so soft are Greenland boots—I followed Anna. I followed her and overtook her in the darkness. She'd gone far.

"Anna!" I breathed.

She heard me, stopped. She faced me. And I saw only the apprehension of her thoughts as she peered past me into the night.

"Anna . . ."

She silenced me. She listened—not to me. She started, and I gripped her arm.

"The schoolhouse: meet me there," she whispered, pulling to get free.

"But why? Why go?" I freed her.

"Salamina," said Anna; and was gone.

As Salamina came up I walked without a word straight past her in the way that I had come. She followed me. I stretched my steps; she hung on close. I ran, and she ran too. Damn it, I *would* get clear! I sprinted. For some distance she kept close to me, then slowly dropped behind. I held on for two hundred yards, I reached the oil casks, hid behind them. Scarcely five seconds after me she came. She was breathing heavily. Straight for the casks she came. As she rounded one end I broke cover from the other. She saw me, followed on. I turned sharp right, ran inland, dodged behind a house. She ran the other way around it, almost got me. A great ramshackle store shed stood near by. I headed for it. Halfway around I doubled on my track—and met her! She'd outguessed me. Leaving the settlement behind, I made off for the hills; still Salamina followed.

It is hard going in the darkness on those sodden hillsides; I wallowed on and up. I reached the shaly crest, ran on a way to put the brow between us, swerved sharp left, sprinted a hundred yards, and dropped down flat behind a grave mound in the hilltop graveyard. Lord, I was winded. A minute passed. Then dark and clear against the starlit sky came Salamina. She reached the hilltop, stopped, and looked around. Behind her in the darkness of the valley glimmered a few lights of the settlement. Before her lay in utter darkness a no man's land of bog and basalt shale and boulder-littered watercourses. She paused for breath; then, *passing* me, went on and into it.

It was some moments before I dared to move. Then without sound, and crouching low so that I might not be discovered on the sky line, I put the hill between us. I was free at last.

The schoolhouse could be reached without going through the settlement, for it stood above it, close to and overshadowed by the mountain's bulk. It was a dark and lonely site. The school itself was but one end of a three-part structure which, beginning with the school, included the church—the dominating central portion —and, corresponding with the schoolroom at the other end, the mortuary room. The whole might well have borne the inscription *From the Cradle to the Grave*. Anna was there.

My approach after the violent exercise of the chase was so leisurely, and its direction spoke so clearly of successful circumvention, that Anna now appeared quite rid of all those fears that had so paralyzed her latterly. She laughed again as in old days, and we entered light-heartedly though still in whispers upon those explanations, mutual condolences, and felicitations which it had rested in my thoughts to make. Nor did my difficulties with her tongue, my pidgin Eskimo, make what was said less touching and delightful. It was a jolly party—hush!

We stood with bated breath: pitch-darkness, utter silence. Then clear as the rustling of a mouse in a still room we heard such crunching of fine shale as the most stealthy footsteps still must make. The crunching stopped. Quick as a thought and quite as silently Anna turned the handle of the schoolhouse door; turned it, pushed in the door, and entered. I followed close. We shut the door; it squeaked. And there we stood in the close confinement of that schoolhouse vestibule, stood, listened, hardly dared to breathe.

Footsteps approached, quite audibly. They paused outside the door. They moved away, came back.

It appeared a minute later as though more feet than two were tiptoeing around outside. Then we heard whispering. Trapped—but not caught.

There was another door behind us; Anna opened it. Making no sound I followed her in through. I shut the door. There was a key in it; I locked the door. *That* made a sound.

It was clear to us now from the scarcely suppressed foot scufflings and voices that reached us through two doors that there were more than two outside, that there were many more. The sounds increased. A crowd, we knew at last, was gathering.

We stood in a cramped hallway no lighter than the pitch-black vestibule that we had left; our legs were pressed against a ladder. With common thought we climbed it. There was a trap door at the top. We opened it, crawled through, and lowered it. And we found ourselves in a dark loft that extended over the entire space below—the school, the church, the mortuary. In the schoolroom gable end was a door flanked by two small windows, in the other merely a small rough aperture at the peak. The starlit sky showed through. But no light entered into that gloomy place.

By this time there could be no doubt that half the population swarmed around the building. The pack had cornered us. And though, God knows, the tryst had been quite our affair, and innocent enough, we had by ill-considered flight to sanctuary, by entering that sacred place, by locking it, not only blazoned our intrigue but violated custom if not law. They had us on both counts. And the fact that they didn't immediately storm our citadel, itself put emphasis on our misconduct in just being there: they waited for authority to enter.

Samuel, the catechist, was in bed when summons came to him. He jumped up, pulled his trousers on over his long woolen drawers, pulled his kamiks on over his bare feet, drew on a sweater, and ran out. It isn't often that a catechist in Greenland, or for that matter clergy anywhere today, get such a chance. Authority?—he loved it. The crowd made way and Samuel strode through.

He opened the outer door, went in. An empty vestibule, of

course; all knew it. He tried the second door: that door—we knew it well!—was locked. Then Samuel thundered: "Come, open up! Come down from there, come out!" But from our loft no sound came back. Believe it: I was thinking.

The gable door over the schoolroom opened out upon a ten-foot drop right into the outskirts of the crowd. The ladder we had climbed led down and out through only that same door we'd entered by: impossible. I crept over the boxes, nets, and cordage with which the loft was littered and climbed to the aperture in the other gable. No use. It had been made for no more than the passage of an arm when one reached out to fix a new rope on the bell that hung outside. The bell!

Among the expedients of nature, or principles, I'd better say, that serve expedience, the *ruse* is much employed as a corollary to concealment. The female partridge, having hid its young, discovers itself to lead the search away; the ruse is half the battle of escape. My young, let's say, was Anna: save her—and myself.

It was not too hard to find in the mess of cordage that littered that dark place a piece of net twine long enough to extend from one gable end to the other. It took some time, of course, and Samuel raved. Well, let him. With one end of the twine in my hand I now climb the mortuary gable. I reach through the aperture, and with the most exact care not to clatter the bell affix a noose to its lever, draw it tight. Careful to keep my bell rope slack I now descend and, approaching with the utmost caution the other end of the loft, pay out the twine along the floor. Rave, Samuel, rave: we're ready.

One has, even in such crucial moments of peril as this, a sense of art, of drama; one feels the need of doing what one must do, splendidly. My conception of the performance that was about to follow required an opening like that of Beethoven's Fifth. No dribbling in. Accordingly, I picked up the rope a few paces back, gripped it firmly in both hands, and, leaping forward as I tugged, achieved at the first stroke a pandemonium of clamor. "Clang, bang, bang, clang!" I kept it up.

At the first stroke of the bell the crowd stampeded for the mortuary end. And as though drawn to fill the void they left, our gable door swung out. Now, Anna, quick!

Anna got on her belly. She wriggled her legs out. She lowered herself—and dropped. "Clang, bang, bang, clang!"—the bell crashed on. Now me. I let the rope go, wriggled out, hung by my hands, and dropped.

"Anna!" I breathed as a woman's arms received me.

"Yes?" said Salamina.

Well—so it goes. She was not unkind to me as, gripping me firmly by the arm, she led me home. She was not unkind at home. Severe, perhaps, not bubbling with good humor—not unkind. One doesn't make a dog love home by beating him. My bed was made. She pulled my boots off, tucked me in. "Good night, Kinte."

XIV. OF TROLLEMAN

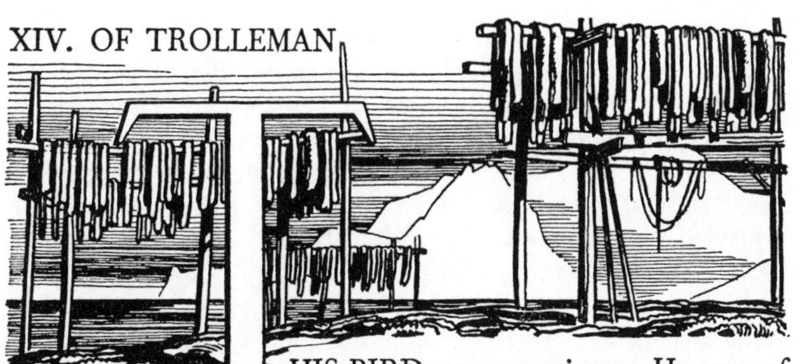

THIS BIRD grew wearisome. He was, of course, a wonderful fellow. He could do card tricks; he could bring whales out of the ocean as they bring rabbits out of hats. He could do lots of things without appearing to do anything at all; and nothing—with a mad man's energy. He was, in fact, a showman; and his notion of *being* a trading-post manager was to look like one. Whew, with what gusto he would greet the mornings —late! "Well, well, well, well!" he'd cry, as though that compensated men for waiting. "Just talk to them," he said, instructing me, "just talk. They like it. No matter what you say, they like it." So, heartily roaring his inanities, he'd slap men's backs and pinch the maidens' bubbies.

His sterner side had better been confined to the domestic circle. His roars of rage when someone bumped his aerial guys were echoed by the mountains and boys' laughter; and his physical violence, although he chose its objects with some prudence, was neither impressive nor always fortunate. Canute was wise to leave the tide alone; not wise was Trolleman with tides of men.

The human tide that nightly strolled the beach adhered as strictly to the line of shore as though it were itself a fluid counterpart of the sea. Where sea was not, it flowed. And just as inevitably as the sea pursues all indentations in the land, would that human element flow out and flood where land indented sea. Such an indentation in the otherwise unbroken waterline of Igdlorssuit was the wharf, a sort of dry-land Bay of Fundy by the tide that ran out there. And Canute Trolleman, the fool, forbade it. He wrote a notice and he posted it; it was to this effect: *Keep off the Wharf.* "That's that!" said Canute Trolleman, and strutted home.

So evening came, and evening's tide of men. They flowed from house doors to the shore, flowed out to loiter, stroll, throw pebbles in the sea, catch little fish, kick stones, do nothing there at all —just be. They sought the level of their mood, and it carried them seaward to the tip end of the wharf. So *every* evening came and went these tides; and at last from the rubbing of innumerable shoulders, from the work of sun and rain, the edict was quite worn away. The tides flowed on.

Now one day Trolleman, sitting at his window reading over again his file of last year's Copenhagen newspapers, getting a bit bored at it, yawned, lowered the paper, and looked out of the window. There before his very eyes were three boys on the wharf. Trolleman saw red. He leaped, tore out, and prancing upon the wharf roared out like thunder that the wharf be vacated. I tell you! Trolleman enraged would scare small kids. At least he did scare two of these, for they went flying as though the devil were after them. But one, the eldest, a boy of fifteen, had a fishline in the water—or a piece of string or something. Anyhow he moved so slowly that the devil got him. "Get off, I say," roared Trolleman, and pounced on him.

Is it because the Greenlanders are a powerful race that they don't fight? That they don't spank their children and seldom beat their wives? Jakob—the boy was Jakob Nielsen, Aron's son—had never in his whole young life been handled so, nor seen another be. He felt a sudden, fierce resentment, struggled back. Trolleman, now more infuriated, shook him, hurled him down; he got him as he struggled up again, and pitched him off the wharf.

Trolleman did a lot of blustering about his rights in this affair, and indignantly refused to recompense the father for the boy's anorak, which had been torn and ruined. But native might and right asserted itself; and upon the community council's threatening action, Trolleman paid up. If only he had now left bad enough alone, had common sense, forgotten it. Not Trolleman. So, watching for a chance—of course it came.

"Get out!" roared Trolleman to loitering youngsters in the coal shed one cold day. "Get out!"

They moved, they got along, but Jakob, sullenly, was last.

Trolleman's assault of Jakob pitched him headlong out; it brought Trolleman himself right up into the doorway, and into the hands of Jakob's father. Those hands, big hands, closed tight round Trolleman's neck. They bore him backwards, they lifted him, they shook him like a rat; they threw him like a sack of dog meat on the coal heap. The Nielsen men who hovered over Trolleman looked black and huge against the light of out of doors. They were big men, and Trolleman, if he could trust their looks and words, might well lie very still. He did. The danger passed.

But just as an example of how unreliable history is, of how there are always two sides to events, I may quote Trolleman about what happened. "I merely pushed him," said he, speaking of Aron Nielsen, "and knocked him over on the coal heap. I didn't want to hurt him." That was considerate too, for Aron was in fact a powerful man.

Two sides, two different points of view: that was doubtless at the root of those troubles between Trolleman and me which led in the end to a complete severance of diplomatic relations. That Trolleman had often met such differences in life was suggested by a characteristic expression of his face which hovered between astonished indignation and indignant astonishment. I think my own face must at times with Trolleman have worn that look—though I came soon to be surprised at nothing. But we *were* different, as different as Red and White: I was an artisan and he a trader. I don't mean merely that he ran a trading-post and dealt out beans for fat, and kept accounts; that was his job. Nor that he did it well; he didn't. He was too much a trader not to profit even in the trade he'd made of time for salary. Buy low, sell high, give little and take much: he lived for profit. And he was far less concerned with his official duties at Igdlorssuit than with the least of opportunities

Igdlorssuit might offer him to make more money. I came, of course, a lamb to slaughter. And despite that contempt which a workman feels for those who, doing nothing, trade in what the workman does, I must still blush for shame at the almost imbecile naïveté with which on my first arrival in Umanak I let trader Johan Lange, assisted and abetted by traders Nielsen and Trolleman and clerk Binzer, sell me seven dogs for fifty kroner apiece. Good dogs were worth just ten.

And what a fool I was in the affair of Tukajak—you know, my hired man. See trader Trolleman in this. "A splendid man," says he, "the very man you want. I'll see him for you."

"You shall pay him," says Trolleman upon reporting the success of his mission, "one hundred kroner a month." (One kroner ten öre a day was the established wage.) "And now," says he, "I have a plan: these people *will not* save. They *shall*. You shall give half the pay to Tukajak, Mr. Kent, and half to me. I'll put that in his savings-bank account." Am I such a bonehead as to fall for that? I am. Months after I had fired Tukajak for sheer stupidity and utter uselessness I learned that he had never had a bank account and never smelled the money. Trade is a funny business.

But let's, to save my face, get on to the great dog-meat coup, for I emerge from that not quite discreditably.

One of the prime necessities of Greenland life for which one makes provision is food for dogs. Forewarned in Denmark, I had brought up with me from South Greenland a fair quantity of dried caplin, yet far from enough to see me through the fall and winter months. I needed more, and shortly after my arrival at Igdlorssuit suggested to Trolleman that I begin laying in a supply of the shark meat which is the staple dog food of the place, and of which the summer fishery furnishes an abundant supply. "Don't buy it now," said he, "not now. It hasn't dried enough and you don't get your money's worth. Just wait. I'll tell you when." Now this was good advice. I waited.

Time passed. And presently I noticed that Trolleman's meat racks were beginning to sag under a growing weight of dried shark meat. "Now shall I buy?" said I to Trolleman, for he was at the time, and sought to be, my adviser in all local problems.

"What, now?" cried Trolleman, looking at me with that indignant astonishment of his. "No, no, Mr. Kent; no, no—no, no, not now. I said I'd tell you when. Just wait."

And so I did. Time passed.

So that at last, seeing his racks fairly groaning under their burden of meat, I ventured once again.

"Why, yes, of course!" exclaimed the fellow in astonishment. "What! you have no dog meat? Why, Mr. Kent, you can't get dog meat now. There *is* none. No, Mr. Kent, you can't get dog meat now. There is none. No, Mr. Kent, no, no; there is no meat. All gone."

"But," staggered, I put in, "you said to wait; you said you'd tell me. . . ."

He fairly gasped with amazement and indignation. "What, *I* told you that? To wait? *I* told you?—Well—yes, Mr. Kent; I do remember something about it. No, no, there is no dog meat."

And there wasn't. Believe me: as I write this I'm ashamed. Damned fool! I went on trusting him.

It so happened that I made a trip, shortly after this, to Nugatsiak, a trading-post distant about twenty-two miles across Igdlorssuit Sound and Karrat Fiord; and that there, praise God! I found Nugatsiak's great, swashbuckling ear-ringed buccaneer of a trader, the Greenlander Pavia Cortzen, to have a surplus of shark meat for sale—for sale, and cheap, for but six öre a kilo while the established Igdlorssuit price was eight.

"I'll take four hundred kilo," said I.

"There's maybe not that much," said he.

"Well, all you have. *Skaal*, Pavia!" (He liked his beer.) And leaving the meat to be taken over by the next supply schooner, I sailed light-heartedly for home.

Of course if I hadn't said anything about it, if I hadn't in my pleasure blabbed about it all to Trolleman, if I'd had common sense, there would have been no trouble. But, having none, when two days later Trolleman asked to borrow my motorboat for a trip to Tartusak—there was a post house there that he as trader had each year to see supplied with coal and dog food—I said, "Of course," and thought no more about it.

It was now the third week in September. Every day more ice came driving out of Rink's Fiord, deploying like a maneuvering army for an advance upon Igdlorssuit by the first northerly gale. And there, with motor broken down, exposed in helplessness to what might come, lay my motorboat. In vain had I besought the authorities in Umanak to lend me tackle that when trouble threatened I might beach the boat. They promised—and sent none. The schooner called again: no tackle came. Now much concerned, I determined to go to Umanak on the schooner, get the tackle, and return by the schooner ten days later. Then, too, I'd get my dog meat, for the schooner's next port was Nugatsiak.

But no sooner did Trolleman hear of my intention than he set up the most extraordinary expostulations. "No, no, don't go. No, Mr. Kent, don't go. They'll send the tackle. No, don't go." Even at the time I was puzzled by the wild agitation of that excitable little man. He was always a talker; now he raved. He was always a good fellow, hail-fellow-well-met, jolly, hearty, put-it-there-old-man; he *loved* me now. "Well, then, now, Mr. Kent, we'll drink. Come! yes, you must. Come in!"

Passing the buck is rather shabby practice. In passing a responsibility to Trolleman I was no less to blame for what occurred—at least as that contributed to the disaster. "I can't go in and have a drink with you," said I, "for I have to put out another anchor from my boat before I sail. There's hardly time."

"Now, Mr. Kent, now, now, now, now, I wouldn't do that, Mr. Kent. She doesn't need it. Come, Mr. Kent, come in."

"You bet she'll need it if it comes to blow. No—let me go."

But he didn't let me go, just clung to me—grand fellow that I had become.

"I'll put your anchor out," said he, "I'll put it out. I'll do it just as soon as you have sailed. Come in now, Mr. Kent, come in!"

Well—like a fool, I went inside. And I had drinks—one, two, three, four, I didn't count. And Trolleman, the jolly boy, just raved good-fellowship. All right now, all aboard; and I got up. No, he must take me there. "I'll row you out, I *will.*"

There was bad blood between Trolleman and the skipper. So while Trolleman, who had come right along on board, poured out to me the dregs of his devotion, the ship weighed anchor and quietly bore away. "Good-by, good-by," wept Trolleman, not heeding this. "Safe voyage, quick return.—Oh! by the way, give this to Pavia Cortzen; it's something that I owe him." And he pressed a sealed envelope into my hand. "Now, good . . . good God! We've sailed!"

The skipper had no mercy. Heave to for *him!*—he laughed. And Trolleman in getting off, and clear, was near capsized.

"Put out that anchor—*sure,*" I called to him.

"I will," called Trolleman.

That evening at Nugatsiak I wrote: . . . *the splendor of the day, the sun, the blue sea, the golden snow covered mountains, the bitter cold clear northeast wind.* . . . I still recall the beauty of that day, that golden snow of which I wrote, its shadows that were violet, that gold and violet against the turquoise of the lower sky. And I recall that wind, a half a gale: how in the teeth of it the motor-driven schooner hardly made Nugatsiak. And how it blew all night. We stayed aboard.

"This is for you—from Trolleman," I said to Pavia next day, and handed him the envelope.

"For me?" He looked surprised. He opened it, found money. More surprise. "For me? What for?"

I didn't know. "But now," I said, "I'll take that dog meat."

"You have it," said Pavia. "That was all I had. I told Trolleman so when he came to get it for you."

My dog meat stocked the post house at Tartusak.

"And now for Umanak," said Skipper Olsen, pushing back his

plate and standing up. "Thanks, Pavia." And we three strolled down to the shore.

At the shore there was a gathering of people; a kayaker had just come in. He stepped out of his little craft, stooped, hooked an arm into the cockpit, lifted it lightly, and, carrying it up the bank to a place of security, gently set it down. Then coming straight to Pavia he handed him a letter.

"This is for you," said Pavia, looking at the superscription. I opened it and read:

Igdlorssuit, Sunday 20th
11 A.M.

Dear Kent: Your boat came ashore last night and there's a hole in it, but we are unable to say where or how large. We are remaining here and will try to pull it out with high water. You better make the Umanak schooner come in here and take it to Umanak. She may not be able to float for long, and we have only a short time on our hands to remain here. *Yours,*

J. O. B. Peterson

(Peterson was a Canadian geologist prospecting for the Danish government; his coming to Igdlorssuit was in the nick of time to save my boat from total wreck. Thanks, Peterson. He left again next day.)

That was a wild dark night. The light of the lantern that someone held out on the remnant of Igdlorssuit wharf danced on the stormy water. It showed a jam of ice against the shore. My boat lay at its anchorage; a dim light burned on board. On shore a crowd awaited us; and Trolleman. They told about the gale they'd had, of how the ice drove in and carried everything before it, of how the boat had lain helpless in that churn of ice and surf. Of how with Peterson's boat they'd dragged her off, of how she'd filled—she'd sprung a leak somewhere; how now she only kept afloat by constant pumping.

I turned to Trolleman. "Did you put out that second anchor?"

"Well, now, you see, well, it was this way, well, I, to tell the truth—no, Mr. Kent, I . . ."

"And how about my dog meat?"

Well, that was different; yes, now he beamed. The trader rubbed his hands. "Well, now that's different, Mr. Kent. You see . . ."

"Oh, go to hell!"

And so occurred the break, the parting of our ways, the war, which instead of leaving me a friendless outcast in the settlement was to throw me into the very arms of the people. The trader was the outcast.

But at the moment, with my boat a hulk and I cast out half-fledged from the official nest, things looked as black as that black night. My rage sustained me; that—and Salamina. If in the past I had resented her constant warnings against Trolleman, and dismissed as inconsequential her repeated complaints of sharp practice, now her proud I-told-you-so spoke not only of *her* loyalty but somehow conveyed the sense of the whole army of her race behind herself—and me. I'd taken sides, I'd joined. "Come, pack up, Salamina, you, the kids, and me. We're off to Umanak."

It was near midnight when we sailed, my boat in tow, two Greenlanders and I on board of her. Two altogether had been plenty. Yet at the moment of embarking Tukajak, my hundred-kroner beauty, struck. "Me, and two more," said he.

"You and *one* more—and I," I answered him.

"No, *two* more, or we don't go."

There was a crowd around and the awaiting skiff was thrashing against the steps. No time for scenes or argument.

"All right. Then stay home, all of you." Fed up with trouble, I jumped down, cast off. They nearly sank the skiff as they jumped in. So three of us kept watch and pumped by turns all night.

And in the morning there came Salamina to the schooner's poop; she had a paper parcel in her hands. She secured the parcel with a loop of string to the tow cable; she released it. And from the high poop it came sliding down to our awaiting hands: our breakfast.

Oh, Trolleman and the dog meat! Well—since all things have their price, I published at Igdlorssuit that I would pay *ten* öre a kilo: I got some. I raised the price to twelve, and plenty came. And when I had acquired the exact amount that had been bought of Pavia, I stopped, I had enough. Then when in course of time I settled up accounts with Trolleman—for this and that, and for his use of my motorboat—I charged him for the boat as we'd agreed: petroleum and oil and crew. *Plus*—just exactly the difference between the six öre a kilo which I should have paid for the meat, and the ten and twelve which I did pay.

"I won't pay it," screamed Trolleman.

"Don't," said I, "and I'll take the matter to the King of Denmark if I have to."

He paid. There broke a trader's heart.

XV. THE SPECK

FROM small to great; from Trolleman and me, and Salamina and the kids, and Anna, Martin, Abraham, Jörn, Joas, Lucas, Tukajak, from whether you pay six öre or ten for dog meat, or whether people love or hate, or live or die, from man's concern with man, look out on that epitome of unconcernedness, the face of God. Look out? What do we live by here, day in, day out, but that?

It has two attributes, that scene: the finite and the infinite. It is the extensive zone of man's activities, the arena of his fight for life; and it is an abyss of incalculable immensity into which man pours his thoughts, his aspirations, pours out himself. Men *lose* themselves in that. And it may be that the whole activity of men's lives serves no end other than the replenishment of what evaporates, without return, to God. What happens when we lose ourselves? What emanates? The artist, poet, makes it his concern to grasp that emanation, realize it, make it ponderable; that is as futile as to stay awake to watch the pageant of our dreams.

In the contentment of merely *being* which comes to all of us at times, and which to many unpretentious ones is daily life, one is perhaps most perfectly related to that cosmic environment which we call God. What our *thoughts* then are, or whether what goes on in us has form enough to be called thought, is hard to say. Perhaps the whole experience is sensual, just that; and yet for being sensual no less sublime. To yield ourselves unthinkingly to that for which, by which, we're made: the sun, the moon, the stars, their light—I'm writing of the North—on snow-covered mountain ranges, on floating mountains of white ice, on the sea; the sound of wind, of waves along the shore; the *feel* of sun and wind and cold; the whole manifestation to the senses of all that is in that whole vast esthetic unity. Give over thought, and yield yourself to that. Or, if the mind *will* work, let thought just drift, float freely in the air like smoke, to lose itself. I think few people wonder about God. Thank God for that.

It is the way of the poor people of Donegal—and, for all I know to the contrary, of the Irish country people everywhere—to lend even the most perfunctory expressions an impressive earnestness. "How *are* ye?" one would ask in greeting. To which the proper answer is no casual, "Good, and how are you?" but something in the line of, "Well, yesterday I had a bit of a pain in me tooth. It was better by night, and I think I'm maybe all right again today." Now while the Greenlanders lack, as far as I have observed, all *form* of salutation, while man passes man with no more than a nod, if that, and while they are altogether given rather to silence than to prattling about unimportant things, a comment on the weather is in order. First thing, they speak of that: they say, "The day is good." And that *good day*, that *sila pinaka*, has about it the intentional earnestness of the Irish salutation. It is a meant remark. To begin with, the word *sila* denotes not only the weather but the whole outdoors, the world, the universe. To so translate it and convey in English speech its tone and emphasis one needs to say, "By God, the world is beautiful!"

By God, it *is*—these cold October days. It's winter weather, freezing, sharp. Less loitering on the strand these days; the shadow of the mountain has reached over us, to stay till March. The sun goes out, the ocean turns to ice: all beautiful—yes, terribly—the huge phenomena of changing seasons.

The little figures on the strand: what are they doing, running so? They launch a boat, pile in. They're rowing now like mad. Two men put off in kayaks; it's a race. Look! there's a third emerging from behind the headland. It *is* a race; he's heading them. They're paddling frantically out to sea. People have climbed

A kayaker

the hill; they stand, a crowd of puppets up against the sky, the spectators—of what? There's something up. I get my glasses, train them on the water. They are powerful binoculars, and the field of vision is small; one by one I pick them up—the boat, the kayaks, one, two, three. If it's a race there's nothing in it for the boat; it's far behind. One kayak leads them all by a wide margin; it's heading where? For what? I search the plain of water on the kayak's course: there's nothing there, no—yes! A dark thing on the water, almost quite submerged. That's it: dead walrus, something of the sort. They're racing out to claim a share in it. But at one end of it, what's that? That whitish thing that moves? No, it's just off one end; the black thing peters out so that there's a space of water between the end of it and—that. Yes, *that.* Good God! I know it now—the fluttering thing. It is a drowning man.

The race was a desperate one, with kayakers and boatmen holding a terrific stroke despite the two miles that they had to cover. It became apparent that the kayakers sitting low in the water were steering blindfold, guided only by such bearings as they may have taken from the land. They veered considerably from the true course. A few more yards to leeward and the leader might have passed his mark. He seemed about to when, coming suddenly about, he made straight for it. How must his shout have sounded to the drowning man!

What happened at the rescue was not to be observed from land; kayaks and men, and then at last the boat, were to the eye one wriggling mass. Nor when the boat detached itself and made for land again could it be seen whether or not a successful rescue had been effected. How slowly to that waiting crowd the boat returned. Who was it? No one knew.

And now they near the shore; the people crowd the water's edge. Men push the ice aside to make a landing-place. The boat rides in through the low surf, and grounds. Down in the bottom, at the stern, held sitting upright between another's legs, is David. They lift him like an inert thing and bear him to the nearest house, the house of Jens. He's conscious; he half lifts his head and tries—no, does it!—smiles.

They strip him of his saturated clothes—and how pathetically little he has on! Kamiks—without their seal or dogskin socks, and he had lost one kamik in his fight for life. Good sealskin trousers, but no underwear. Two sweaters. His body is like ice; ten men are rubbing him from head to foot. And from the fat face of Martin across from me the sweat drips off like rain. The rum I poured into David's mouth he hardly could contrive to swallow. But now he's coming round; we watch that pallid face come slowly back to life.

David had been in the water about forty minutes, and the boat took half an hour to come back. This was his third close call. This time he'd shot one seal, had it on board, behind him on his kayak, when a "saddleback," a large variety of seal, showed up off his port bow. David drove his harpoon into it; the rawhide line paid out—and caught; the kayak was capsized.

The Greenland kayak is perhaps the finest craft that mankind has devised. It is less a boat or canoe than an extension of man himself to be amphibious; the kayak and the man are one. One literally, for in the "full jacket" which is worn by the kayaker in rough weather he is united to his craft, bound into it. His hooded sealskin garment is tied tight around his face, around his wrists, around the kayak's cockpit. Seas may break over him, they do; only through mouth and nose can water enter. He may capsize, he often does; his skill enables him to right himself again. In ordinary weather the kayaker wears only the "half-jacket." That is a cylinder of sealskin which is tied around the cockpit and supported up under the armpits by shoulder straps. It is as though the kayaker sat with his head and shoulders sticking out of a conning-tower. So David was equipped this day that he capsized. Once upside down he couldn't right his craft: the seal was tied to it. And the saddleback struggling in his death throes was fast to it by that harpoon line. And David was fast to it—and upside down. How he got out of it, who knows; maybe not even David.

Well, David lived. They *made* him keep indoors that day, next day he got another seal. Such is the Greenland hunter.

XVI. PASTIMES

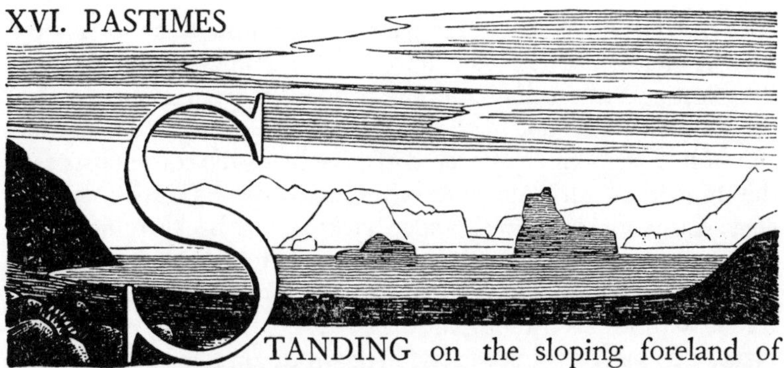

STANDING on the sloping foreland of Igdlorssuit, one looks out as though upon the stage of a great theater. Of that stage, the level plain of the sea is the floor, the great circle of the heavens is the proscenium arch, the two headlands are the wings. Sea, mountains, ice, are its one set; sun, moon, and stars the light. And of the drama endlessly deploying there, the theme is the inconsequence of human life to God. Yet *that*, brought home by the unfeeling immensity of the scene, only deepens in men their sense of the vast consequence of man to man. Despite man's littleness out there, let him just *be* there, enter on that scene, and as far as eye can reach all eyes have found him. The speck is an event. A speck to eyes on land was David fighting for his life. Eyes read its meaning.

Eyes see while far away, and throats proclaim, what's news. The return of the successful hunter; the capture of a white whale, narwhal, walrus, bear; the return of reindeer-hunters, of campers in their laden umiak—men, women, children, kayaks, dogs: all these are news. And all arrivals from the outside world: a motorboat, the schooner, the post in winter time—great news! For just as the immensity of the environment brings into visual prominence the speck, so does the vast monotony of time enlarge the moment's happening.

If houses had not been contrived in order to shelter man against the elements, they might still have been thought of for the diminishment in times of need of man's environment. They serve both ends. And as great space is sometimes unendurable, so too is time; for the defeat of that men have their pastimes. We who spend the great part of our lives indoors, who even drive about in heated rooms on wheels, and who make pastime almost be the end and aim of life, have maybe fostered in ourselves such consciousness of the impending ultimate as to have *had* to flee its terrifying presence. Certainly the Greenlander, lacking our background of romantic thought, does not incline to see with us "upon the night's starred face huge, cloudy symbols of a high romance." He is, I think, without such thoughts; and, lacking them, he can contemplate immensity as children not brought up on ghosts can face the dark. At least he does, and likes it. And so it is, perhaps, that neither houses nor pastimes have the place in Greenland life they have in ours. The very smallness of the houses, and their total lack of the accessories of comfort, is evidence, in part, of that; and the very fact that such indoor games as cards and checkers, with which through contact with the whites many Greenlanders are familiar, are rarely played does show that people do not need to pass up time, at least to that extent. Their pastime indoors is the social gathering; and that, whether it be the kaffemik or the dance, is so essentially the expression of social gifts and energy as not to be quite comparable to such time, place, and self annihilating games as cards. Not that their social gifts achieve much—to our taste; or that their dances show much art: they don't. They have the kill-joy priests to thank for that. For in place of what must have been in pagan times real salutary orgies of conviviality, of feasting, dancing, song, they have—well, come to one: the kaffemik.

First must come the invitation; you can hear it coming. It fumbles at the latch of your entry door; it shuffles its feet in the passage; it gets its hand on the doorknob, turns it timidly, and slowly opens it. It comes in like a mouse prospecting in a roomful of cats. And there at last it stands; its face is washed, it's all dressed up: a little girl. It is her birthday. Almost inaudibly she murmurs that and asks you to a kaffemik. Now this is not the time when you'd like to knock off work and go and have a good time at a party. It is ten o'clock in the morning, or two-thirty in the afternoon, or just noon—and you're about to sit down to your dinner. But whenever it is, you stop whatever you are doing, and go. But first a present—what do you think they've asked you for? Your present—go easy now, there are one hundred and eighty or thereabouts birthdays in one year at Igdlorssuit—your present may be anything: a cake of soap, a cake of chocolate, a tin of sweetened condensed milk, a piece of ribbon, a pair of mittens, a necklace, almost anything. Take it and *wrap it up*. That's held to be good form. Oh, any scrap of paper not too soiled will do. Newspaper? That's fine. Wrap it and hand it to the child. She'll thank you—maybe; but now follow her. She leads you to her house. You'll see no more of her: the party is for grown-ups.

Shooing a couple of dogs out of your way in the narrow entrance passage, you grope your way in, feeling as you go for what may be a door; that found, you push it open and walk in. It is, let us say, one of the better houses. The room—the house—may be, therefore, as large as twelve feet square, or even more. You can just stand up straight in it. The house is clean—well, clean enough. The floor, the sleeping-platform, the chair—if there is one—have all been scrubbed. The walls and ceiling have been painted, not too recently, a pale blue. There's an old chest of drawers, and on the top of it is a museum collection. There on a cross-stitched tidy is arranged everything in the line of knickknacks that the family owns. It's sad, this stuff, this treasured shabby, tawdry junk; these faded photographs in nasty frames; these arty ash trays, all these fake, pretentious cast-offs of the worst that whites turn out. And as though the bureau were an altar—and there are little Christmas candles on it—over it hangs a vile chromolithograph of a vile imitation of a vile green Guido Reni—a weeping Magdalen, or Christ and Lamb. This picture is not an idol, not a symbol; it's not there because they worship it. It's worse than that: they *like* it. And on either side of the altarpiece, in duplicate and arranged with geometric precision, are all the remnants of old lines of picture postcards with which the store is stocked. The sleeping-platform with a flap of it turned down takes up one third of the room; there is a stove in the corner, and a small table in the center. On the table is a cloth, and on the cloth three cups and saucers. So much for the house.

Seated along the sleeping-platform, seated everywhere that there are seats and standing where there aren't, are people. It looks, as you walk in, as though a business meeting were in progress; the business, it appears, is silence. It has the feeling of a constrained silence, for the occasional interruptions to it, being mostly such personal remarks by one woman to another as, "That is pretty work on your kamiks; what do you think of mine?" are in undertones. And although there may be a ripple of laughter over some occurrence, or a burst of talk from three or four, there is rarely general conversation. Yet it is a good-humored silence: they're nice people, pleasant people, always ready to return you smile for smile.

The coffee-drinking may have been in progress for some time, for the stove is laden with coffee kettles brought in from the several houses that are contributing to the event by roasting and making into beverage the raw coffee beans and barley that our hostess has supplied. At any rate the coffee is ready for the new arrivals. And the cups: they've just been rinsed in a bowl of dirty water and wiped with a dingy rag. The hostess fills two cups—no, three; another guest has just come in. She fills the cups so that they overflow into the saucer. "*Ak*," she murmurs, and goes back to the stove. You reach over, or walk over, and take your cup and such sugar as you want from a dish of it—yes, that too was on the table. Seated again, you toss a lump of sugar into your mouth, pour the saucer full of coffee, and from the saucer drink it. When finished, you put your cup and saucer back on to the table, sit down again, and become as the rest—silent. Meanwhile a number of the guests who, having had their coffee, have sat their time out, have gotten up and left. You bide your time, and follow. The party lasts like this most of the day. Guests come and go, until at last the whole settlement has been entertained. And then, that night, the dance.

In ancient times when Greenland was isolated from the world the people's way of life, their manners and beliefs, formed a homogeneous culture in which men's desires and the means of their fulfillment were commensurate. (That *is* a happy state. We worry about happiness: in homogeneousness lies the key.) There was, in those days, a place for everything, and everything was suited to its place. And such an emergency as wanting to dance and lacking room for it could not have been. What troubles Progress brings! It taught them in Greenland to own things: "A poor thing," runs the saying, "but my own." The poor thing came to be the little coops men built themselves to sit and own things in. It taught, or tried to teach, them virtue; and for the obscenity of solo dancing to a chorus it substituted the mass dance of embracing couples. It taught them how to kiss; it taught a lot of things that we are not concerned with here. On with the dance: but where? Undoubtedly the missionaries of the early days invited the more chastened of the natives to the parsonage, where, in their ample rooms, they and their lady wives, both setting an example of refined deportment, instructed the agile primitive in the measures of the European folk dance. Possibly then, as now, some empty floor space of the trade administration's premises was put at the disposal of the crowd, that all might dance. That's done invariably in the colonies, the trading-centers. But it is not of such privileged show pieces of the administration that we are writing. We're at Igdlorssuit, an outpost, a producing center of the North, out where men are hunters, where they stand on their own feet, dance on their own feet, and are presumed to have a place to dance in. Well—they have. And Trolleman, the trader, has the key. He is a little strict about his premises, and moody in his strictness. You never knew. This night he gives the key.

Down near the shore stands a very dilapidated turf hut. It has a large doorway, and a window with no glass in it. The turf walls have shrunk and settled, and the roof being supported on wooden posts, there is a space of several inches between the turf walls and the eaves. Through this the stars blink down, or snow or rain drives in. It is a dark, damp, dismal hole, this hut of turf: it is the cooperage.

It is a small place—ten by twelve inside; and not only is part of it occupied by the cooper's bench and work materials, but exactly one-half is taken up by bags of salt piled to the rafters. There is no necessity for the salt to be here, but here it is. And from it moisture oozes out and puddles on the floor. Six feet by ten of wet and filthy floor space in a drafty hole: Welcome, you hundred people, dance, enjoy yourselves! The pity of it is they do.

Dressed lightly for the dance, on winter nights they pack that icy cave and crowd outside. The place is foggy with the vapor of their breath and steaming bodies, and the feeble light of the guttering candle glistens on the dancers' sweat. Crowd in and dance, dance, dance. Forward and back, and whirl around; one, two, three, four: their feet embroider a quadruple beat, play trap drum to the march. Dance on; play on, accordion. Outside the moon and stars are shining; the aurora drapes its veils. The wind is cold; it pierces you: the wind, the stars, the night—so beautiful!

XVII. WATCHMAN?

ONE NIGHT, one late fall night when newly fallen snow was on the ground, when the full moon shining from a sky just thinly veiled with cloud diffused a brightness like unearthly daylight, when it was breathlessly still, hushed as though in expectation of an event, the young people strolled in a great band along the shore, and sang in harmony. That was as lovely as the night itself.

One late fall night when a bitter north wind raked the settlement a waning moon stood in the wind-swept sky. Seawards, against its light, were reared the ghostly forms of stranded bergs; they cast black shadows on the moonlit sea. Then suddenly great shafts of light flamed in the sky. The waning moon, the stars, the northern lights; the tossing, moonlit sea; ice, ice; and far away high snow-covered mountain ranges seen through the vaporous light. The people, huddled close for warmth, stood looking at it.

One night—November becomes mostly night—as twilight faded leaving the southern afterglow still lingering on the mountains, there suddenly appeared above the mountains in the north, extinguishing their light, the moon. Night deepened and the wind-swept bay grew black; and icebergs glowed like jewels in the moonlight. A planet rose, enormous, red. Incredible to eyes, it hung there like a lantern on a mountain peak.

Well, what of it, watchman? Lord! I don't know.

XVIII. MUCH ADO

ONE NIGHT—it was a blustery night, and dark and cold—I went as usual to promenade the shore. There, pipe in mouth, I strode along. And presently who should appear and greet me but midwife Martha and the young wife of the young hunter Boye, Sahra by name; and Martha carried on her back her year-old son. So, falling into step, we marched together—up and down and up and down, until my pipe burned out and I got bored. "Now," said I, stopping where a path led from the shore to my house, "home." And having thus conveyed to them, I thought, good night, I walked away.

Now my Greenlandish was at that time—it still is—preposterous, and my friends are not to be censured for having taken my dismissal as an invitation. So they did take it, and when I found them following at my heels I just hadn't the heart to send them back, to send them home as one sends home a dog. And why shouldn't they come to the house with me if they wanted to?—But gee! I thought, there'll be the devil to pay when I come marching in with them! For Salamina was of course at home; I'd left her there. And her devotion to me—I guess you'd call it that—had become extraordinary. So then, if I quavered as I turned the knob, what was my thrill on walking in at finding—nobody! Come in, you girls, come in! And shut the door. Sit down. Well—here we are. And that, just being there, seemed all there was to it. They're rather taciturn, these Greenland women. So Sahra, and Martha with her little boy on her lap, sit down on one side of the table, and I sit on the other. The lamp is lighted and the house is warm: not gay, the party, but it's comfortable indoors. Enough on such a night.

What's that! The house is still, we turn at the slight sound. There, peering in across the window ledge, are eyes innumerable. My fatal blunder was that in instinctive reaction to impertinence like that I did as we'd all do: I drew the curtains. Now things start.

It was as though the darkness out of doors, content enough with contemplating us through windowpanes, had suddenly been roused to fury. Like the storm's first sudden gust of wind that rattles blinds and howls around the eaves, a roar of mutterings swept round the house: the mob was there. One heard the pattering and scuffling of innumerable feet, the rubbing and the bumping of a crowd against the walls: the mob—its muffled thunder. My guests are terrified. Don't go, sweet guests, be calm, sit down again.

Suddenly we hear the entry door opened and slammed shut; quick footsteps in the passage. The room door is flung back. Ah, Salamina: thunder-brow; What's up? What's wrong? Why stand there glaring so?

"Salamina," say I, "you will please serve coffee."

It must be rarely that true hospitality suggests the throwing out of honored guests. Yet it was hardly the part of kindness to the two bewildered, frightened women to have detained them there to drink those poison cups that my virago served. Yes, she obeyed. She served us coffee: how! She bumped the furniture, she crashed down cups and plates. She stamped about, she glared. And silent all the while? Ah, no, she raged. Oh, stop it, Salamina, stop, shut up! She raged. "What," I made out at last in her bewildering flow, "what if I should bring in Martin and Peter—and Boye?" What Martin and Peter had to do with it, unless they were both her suitors, I don't know. But Boye—yes: "Good, send for Boye." And actually, as Salamina rushed off on that errand, my guests grinned. It was getting funny.

Whatever message got to Boye, it was an urgent one: come quick. For quick he came. It was a wild and desperate one, for wild and desperate he looked. I greeted him with warmth; he looked surprised. "Sit down," I said, and put him next to me. "More coffee, Salamina."

Boye spoke across to Sahra in tense undertones; he was excited, angry, but he controlled himself. I marveled at his manners. He accepted coffee, but refused the cigarette I offered him. The cigar that I laid down for him he left untouched. Now silence fell—with Salamina pacing up and down. That helped! Those footsteps, and the mob outdoors; that burdened, agonizing silence. But how end it? How? Of course! By concord of sweet sound, by music—of harmonica and flute.

As I laid the harmonica before Boye, urging him to play, a doleful smile showed on his tragic face. "No," said Boye. No, no use; and silence fell again.

Now Martha's baby, having already wet the floor and her, began a peevish whimpering. And under cover of that melancholy sound and of the diversion which the consequent suckling of the child occasioned, I ventured to tune up; I played. O silver flute, it's little pleasure that you've given ears, and yet you've had your hours. This was one. Sit, guests, and brood and sulk; pace on, old termagant; *be* silent, all of you, and think your thoughts—you'll listen. And as though my life hung on the fragile thread of melody, I played. Played what? No matter what, played on. Ears like what they're accustomed to: I played to *them*, played tunes they knew. Played "Home Sweet Home," "Nearer, My God, to Thee," "Ach, du lieber Augustin," "Shall we Meet beyond the River," "I'm Tired of Living Alone"—the irony of that! I played; I might not stop. And when my repertoire of such tunes was played out I plunged desperately into the recesses of my memory and dragged out "Elsa's Dream," and "Träumerei." Once Salamina, to turn the spotlight on herself again, made a dive at the drawn curtains—as though she hadn't noticed that outrage before—and drew them back. I stopped "Sweet Moon of My Desire" and shut them tight again, and smothered her infuriated protests with "The Rosary."

Sahra, meanwhile, had begun tempting Boye with the pile of photographs which, earlier in the evening, I had submitted for the entertainment of herself and Martha. Among them was a photograph of me, a dreadful thing, but Sahra fancied it. "Good," I had said, "from me to Boye." Sahra now chose that one out. "This one," she said, "Kinte has given you."

Boye, who had so far made no response of any kind, now reached and took the picture, looked at it. He's going to tear it up, I thought, and played a merry tune. Boye looked at the photograph, then he laid it back. Again he picked it up. He looked at it a long time, and then he put it down beside his cap. He'd taken it. As I switched back to "Nearer, My God, to Thee," Boye quietly picked up the harmonica and played. He played; then Martha played. *We* played, and Boye sang. A Greenlander, a catechist, I believe, or pastor at Godhavn, saw as he slept an angel come and stand before him; the angel sang to him. And so moving were the melody and the words of the angel's song that they awoke him. Then he wrote them down.

Guterput kutsinermio nalangnarssingardle nuna erkigssinekardle!
(*Glory be to God in Heaven, peace on earth!*)

So the words of the song began; and its melody was this:

It was the angel Schubert, maybe, who had at last done that in Heaven which he'd left undone on earth.

This, Boye sang; we played. Peace *came* to earth, and so the night was saved.

XIX. PEOPLE

ONCE, years ago, bound for a visit in the country, I was met for the last leg of my journey by a small boy in a buggy. So we drove along. Presently we passed a little gabled house all overgrown with, probably, wistaria. It had about it such unusual charm, and the air, somehow, of sheltering particularly nice, happy, cultured people, that I cried out, "Look! in that house—what sort of people live in there?" And the boy, looking at me as if I'd suddenly gone crazy, said, "Why—just regular people." It was a rebuke to all of us who let ourselves get tourist-minded.

The tourist mind sees *differences*, and magnifies them. It observes the cut of clothes, the twist of hair. It delights in the picturesque and quaint, and feeds on novelty. And concentrating upon the contemplation of exotic detail, it yields us in the name of science a picture of the vast divergencies of man. To what lengths won't minds go to find significance in little things!

It is to be observed that Greenland women incline to sit with legs straight out or, sometimes on the sleeping-platform, on a table, or a bench, with legs up on it. "I am told," said a traveler to me, "that they do this because of an ancient superstition that demons lurk under the platform." Would it not occur to one that, possibly, the stiff hide of their boots wrinkling below their bare knees would prove uncomfortable? Nor be observed that the vermilion paint with which the women's boots are coated cracks where the leather creases? And that women like to keep fine kamiks new and straight and shapely? Nor that the floor is cold, and underneath the sleeping-platform drafty?

The trouble is that we, taking for granted the rational nature of all that we do—even when it isn't rational—incline to find irrational and strange and on deep grounds to be accounted for, all different ways of other folk. And in direct consequence of all that we have read of *mores* and *taboos*—itself a nomenclature not applied at home—we embark upon our proper study equipped for little but misunderstanding, and approach our goal, the heart, mind, soul, of fellow man, via the far-flung periphery of his table manners.

I may now, I trust, with this preamble off my mind, confess to having been far less interested in Salamina's hell-raising as an expression of primitive woman's unique conception of property rights in men than as evidence, if I needed it, that she was just a regular girl. And to have conducted myself in the reckoning that followed not at all with the dispassionate restraint of a museum curator, but with all the blustering and pompous wrath of injured manhood. And that, of course, it worked. Oh, but we had great times!

Take, for example, our social gatherings, such as, for the limited circle of our set, became events of often more than weekly occurrence. That "set" was determined by Salamina; it was reasonable that I should rely upon her knowledge of her own people, and the part of prudence that I should introduce among our guests at least no woman of my own choice. So Salamina settled things. And it was consistent with her character and taste, her snobbishness, that her choice fell upon the undoubted aristocracy of the place. The best men and their no doubt noble wives became our friends. Thus for my avoidance of the many pitfalls in the adventures of friendship I have her innate common sense to thank. To name our set is to compile Igdlorssuit's social register.

First of our friends in time, in favor, and in fortune were Rudolf and Marghreta Quist. The highest distinction of birth, in Greenland—next, possibly, to illegitimate descent from Danes of consequence—is trader stock: that constitutes the Greenland peerage. Both Rudolf and Marghreta thus were peers, Rudolf's father having been by trade a cooper and, in an interim, a trader, his mother having been the daughter of the foretime Danish trader of Igdlorssuit, old Nielsen, and Marghreta being not only a trader's daughter but the sister of Johan Lange, the most astute trader in the district of Umanak. Good blood: they, strangely, showed it. Rudolf was handsome, with extremely beautiful dark gray-blue eyes set under heavy brows; he was broad-shouldered, straight, and tall. He was reserved and proud. He owned two whale nets and twelve dogs—the crack team of the place, perhaps the best in all the district. All of Rudolf's enterprises prospered. He held the job of cooper to the post. Marghreta was not beautiful, but she had style and bulk. She had three chins and when she sat, two lifebuoy rolls of belly. She didn't like to be so fat, but laughed about it. She dressed well, kept house well, kept everything about her orderly and clean.

Of Abraham Zeeb I have spoken. He too was a grandson of old trader Nielsen, that little black-haired Dane who by his native wife begot a clan of strapping men and women for Igdlorssuit. Louisa, Abraham's wife, was Rudolf's sister and her husband's cousin. She was fair to look at, good to dance with, impossible to talk to, and completely stupid.

Then there were Hendrik, Rudolf's brother, and his cousin-wife, Sophia. Rudolf seldom, Louisa rarely, Hendrik never, spoke. He was short and immensely powerful; he was capable in all things—including the procreation of children. Yet he was not one who prospered. But much in Greenland life hangs on the woman's management, and Sophia was not only always having children, she was lame. She was, in my eyes, the most lovely of the women of Igdlorssuit, the only lovely one perhaps. She had less beauty than the *quality* of loveliness.

Sophia's mother, Elisabeth, and her husband Jonas were among our friends. She was a daughter of old Nielsen, had the physique and stature of a man, the character we like to think men have, and all the marks of forty years of it carved in her features and graven in the seams and furrows of her weather-beaten face. Great, raw-boned, plank-backed Amazon; her Jonas worshiped her. And she could pride herself on having the best-looking little lad in all the settlement as hers. A good man, Jonas, and a gentleman. At the time of my first arrival at Igdlorssuit I had used, with the consent of the community council, the then vacant house of Jonas as a storehouse for my goods. Jonas and his family, returning unexpectedly soon, found their house thus occupied; and Jonas came to see me straight away. "I have come," he said, "to thank you for having used my house." And absolutely refusing to allow me to remove my goods, they went to live with others.

Severin Nielsen hardly looked like a Greenlander. In fact he bore such a striking resemblance to a friend of mine at home that just for companionship one night I picked him up on promenade and brought him home. I got out whisky, poured us drinks, and drank "Here's to you, Jack!" He was small and slight, good-looking, sensitive—extremely so. His cousin Salamina, Rudolf's sister, was his wife. She broke the spell of Quistian silence: she was alert, gay, talkative, a charming, sprightly little woman.

And there was Martin, but, alas! no wife. Only his persistent, melancholy devotion to the Salamina of my house and, in strange consequence, to me. Martin had a face like the full moon, a smile like the rising sun, and tear ducts like Niagara Falls. We were to see him more than once at some unfortunate reminder of the hopelessness of his love get up from the table and go out, to hide from us the tears he couldn't stop.

Our house was really fitted for fine company, for next to Trolleman's executive mansion it was by long odds the best house in the place. To begin with, it was built of timber; that impressed the people who, like people everywhere, would rather freeze in style than keep warm out of it. The house was cold; but it was in many ways convenient, having such ample room for storage as to leave its main room unencumbered. It was a pretty, cheerful house inside. The walls were pink, the window curtains and the sleeping-alcove were deep blue, and the alcove curtains were a royal purple. And all the furniture having been made on the spot, all rough, substantial, plain, and sensible, gave to the place a homely, free and easy look that put the guests at ease.

We did not entertain our guests in the style to which they'd been accustomed. It would have been no thrill for them to eat boiled seal ribs from the pot, nor, coming all dressed up as to a function, to meet with manners like their own at home. As our guests entered they beheld a long table laid with a white cloth, bright with lamps and candles, glittering with silver (or what passed for it) and glass and china, and groaning with good food. They entered—how? Well, sheepishly, not knowing, naturally, what to do. That mustn't worry you; just let them be. Be guided by the native diffidence, and in new manners simply lead the way. Seat them: You here, Louisa; Marghreta, you sit here. You, Rudolf, at the end; Sophia next. Now, Salamina, pass the food—to me, me first. That is important: lead the way. They're watching every move.

When all have had their fill, the table is moved back. It now becomes a bar, with beer stood out on it. Now dancing starts; it lasts until the beer is finished. Time isn't much on dark November and December days; no work, no work to do. The sea is neither water nor firm ice, the storms are violent. Sleep long, eat seldom, stroll, and dance: that is the order of the days. We dance. Somehow, by virtue of the food, the beer, the lamplight and the cozy room, the crowd, the heat, the stifling air, tobacco smoke, and sweat, the incessant rhythm of the accordion, the dizzy whirling of the dance, and most of all the whole-souled carefree gay warm-hearted natures of our guests, there was achieved a rare conviviality. And always when at last we stood at parting on the hillside and felt the cold, clean, early morning air on our hot faces, and sensed the dawn of twilight, always to all of us there'd come the thought: How good it is! We'd put our arms about each other's shoulders, loath to part. Good night, dear friends.

XX. TEARS

YES, take our social gatherings: who contrived them? By what power could I sit back, exactly as I did, rap my knuckles on the long home-made deal table, cry out, "*Tischlein, deck dich!*" and *have* it as by miracle bedecked with food? And then having regaled myself and guests cry, "*Tischlein weg!*"—to have it cleared, the litter swept away, the room transformed for dancing? Who filled our glasses, kept them filled? And passed cigars, and waited on the guests, dumped ash trays, kept things orderly, did every last least thing there was to do? No one but Salamina. The whole performance from its start to finish, from scrubbing the whole house that afternoon to scrubbing it again next day, beginning, end, and everything between, she did. And how! With what precision and dexterity, what unflagging energy, with what perfection! Not as a servant but as hostess, not giving herself up to work but somehow working as she dined and danced. Well may I thank the beer and food and this and that for those good times: thank God for Salamina! And Abraham speaking, as was his way, in thought of all the people of Igdlorssuit, speaking for them as to an instrument of their good fortune, said, taking my hand, "Thank you, Kinte, for bringing Salamina to Igdlorssuit."

Yes, she could work. Well, look at her: straight as a whip, strong as an ox, lithe as a cat. Her hands were rough and hard. When she crooked her arm the muscle bulged up like a baseball, round and firm. They're built for work, these native women, some of them. They like it—some of them. We know that sort; work seems to be their life. One doesn't think of them as of the gentler sex; they haven't, it would seem, their sensibilities. It's hard to know.

One day—I don't know what the trouble was—I'd had that miserable Karen at the house and given her the devil for some one of her petty sneaking underhanded tricks, some swindle that my kindness to her husband, David, laid me open to; and she'd been properly told off and sent away. And Salamina felt the miserableness of it all. She put supper on the table, and we ate it. Salamina was very quiet. Then she came over and sat next to me, and rested her hand on my shoulder. After a time she spoke:

"In twenty-seven my husband died, and it was terrible for me. And twenty-eight was bad, and twenty-nine was little better. In nineteen-thirty I was contented, and there was no man in my life. In thirty-one Kinte comes to Umanak and asks Salamina to go to Igdlorssuit and live in his house. In thirty-two Kinte goes away to America and never comes to Greenland again. And oh, I can never bear it, for there can be nothing more in my life."

And as I held her head against my breast her tears poured down over my hands.

XXI. SALAMINA

THIRTY MILES from Umanak in the interior of Umanak Fiord is the little settlement of Ikerasak. Like most of the settlements of the district it is on an island, and, like Umanak, it is shadowed by a mountain peak, a peak like Umanak's, but smaller. A little settlement, a little peak; there reigned a little man as King. It seems that kings *may* be quite little men; for the fact of majesty is of itself a worshipful matter, as we of America all know who yield our headlines to the least of princelings. This little man, accordingly, by virtue of his shrewd intelligence, by his ability as a hunter and dog-driver, by his authority as outpost manager, by his royal hospitality, good-fellowship, and open-handedness, and by, not least of all, his own conviction of a Viking lineage, was king almost in fact. His lineage, whatever it had been, did count. It was a dynasty whose sons held power, whose daughters by their charm and character were allied with distinguished Danes, and whose hatchet-faced descendants are today the district's native aristocracy. Blood counts, we say; but the conviction that it counts counts more. And that conviction of the little half-breed King's at last in his old age blazed out: he raised the flag of Norway on the ramparts of his turf-walled castle. Mad? Just a bit; but it was, by all accounts, a charming madness. And although his royal requisition of the royal stores (the King of *Denmark's* stores) led finally to his relinquishing the throne, he continued loved and honored to his death. And long will live the memory of "Uncle Jens."

What is of more importance than Uncle Jens's ancestry is the fact that he played the fiddle, that he played it nicely, that he played Schumann airs and German lieder and the Beethoven Minuet, that he owned a good old square piano and played on that a bit, that he was finely sensitive to cultural things and showed it in himself, his house, his way of living; that he was, in short, in a most real sense a gentleman. For when his wife's little niece, Salamina, came to visit him from Karajak, far up in the fiord, she came under an influence that was a perfect complement of her good, poorer home.

Little Salamina was herself of what even in Greenland is distinguished as good family. She was by blood of distant kin to Uncle Jens, she was the daughter of one who was both a good hunter and a catechist (a rare phenomenon); and her people were of that fortunate class which, living in the outposts, could acquire some of the virtues of Danish culture without succumbing to its metropolitan vices. Such things do count. What counted more was that her father's precarious livelihood as a hunter was backed by his small but dependable competence as schoolteacher: she got enough to eat. Sturdy and strong, she'd turn from playing house and making mud pies to chasing with the boys and cracking her small whip. She was a tomboy. She shot at the snow buntings with her bow and arrow, creeping up on them again as they flitted from boulder to boulder—to shoot, and miss, again. She climbed the rocks and roamed the hills. She led, like other Greenland children, a free, unhampered life. She took what bumps she got, and didn't cry. They do, in Spartan Greenland. She worked. A winter morning, dark and cold. "Get up!" her mother says, shaking her out of her dreams. "Get up, and light the stove." Barefooted, yawning, up she gets. She's ten years old.

Dressed in boy's clothes—skin breeches, anorak—she accompanies her mother off into the hills to gather the scrub brush for fuel, and carry staggering loads of it back home. That's daily work all summer and in early fall. And when the snow comes and the ptarmigan in search of food move down from the mountains, Salamina takes her father's gun and, in boy's breeches, tramps the hills to hunt them. Yes, she could shoot: gulls, ptarmigan; she'd even shot some seals—but on the ice. She tried a kayak once; got in, got pushed afloat. And then in panic dropped her paddle, screamed, clung to the cockpit—and upset. For all her breeches she was still a girl. But dogs she handled well, and in the light, late winter days she'd drive her sledge beside the best of them.

Her visits to Ikerasak were always fun. Mostly they'd drive there, in the winter time, bowling silently along over the smooth, snow-covered plain of the frozen fiord, westward down the dazzling pathway of the sun. Those drives! The world all gleaming white, the sky so blue; so beautiful! And there: that rambling five-room wonder house of turf, with all the things it held! And Uncle Jens and Nikolena: they adored her. He'd sired innumerable sons and daughters; the house was full of them, of children, always. And Salamina now became that pet, the youngest. And the chocolate with which Uncle Jens would get the child's mouth smeared Nikolena would rub off with a wet rag. That was her rôle, unspoiling her. Grand dame! She made them mind their p's and q's: work, and keep clean; be in at night, and don't go flirting round. Wipe chocolate off her *mouth?* One day the child, not satisfied with eating it, stuffed chocolate down the leg of her long kamik, then ran out to play. The day was hot; she played about and clean forgot her bootlegging. Her bare leg was a pretty sight at bedtime.

So, as Salamina grew up, grew from childhood into maidenhood, she came to be at frequent and for longer periods a member of that household. She helped with everything; their ways became her own. And Nikolena's skill and standards, her requirements of perfection in all the native household arts, were transmitted to the child, to serve her all her life.

Such things as Nikolena taught, and how to read and write, and all her tomboy stunts, it may be said she *learned;* and all the rest of knowledge she grew into. Knowledge comes easily where there is no restraint. It is partaken of like food, like mother's milk, in just the measure of the child's capacity or need. It merely comes to be

—like sense of balance, power of speech. And all those things that we write books about, suppress books for—advice to girls, advice to boys, advice to newly-weds, advice, advice—the Greenland child just grows to know about. What fools it makes us out to be! There in one room they lived, the family. Life in a nutshell, one might say. One would be used to life who lived like that, grew up with it. The Greenland child grows up on facts, and builds its play around reality. What child would need a doll that had a baby to play mother to? So Salamina mothered her small sister when she came, dressed and undressed her, toted her around. And then, just when, if it *had* been a doll, she might have tired of it or with much handling broken off its jointed legs or glued-on head, the baby grew to childhood and became a playmate.

Salamina loved her little sister; so did everyone. And every year she became prettier, so that everybody knew and spoke about how beautiful she'd be when she grew up. She grew so fast: how years fly by! Why, she'd be nine years old in no time. And what appetites growing children, good, healthy, growing children, have. She'd eat her fill of seal meat at home, and then go over to the neighbors and fill up again on porridge; for the neighbors were good people, and made a great fuss over her. There was often a pot of oatmeal porridge there, and always the spoon and plate where Job, perhaps, had left it when he'd finished. (Poor Job! he wasn't well. He died quite suddenly. The doctor said it was t.b.)

Then in the very bed where she'd been born, that bed of all of them, Salamina's little sister died. It was t.b., they said. Children grow up with death, in Greenland.

Salamina was only twenty when her father died; and in the same year died her mother. It was as though they had been too much used to live together to endure apart. Then, too, going hand in hand in life they'd shared their malady: t.b.

Salamina's brother had married and had moved to Ikerasak, and Salamina herself now went to live with Uncle Jens and Nikolena. And it was a fine thing all around when she took up with her cousin Frederick, their son, and married him, and so became in *fact* a daughter of the house.

Uncle Jens was not one to have neglected the education of his sons. His own culture, and the European connections of his family, had shaped his inclinations: he, naturally, would advance the boys that way. That's progress, they are told in Greenland. And a benevolent administration furthers it by providing schools and higher schools for the conversion of first-rate hunters into third-rate clerks and lazy catechists. And one suspects that the remuneration of the trading class, from clerks to bankers, is God's just way of compensating men for what the folly of society has done to them. At any rate here's Frederick, a clerk at Umanak, a life-long job with steady pay; and Salamina for his wife. Life starts for them; they settle down to it. He was an even-tempered, quiet man. "If there was ever any trouble, it was my fault," Salamina told me. "He was always the same, always good." And with the coming of the children—first Regina, then Frederick, then little Helena who is with us now—marriage took on its form and substance, family. *Now*, we may surely say, life starts. It ended soon for Frederick. He died of tuberculosis just after the third child was born.

But anyhow, life starts for Salamina.

"What is it, Salamina?"

Salamina seated near me in the lamplight has lowered her sewing and is looking at me quizzically.

"*Salamina ajorpok?*"—"Is Salamina bad?"—she asks me in my pigeon dialect. How in the world does she know that I've been writing about her!

"No," I tell her laughingly. She smiles and takes to work again.

XXII. FOOTBALL

"HERE! pass it, Martin!" The little seal-hide bag of grass comes sailing over; I kick it on the run: kick, slide, slip, bang!—and hit the hard ice with my tail. Up, up again and after it! There's a dense scrimmage round the ball: plunge in. Kick, kick, be kicked; fall down, get up again; butt, shove, trip, hold: no rules; just fight. Peter is greased lightning, Niels a roaring lion, Paulus a tower of frozen turf: butt that! They're strong and fast, these boys. "There, take it, Samuel!" But Niels roars down on him: You will? You catechist! God, look at Niels! He picks the preacher up and slings him to his shoulder like a sack of blubber. He's down the field with him, the preacher kicking heaven. He's got the ball. God, look at Niels! A goal.

Twilight of early afternoon, the full moon in the north. And now and then the foolish little bag of grass goes floating up across it as though small boys were throwing stones at Heaven's window.

XXIII. OLD TIMES

HERE! pass it, Olabi." Olabi, with a charming, rather sickening smile and mincing manner, takes the brimming cup from me and hands it to his mother. She can't well help herself, poor soul, bedridden now for weeks. Hard luck to be bedridden in a house like hers, a den, low, cramped, and black with dirt. There is an elegance about Olabi that, as maid of all work, he doesn't communicate to the house. Ashes are piled up on the floor around the cracked old stove, the cooking-pot is caked with dirt. Well—Olabi himself is not too clean: he needs a shave, he needs a wash. It isn't that he doesn't know that cleanliness is virtue; his fancy needlework and crocheted lace that he has shown us is spotless. His heart is in that work; his heart is maybe spotless pure.

Charlotta drinks from the mug and puts it down. "*Aja, aja, aja, aja—kuja, kuja,*" she sings in her old cracked voice. She roars with glee and goes off into spasms of asthma. "*Kuja, kuja, kuja,*" she sings on, old die-hard crone. Half dead of asthma, heart disease, t.b., and God knows what, she's got more guts, more joy of life, than any living thing in the whole settlement. She knows it, lays it on, shows off—old relic of old times. "*Kuja, kuja.*" She rocks her body, rolls her head; stops suddenly; puffs with grim fury at her sawed-off pipe; bursts into a roar of laughter, and collapses in an orgasm of coughs. Good! Crack your lungs, old girl, and burst your sides; roar on, be happy, choke, and die. You've long outlived the world.

We were good friends, this bent old crone and I. I liked her stuff: she laid it on for me. She liked my stuff: I poured it to the brim. You *grow* to know most people; Charlotta burst on me.

Shall I ever forget her on that July day I raised my roof! How as the people were all quietly wending their ways up hill to my house, all with cups in hand, all set to decorously celebrate the day, how, suddenly, the roof of heaven was shivered by a cry: good God, what's that!

There was Charlotta midway on the hill, crouched by her bent old back and legs, but chin in air: "*Aja, aja, aja, aja*," she cried, wriggling her belly, waving her arms and coffee cup and pipe. "*Aja, ajaja, ajaja, aja.*" The crowd roared laughter. "*Aja, aja, ajaja, aja*," wild and loud. Then suddenly she stopped, turned, and with desperate effort—poor old thing—resumed her spider-legged progress up the hill. She had proclaimed her joy.

That was her day; she made the most of it. What songs she poured out sitting on the hillside! God shrank away; Tornarsuk woke, trolls listened from the mountain tops and grinned. Wild, loose, free stuff: the people roared, girls covered up their ears—or cupped them. What power had that ancient hag to shatter centuries!

It is delightful to refresh the memory
It is delightful, ija, aja.

Mana ajaja, ejora, aja-a,
I, I am wicked; I, I am wicked; I, I am wicked.

Aja, the one who has never had a bastard,
Aja, the one who has never had a bastard,
Aja, the one who has never had a bastard,
The little one who has never had a bastard,
Aja! it is only I, aja!
Who is all men's toy.

My playmate always touches me;
He pulls my wristlets off,
He pulls . . .

Mala – poor old half crazy thing ; fine artist

We can't go on with this. We can't have old Tornarsuk rocking the foundations of Manhattan, nor mountain trolls smearing their paw prints on the tinfoil of the Chrysler building. We can't have old girls telling all they know. "*Aja, ajaja, aja*": what fun life is! *Old* girls: they know.

Take old Beate—not so old, in fact; old-timer is more accurate. Dear, quaint, vivacious, charming soul. A tiny thing—big head; two-thirds of her was head and body, one-third legs. Her legs were bent from habit, not infirmity; but they seemed grotesquely inadequate to support the wrigglings of her eel-like trunk. *She* felt the joy of life! She squirmed with it; she danced. None of your linoleum-pattern steps and mission-parlor posturings for her, none of your blasé nonchalance of modern youth: she *danced.* And the rhythmic windings, spasms, and contortions of her sinuous body were as a pantomime of lust and laughter. Fierce, wild, grotesque, abandoned; and controlled: consummate artist. She danced alone, of course; this was the past become alive again one night at my house: the drum dance. Beating the tambourine-like drum she sings; her voice is passionate and deep.

My drum—jajïja-ja-ja-ja,
My drumstick—jajïjaja,
My voice—jajïjaja.
Ajïja jaja kanarrajaja a—ajïjarra.

It grips you, hypnotizes you—that rhythm. You stamp your feet and sway your body to it; your mind is leaving you. Well, let it.

Beate stops. Emanuel, her brother, takes the drum. He's an old hunter, one of the greatest of them. Short, stocky, wrinkled in the face, and dark; light-footed as a youth. He boasts an angakok as grandfather; if there were angakoks today he'd be one. He's a man of authority, and a lusty lover. Dead silence; he begins:

"*Aja!*" (He has pitched his voice high for comic effect. He holds his drum as though to hide his face and peeks out coyly from behind it. He handles the drumstick with affected daintiness.)

Aja! from the North and from the South,
When I was young
I began to long for women;
Aja, ajijaja.

Suddenly like a wild man he leaps out into the circle. "*Aja, ajija,*" he shouts. Right and left in sudden shifts he moves his drum: tum, tum, tum, tum, "*aja, ajaja.*" He wriggles his body in contortions of ludicrous obscenity; he grimaces like a demon. Now stooping over, chin in air, he sticks his drum behind him like a tail: ferocious clowning. The crowd is beating time and punctuating the refrain with "*Huh! ha!—huh, huh, huh!*" Excitement mounts; the house is bedlam. If Emanuel ever had any inhibitions he's rid of them now. No symbolism to his dance; it's it. Finally as a climax of realism he throws himself face downwards on the floor, and without a hitch in time completes his act.

And Mala danced. To Beate, to Emanuel, and to Charlotta the song and dance were acts. They played a part. They had the artist's gift of assuming it without embarrassment, completely, instantly; and of emerging from the part as though they merely laid aside a mask they'd worn. Mala was different. She was a poor suppressed old thing, half crazy all her life, to whom the dance was just an outlet to her crazy self. She danced with terrifying fervor, her face distorted with half make-believe, half real ferocity; her voice was like the baying of a hound. She was superb, and tragic.

And Abelone danced, and Peter Sokiassen; only the old knew how, though all of us from envy and excitement had a try. It was the old one's night; their vindication of the outlawed past, their resurrection and their glory. Pride displayed itself. This, Greenlanders, they seemed to say, is what your fathers were.

"You're magnificent!" I said to old Beate. She beamed; put out her arms to me.

"Some night you come and sleep with me," she said with fierce mock passion. Phew! Think quick.

"I'll have to ask Justina," I replied.

"Justina!" She fairly snorted her contempt. "Those young things know nothing." And leaning her funny body far over she went into roars of laughter.

So, for a night, old times had lived again. The trodden embers of old fires flamed. By the light of them, and by the stars and moon, the crowd dispersed. Emanuel went home with his little old wife; Beate went home to her daughter and the children; Mala, slave of all work in the house of Knud, went home to curl up like a dog in a corner of that dirty floor; all found their homes, and sleep. And waking in due time to gray reality they might have felt that old-time orgy to have been a dream—but that that pompous ass, the catechist, his wind up, was running around threatening every living soul with hell fire that should dare to dance an old-time dance again.

XXIV. FRIENDS AND FINANCE

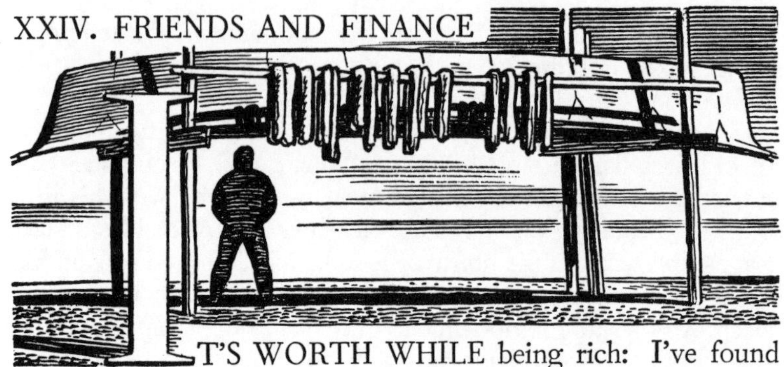

IT'S WORTH WHILE being rich: I've found that out. If it had never dawned upon me before going to Greenland, it burst upon me there. It's thrilling—money. Not that I made my wealth, or mined it there; I merely woke to find myself, in Greenland, rich; the richest man by far on the whole of Ubekjendt Ejland, and one of the most wealthy in the district. I used my money to buy friends.

Buy friends! That's crude, perhaps; let's say to win them. And it is done so easily, and proves the source of such unlimited pleasure and self-satisfaction, that I can only wonder why hardly anybody ever does it. It is not, of course, a new idea, the Eskimos themselves having practiced it in the old days—at least in America —in a magnificent way, hoarding their little wealth that they might buy, or win, the whole community at one great spending orgy, *potlatch*. That must have been great fun, to corner the whole friendship market at one swoop. I'd like to have the nerve for that; the Christian, somehow, does it timidly.

It must be pleasant, too, to have your friendship bought, to have a rich man say to you, "Here, take this check; my compliments." How friendly it would make one feel! A fair exchange in pleasure. There is much friendship pent up in the world that no one wants.

In Greenland—here the timid Christian speaks—friendship is cheap. Friends can be had for a plug of tobacco, and up. Good Lord! in America people will pay out ten thousand dollars—and only get a string of beads, and then you never know for sure they're genuine: friends mostly are. At least you take them on trust, not feeling them to see if they're all wool, or looking at their bottoms for the sterling mark. You merely hand your gift out, and go home to write a new friend's name down in your book.

Besides speculating, to a limited extent, in friends in Greenland, I became a banker, ran a bank. One does, when one first goes there. People, beginning in late October when the fall gales blasted hunting, through October and dark November and December, on more or less till March, when they were pinched for food and without cash to buy it, people would come trooping, one or two a day, to borrow at my bank: I lent. One kroner, two, five sometimes, sometimes only fifty öre. I kept my records on a slip of paper first, and then I used a book. It was, of course, only play banking, for there was no security put down and no interest paid, and the president got no salary and no bonus. I wouldn't like to be the first in Greenland to suggest that people pay you back more than they have borrowed. In fact I was so grateful when they paid me back at all that I'd pay *them* interest in cigars and beer. That was expensive in the end: they all but one paid back.

As Christmas approached it began to look as if we'd have to suspend business, close the doors. There was virtually a run on the bank, due not to panic lest the bank's funds might run out, but to the growing rumor that they wouldn't. And I couldn't well combat it with any plea of poverty, living as I did, in such a house, with two brass student lamps, a dozen or more pots and pans, and food in plenty. The simple logic of their attitude, that those who have should give to those who haven't, was as irrefutable, it appeared, as physical law: that nature hates a vacuum, and water seeks its level. Why shouldn't gold? It does, of course, in time. We pile it up, taking from those that have little—I'm not moralizing, it has to come from somewhere—taking from those that have little and stacking it for those that have, deepening the valleys and piling on the mountain peaks, till crash! there's a cave-in and a landslide, and it all has to begin over again. At any rate, in

Greenland one is confronted by the relentless logic of communism, against which to maintain oneself in the enjoyment of a sufficient—and, I may say, considerable—residue of one's wealth one has recourse to his Christian sophistry: he will not pauperize the poor. In consequence, I *lent* them money, reserving the giving of it to such special occasions of need as the sickness of the breadwinner of a house, or death, and festivals. The wonder is that anyone paid back; the marvel is that all did, as I've said, but one. That one! That miserable, whining, whipped cur Joas. Let me tell about him.

He, and a female of his kind, his wife, their children, and Cornelia and hers, inhabited one lair-like den. There Joas, who was able-bodied, in the prime—if one could call his that—of life, maintained them in the filthy squalor to which they were no doubt accustomed, and which they no doubt liked. They lacked the energy, the will, to even wipe their noses on their hands. Cats preen themselves, hogs given half a chance keep clean; not they. That stinking outfit—phew! Who cares?

I didn't, at the bank. They'd come: one day a half a kroner, next day a kroner, then two, then five—and so on. And always, so they said, *Cornelia* needed it. Now Cornelia was one of those unfortunate creatures to whom the heart of man—or, more particularly, men—goes out. She had no family, no standing, no character, no morals, and no charm. She was the sort of amiable girl that would lend herself to any man, and one whom a surprising lot had borrowed. So when it came to naming the father of her child she picked—on, doubtless, grounds enough—a good one, Severin. Five kroner a year: that's the indemnity the law secured to her. And Severin, obeying law and custom, pays the cash and cuts the child and mother dead. It seemed a bit severe. I used to hand out for Cornelia.

"Why," asked Salamina in some indignation one day upon returning from the store, "why are you giving all that money to Joas and his wife?"

"I'm not," said I. "It's for Cornelia—poor thing, she needs it."

"Cornelia! Why, she hasn't been living in their house for a long time. They've been buying coffee and sugar and crackers with it for themselves."

And that was true. I bode my time. Not long, and Joas came again: five kroner for Cornelia.

One feels at times like that, the need of words, the lack of words in Greenlandish. How eloquent my English would have been! I would have told him off, concluding splendidly, "You God-damned lying sneak, get out!" In Greenlandish? The best I knew, the best, I think, they have, is what I said: I told him how he'd sinned and then in wrath cried out, "Bad man, you're very bad. Go way!"

Joas stood still, looked black. Then he turned round, strode out, and crashed the door shut back of him.

Good riddance, worth the price. No more of him, thank God. Oh—no? Not right away—ten days or so—he's back. No, Joas, none for you. Good-by. For never—now in '34 I'm writing this—never shall Joas or his tribe—Wait, please, excuse me, Reader, just a moment. I'll be back. There's someone knocking at the door, outside somewhere.

Funny coincidence: it was that wife of Joas's. She was afraid to come to the house door, scared of the dogs. "Why, they're all right," I said. "No, that one there," she whimpered, "I'm afraid of him." I thought that only dogs feared dogs in Greenland. "What is it that you want, Louisa?" "I want to borrow money." She was shocking to look at: filthy, of course, her clothes just black with grease. And such miserable, wrinkled, worn-out kamiks without stockings; bare knees in winter time! And that half-wit face with wisps of feather-dusted hair across it. And she had had a nosebleed; it was caked all over her upper lip and chin. Oh, well, I gave it to her.

XXV. ON WIVES

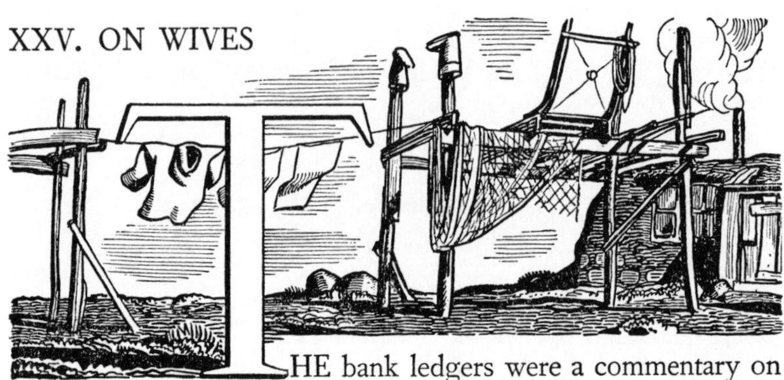

THE bank ledgers were a commentary on the domestic economy of the families of the settlement; they were less a reflection of the earning power of the hunters than of the spending wisdom of their wives. Of this no family among my clients furnished a stronger example than that of my near neighbor and employee David, and his wife, Karen. They were my greatest debtors, having had only to become aware of my leniency to take constant and almost unlimited advantage of that special credit which as the man's employer I stood ready to extend. The bank may well investigate their case.

David Lövstrom was the son of that most lovable old Thomas to whom I paid some tribute in the early pages of this book. David was himself, in looks and disposition, the best of tributes to his father. He was moreover the most brilliant hunter of the settlement and, by the records, the leading seal-killer of the district. For that and for his amiability he enjoyed the respect and affection of the whole community, including—I really think he did enjoy—the love of his peculiar wife. Hunger and cold, fatigue and danger, and his wife: David was one to take things as they came. Complain? He didn't know the thought. Come hardships one and all: "*Ajungulak!*"—"It's good!"—said David. And Karen *was* peculiar.

She came by it. Not that one inherits one's behavior; Karen didn't. Give her the credit for that specialty. But character and temperament: in these she was her father's child, Emanuel's. It is noteworthy that in a small community of an unpopulous district in which there must have been through countless generations unlimited inbreeding, in which the means of livelihood and way of living are the same for all, families should show such markedly divergent traits. Zeebs, Nielsens, Lövstroms, and—Emanuel's family—Samuelsens, all were distinctly marked and different in character and looks. The Samuelsens, even the younger generations of the family, appeared somehow to represent an older Greenland. They were old-fashioned neither by sloth nor by stupidity but by tenacity. As old Emanuel boasted of an angakok grandsire, so, one felt, they all, down to the youngest of the lot, took pride in what their race had been and what, in them, it still continued being. An unregenerate lot. Physically, the Samuelsens were sturdy, small, compact. They were great hunters and men who didn't spare themselves. Even Karen could handle a kayak like a man. She'd killed her seal. Few Greenland women could match that.

Karen was quaint-looking rather than pretty. Her face was round as the full moon; it could beam all over with elfish good humor, and it could go hideous with rage. Her little eyes would then become mere slits, her skin get blotched like moldy cheese. That was when people hindered her; they didn't often. And if one started to—if David did—he'd quit; he knew too well what followed. That was enjoyed by everyone with mingled shame and pleasure, and a thoroughgoing pity for David. He, poor devil, would like as not be in the house with her, she on the bed there kicking everything in reach and howling like a dog pack. You couldn't help but hear those dismal yowls, they filled the settlement. And the nearest approach to retaliation that David ever made was just to walk out quietly—to lean against the house and wait, for hours if need be, till she calmed down.

Living with them and their little family of two children was one Anneke and a fatherless child of hers. Anneke was a poor, half-demented nondescript, useless to everyone, and very dirty. She lowered the tone of the household, and probably contributed by her shiftlessness to its low morale. It was a crowded dirty place, that little house, and what those women did with time nobody knows. Karen was smart enough; she could work, but she wouldn't. She was skillful with her needle; but one who intrusted work to her could never count upon its being either well or ever done. She was a gadabout and a glutton, and most of David's substantial earnings went for fancy store food for herself and Anneke. She dressed quite well enough, while David often went in almost rags. It was common to see her little children floundering about in worn-out kamiks of their father's. There is a Greenland saying: Judge a girl by her kamiks, a woman by her husband's kamiks. Thumbs down on Karen.

Or pants down; and give it to her good and plenty with a stick. That is what people thought would stop her fits. It might have; certainly worth trying. But that seal-killer, David, was too gentle for such measures.

It is told of a man at Skansen, on Disko Island, how he married a pretty girl from the great capital, Godhavn, and how she, becoming discontented with the confinement of rural domestic life, took to gadding about and to making prolonged visits to her family and friends at home. So that with incessant fetching of her and carrying of her back, and being more and more left to shift for himself, his married life was not quite what it should have been. Fed up with argument, at last he beat her. No use, it didn't work. Ha! cry the tender-hearted, it never does. But wait. He waited, went one day and fetched her home. There, taking her outdoors in full and glaring view of everyone, he beat her with a stick. And it is said that from that time—and that was years ago—she has remained a model, loving wife.

Once every year, in spring when seals were plentiful, David and Karen, with their memories of the winter's cold still fresh, would form and act upon a resolution: they would improve their miserable hut by building on a vestibule. So David would touch the community chest for requisite credit at the store, buy boards, and put up the addition. Summer would pass, and fall come round

his is Sahra — wife of Isaac,
other of Abraham, Johan,
d Martin, sister of
lisabeth the wife of
nas.

again; they'd need their vestibule at last. Especially since Karen hadn't gathered brush, nor stacked up turf, nor saved her money to buy fuel. Not saved up fuel? Of course she had: the vestibule. So, as the winter nears they burn it stick by stick. Their good resolve goes up in smoke.

Well, there's *that* pair: great hunter and a spendthrift wife. They live in squalor.

Jonas, that little gentleman of whom we've told, lived with his old Elisabeth and two grown children in one of the largest and best-kept houses of the settlement. Of the children, Isaak was prevented from hunting by occasional visitations of epilepsy. He brought a little money in by catching shark—not much. Dorthe, his sister, aged sixteen, was a good industrious girl and helped when needed with the housework. She brought no money in, and ate a lot. Jonas was a thoroughly good man but, owing to eye trouble, a poor hunter. The sum of earnings in that household was not more than half of David's earnings. They lived well, dressed well, had fuel in winter and food the year around. But how? Just by Elisabeth's good management and skill.

To see in Greenland how many families that are poor live well, and how many that are rich live squalidly, the most confirmed misogynist would get himself a wife.

XXVI. ON THINGS

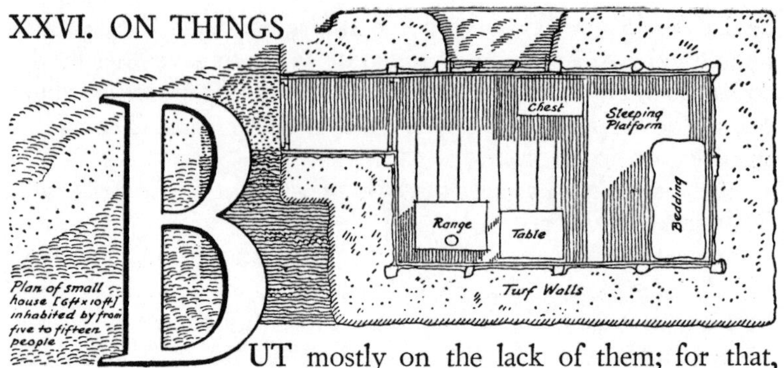

Plan of small house [6ft x 10ft] inhabited by from five to fifteen people

BUT mostly on the lack of them; for that, observing Greenland life from ours, is one of its prime elements. *Things*, there, don't count; and most comparison of homes, and lives, is qualitative. There is no progress without commerce, no commerce without *things*. That Greenland thinglessness must go.

But the Greenlander is curiously stubborn or slow-witted about quantitative values. He doesn't readily see the advantage of having more things than he can use nor of using more things than he has to. It was simple enough to get him out of the habit of making—at great and loving labor—wooden water buckets inlaid with carved ivory by offering him galvanized iron pails. The iron pails were better, and cost—in labor—less. But to make him use two pails instead of one—that's different. A gun, of course he wanted it. But not two guns. A pail, a gun, a coffeepot, a pot to boil things in, a chamber pot, a stove, a cup; just one of each in place of what he used to make. That's well enough, but still you've hardly started commerce. You've got to get them wanting things in quantity, get them to want to sit on chairs, and eat off tables, and own tool chests of eating implements. Good Lord, you've got to civilize them: that means things. But they *are* stubborn.

They don't appear to grasp the principle of ownership for owning's sake, even when as at Igdlorssuit they have before them in the house of Trolleman an example in epitome of the culture that we sponsor, the splendid knick-knack gimcrack gadget culture of today. His living-room, consider it: it measures ten or twelve by fourteen feet; it holds the following:

Two couches; a small dining-table; a set of 4 chairs upholstered in red plush; a set of 4 Victorian-patterned chairs upholstered in ornamental yellow plush and hung with tassels (these are kept piled in twos against the wall); a set of 2 large ornamental wicker chairs and settee to match; 1 large, round, polished, grilled, and jigsawed walnut table, very fine (and on it: 1 green felt tablecloth fringed and tasseled and embroidered with daisies; 1 crocheted centerpiece; 1 beadwork supercenterpiece; 1 jardinière containing paper flowers; 5 assorted vases; 2 German silver urns; 2 brass standards flying Danish flags, these wrapped in tissue paper; 2 ash trays—butterfly and polar bear; 1 paper weight); 1 small table holding gramophone; 1 small table holding radio; 1 jigsaw corner bracket holding ornamental loud-speaker; 1 child's wicker table with 2 chairs to match; 1 seaman's chest—a beauty; 1 walnut bureau with mirror, and on it—oh, never mind; enough . . . ; 1 stove.

I think that's all. Oh no! the walls! On one wall 5 oil paintings, done, Trolleman says, by hand; and on all the walls, covering them everywhere, lithographs, colored prints, photographs of pretentious-looking people whom T. didn't know and of sad-looking people whom he did, a crayon enlargement of T. with whiskers (not good), and one of T. without them (worse), and a beautiful photograph of Regina and her first-born baby—taken at the hospital. And with lace curtains and countless plush sofa pillows with American Indians painted on them we conclu . . . no! no! we *don't*, not yet. The ceiling, with its chandelier. That, just by sheer magnificence, outshone the room. It was the jewel; the room was but its setting. It was the most amazing *tour de force* in brass that human fantasy and human skill perhaps had ever realized. With its labyrinth of scrolls and chains and dangling things diverging as it were from its own object, light, it appeared as a symbolic realization in that symbolic metal, brass, of the eccentric mind of Trolleman. By God! it was just that. For in its very midst, concealed almost in verbiage of brass, there hung that abstract of the mind itself, the lamp. This lamp shall never give out light. It isn't filled; the law won't let it be. It's for petroleum.

So there's the room; most people at Igdlorssuit had seen it. And on Saturday mornings the women of the settlement, having washed, or probably not washed, their pot, not having scrubbed their floor, stand loitering round the store and watch Regina and Helena dust and clean those things, all brought for that outdoors. The women loitering in the sunlight watch Regina work, and there is no envy in their hearts. And they see her wash, and hang her lines of clothes to dry—so many clothes and sheets and pillow slips and things. And they don't envy her. They live on in their little one-room houses quite content. They have most things they need; their needs are small. So scant their property that we can list a household's whole possessions in eight lines:

A stove, a lamp, a pot to boil in, a coffeepot, a frying-pan for roasting coffee, a chamber pot, a wooden spoon, a mirror and a comb, a cup and saucer (maybe two or three), a bowl, a gun, a kayak and appurtenances, a shark line and a fishline, a change of clothes per inmate (or more, or less), a table and a chest of drawers (perhaps), a wooden chest, some old tin cans, a saw, a kitchen knife, a pocket knife, a watch (perhaps), a sledge, six dogs, bedding—that's all.

Such may be the possessions of a household of moderate means and one breadwinner. David and some others have much less than that; several have more. More people don't imply more things. The house of Peter Sokiassen measures about eight by ten feet inside; I can't stand up in it. In that house live fourteen people; they couldn't have much room for things. There are three hunters in the household; each has a kayak. They have, however, but five dogs and one sledge.

Yet little as the possession of *things* appears to count to Greenlanders, their very penury, and the squalor in which many of them live, and the smallness of the houses of them all, is evidence of change, of Progress, I may say. They've learned the first great principle of Progress: *private* ownership. And all these little houses are expressive of the people's will to get apart to own and to enjoy alone what in these modern times they're privileged to possess. To this let one of them bear witness. I present a young Greenlander who, in the third quarter of the last century, wrote of it as follows:

"When I was a child I never visited other inhabited places but always stayed at Kakertok, and I grew up quite unaware of the conditions of people in other places. Therefore I had for a long time no idea of my countrymen's poverty. But having now arrived at manhood, and having traveled round to other inhabited places, I have observed the following facts: The Greenlanders have commenced to live more separately, reducing their houses proportionately, and that, I think, is one of the causes of their decline, on account of which I have written this, wishing that they may reflect well on again congregating together and mutually loving and assisting each other. When I was yet a child at Kakertok there were very large houses with three windows, and the inmates all loved and assisted each other in procuring the chief necessities of life. Sometimes when kayaks had become leaky, three might be seen to be brought into the house at the same time to be sewed and dried. And when a kayak had to be covered with skin, they used to do it in the house; and all the inmates assisted one another without applying to the Europeans; they had a storehouse and engaged one of the oldest women to take care of their stores. They possessed beautiful tents for removing to in the spring, taking to the outer islands or to the fishing-places. When, during my boyhood, I saw my countrymen thus well off, I believed that people dwelling in other places were in similar prosperity. This was also the case when the ship arrived. All the people from the environs repaired to Kakertok, where they pitched their nice tents all around the harbor for the purpose of looking at the ship.

"The decline of the Greenlanders is the result of their having given up their former mode of living together in big houses, and this is the cause of their shortcoming; although some, on the other hand, believe this to be the cause of their separating, that when they commenced to make use of European dainties and articles of clothing, the housemates did not like joint possession and mutual assistance as regards these things, which only yield an enjoyment of short duration. When then, for some of them, this enjoyment had come to an end and they had to witness others leading a luxurious life, they would grow angry and take offense, and this is perhaps the reason why they separate. But this we disapprove of, because such people do not take into consideration what follows after rejoicing and what follows after need."

Nor what follows after what we call civilization. Though I used to try to tell them. "In America," I once began to those friends around my table who, as they often did, had been asking many questions about our life and what we have and what things cost, "in America almost everybody works for someone else. There is one man, let us say, who has an automobile factory, and he has a hundred thousand men working for him. These men are only automobile makers, just as you are only hunters. Now, one day that man's storekeeper comes to him and says, 'The people aren't buying any more automobiles. They have enough.' 'All right,' says the man, 'go and tell ninety thousand workmen that I don't want them any more.' So that is done. Now these workmen try to get other work, but they're no good at other work. And besides that, there are hundreds of thousands of other people looking for work, and can't get it. Well, they go home. They get hungry. Now in America you can't go out and kill a seal or a reindeer; there aren't any. And besides that, all the land belongs to somebody. You can only walk on the paths. The men can't shoot anything, so they go to the store to buy food. The storekeeper says to them, 'If you want food you must pay me for it.' 'But,' they say, 'we have no money, for we haven't any work.' 'Then you can't have food.' So they go home. And there they find a man waiting for them; he says, 'You must pay me if you want to live in this house.'"

"What!" someone asks, "don't the houses belong to the people?"

"No. Well, so they have to go out of their houses. And they can't go onto anybody's land."

"What *do* they do?" asks someone.

"Oh, people give them a few öre, or they get a little from the community chest. That's all. They're just finished."

The people stare at me and at each other, aghast with incredulity. "Well," says one for all, "I guess that Greenland is all right."

XXVII. ON MUTUAL AID

THAT love and mutual assistance of which the young Greenlander wrote must in its day have been affecting. Both are primarily components of the life of primitive communities; they disappear with Progress. And in the Greenland of today there are but remnants left. Nevertheless the stranger in Greenland will do well to temper the pride that he may take in his own munificence by reflecting upon the innumerable acts of free assistance for which he must at last become a debtor. Let goods be landed at Igdlorssuit for me: they're shouldered by an eager crowd and in the twinkle of an eye deposited at my house. And if the opening of my crates and boxes and the conveying of their contents indoors is fun for the people, it is not the less a service to me. It should be fun; and it amounts to an obligation for the beneficiary to make it so. An obligation, yes, but in simple communities where those who come to help are friends and neighbors it is less that than opportunity. The guests are met; it is natural that a feast should follow. And such a celebration as that which attended the raising of my rafters doubtless had its origin in the entertainment which must in old times in Europe and America have attended the completion of the communal labor of raising the house frame. My own house-raising at Igdlorssuit was just such communal work, for on all days, and on the last particularly, my little force of hired labor had been augmented by numbers of free hands. And how the girls and women flocked to help clean up on that last day; how eagerly they climbed the hills to gather creepers and bright flowers to weave the garlands of! What pride they took in dressing up the place! It was their festival.

Unfortunately, however, that popular interest in house-building which was of such practical service, and trial, to me was due to curiosity, to pleasure and profit in seeing how an American carpenter worked, to amused interest in me, to cigarettes and tobacco, to almost anything you like but general communal spirit. For their own kinsman putting up a little house in sight of mine was left to dig his heavy sods, and lug them on his back, and pile them on the walls, without another's hand to help him.

But such work as cannot be done alone is undertaken without pay by whatever numbers are required. All lend a hand to haul a heavy boat on shore, or to stave off the ice when in the early fall a boat at anchor, or the wharf, is threatened. And the work of covering kayaks, of which the young Greenlander wrote, is still undertaken by a chosen group of women without charge. It is pressing work; the skins are wet, and the stitching must be completed before they dry and shrink. And to the workers there may be furnished such a repast as, say, a great pot of lumpy, tepid oatmeal porridge. That makes a festival.

But there is on the whole very little more mutual aid practiced in Greenland than in the rest of the world where time has become dimensional, and the scale for measuring it, money. Yet the unaccustomedness of such a concept as that "Time is money" to a people hitherto unfamiliar with even money itself is suggested by their selling you their *time*, when you employ them, without, apparently, the thought of work to be performed.

The Greenlanders are, in fact, in many respects a bewildered people upon whom new concepts have been foisted which are not only at variance with the old but incommensurate with Greenland life. It is all very well to set a value upon time, to figure it in öre per hour and print it in a price list of commodities—who is going to buy it? And while it is plausible enough to have said, as Progress in a sense does say, Why waste your precious time in making ivory-inlaid water buckets when you can buy a bucket for a kroner? the fallacy lies in that time in Greenland was only precious when there were ivory-inlaid buckets and such things to make. And while, God knows! it's better to be idle out of doors than pulling levers in a mill, it is infinitely sweeter—ask the artist that—to be fashioning beautiful things than to be idle.

A divinely wise administration would have said to the Greenlanders: "We'll buy from you those things we need that you can spare, and sell you what you need and cannot make yourselves." What did they need—if anything? What do men *need?* Who knows! And anyway, it's too late now.

is is not Karen – David's wife; but one day when she was doing just this – skin-
ng a seal which her accomplished husband had brought home – she was drawn
ay by some excitement on the shore, ran out, and – left the door open. Within
ty seconds there were sixty dogs inside. Men came up on the run, with clubs; they
aded in, waist deep in dogs. For full ten minutes they were pitching dogs outdoors.

XXVIII. TWILIGHT

THAT which is called the polar night is less a night than a daylong prolongation of the twilight; in fact it steals upon the North not so much by the increase of the full day's normal period of darkness as by such a progressive lengthening of the morning and the evening twilights as to bring them finally to meet. The meeting of the twilights at high noon is polar night. The fancied winter darkness of the polar regions as contrast to the fact of their summer's midnight sun has such a hold on the popular imagination that that phenomenon the winter's mid-day moon is popularly little known; our poets' symbol of inconstancy is steadfast day and night in winter polar skies. The Northern winter nights are moonlit twilights on a scene whose darkest element, the still unfrozen sea, may be no darker than the twilight sky itself.

Igdlorssuit faced north, and mountains, as we have told, inclosed the settlement upon three sides. Even the summer sun in transit stood as it were on tiptoe to peer over them. It tired soon. In mid-fall by the calendar our "night" began. Yet we were to dwell a whole month more looking out as from a darkened auditorium upon a lighted stage; to see its shadows lengthen and the great two months' eclipse creep up its mountain sides. The last day comes. The last peak flames a moment, and goes out. Now is the polar night.

And now, owing less to darkness than to the coincidence of other seasonal phenomena, men enter upon such a period of inactivity as, if the long nights were in fact as depressing to the mind as they are sometimes said to be, might drive them mad. The sea, their hunting-ground, is in the birth throes of a transmutation, and not until the accomplishment of its metamorphosis into solid ice does it offer the hunter more than an occasional chance to leave the land. Twilight and idleness. To these add threat of famine, a threat so real, in the cases of the more improvident, as to be only staved off by small doles from an impoverished community chest and, during my short stay, the bank. So real that at Nugatsiak, our nearest neighboring trading-post, many people as December advanced were driven to devour their dogs, their kamiks, and the skin coverings of their kayaks. Surely they are enough, these troubles altogether, to cause depression if it lurked. Yet winter is the people's gayest season, their good times mounting with the darkness, to reach their peak in the festivities of Christmas.

Depression? No. Unless old Trolleman, now sealed up in his mansion house, his red nose buried in last season's scandal sheets, got sad. He read, he brooded, nursed his wrongs. They got him, those dark days. He fell to plotting; he devised a scheme to starve and freeze me out. He used the well-established shortage of the stock in trade to deny me at the store such prime necessities as lamp oil, coal, and staples in the line of food. A foolish scheme; he might have known I'd circumvent him through my friends. Here Rudolf stood us in good stead; he was assistant at the store, he knew the stock and kept us posted. Not only that: he bought for us. It helped to make the dark time gay—our laughing at it all.

Of course old Trolleman did have his grievances: for one, I'd raised the price on ptarmigan. That hurt. There in the past he had been getting them for fifteen öre apiece; I jumped them up to twenty-five—the list price, by the way. "Not playing the game," said trader Trolleman. "Whose game?" I asked. So all the ptarmigan the boys brought in that fall came in my door. And ptarmigan are good. And so it was with crabs: from five öre up they went to ten; and cheap at that. The monster sea crab of the North:

delicious food. Yes, it pleased everyone but Trolleman, our great price war.

And then the narwhal tusk. (Do let me tell it all; these are the dark days' pastimes.) Back in our friendly days I'd said to Trolleman, "I'd desperately like a narwhal tusk to take back home." "Well," had said Trolleman, "they never get them here; but if they do, all right." And now one late November night, a pitch-black clouded night, as we were sitting cozily at home, Salamina, young Helena, I, eating our oatmeal supper, suddenly there sounded a many-throated cry from the shore. We dropped our spoons and ran outdoors. "Emanuel," the shout proclaimed, "has got a narwhal." And, with the shout still echoing, I sent off Salamina to the shore to buy the tusk; I'd learned not to trust Trolleman. "Stay there," I said to her, "and meet Emanuel as he lands. Wade out to meet him if you have to. *Get—that—tusk!*" In half an hour's time she came back radiant. Emanuel—it wasn't our old grandson of an angakok, another one—had promised it. "And," added Salamina with some glee, "just as I was leaving, Regina came running up excitedly." "I think," I said to Salamina, "we'd better go back down." We did.

It was a wild scene there: the crowd, the men stooped over cutting up that monster carcass, that black blood on snow, the encircling dog pack. And as the flashlights lit but portions of the scene it seemed as though the night and the whole world were full of crowds and dogs and butchery. Yes, there she was, Regina, in the thick of it. And Trolleman, aloof, his nose in air. O barometric beak: there's something up, I thought. Bore in and ask.

Salamina is, to her credit, no pusher; I wished she'd been that night. For when at last, after waiting with proper consideration until the work was finished and Emanuel free, she ventured to address him, she learned that the tusk was after all, despite Emanuel's promise, Trolleman's. He'd claimed it as his trader's right.

I don't think that Trolleman, buried again within half an hour in his old newspapers, learned until next day that I'd outbid him for that tusk. And that I took it home with me that night.

XXIX. HELENA'S BIRTHDAY

AND DANCES in the dark time! It made no difference how cold the night or how beset with wind and driving snow, how dark; when they were *let* to dance, they danced. And although the people's use of the dance den was restricted to birthdays, and dancing days by order of the church were closed with Advent, still November babies seemed quite plentiful; and one was small Helena. November—I consult my book—the twenty-eighth. And it was Saturday, and she was five.

It was a great party that we gave for her. Not exactly, to our notions, a child's birthday party, but rather, a festival given in her honor so that all, and incidentally Helena, might have reason to rejoice that she'd been born. And surely she took pleasure in it too, though it was always hard to read in the self-contained and placid face of that little mouselike child just what she thought of things. She liked, this day, her cake with candles on it, she liked her presents—though a lot of them were cakes of soap or handkerchiefs—and she liked the brand-new kamiks and the clean best clothes that she was dressed in all that afternoon. Then she was hostess in a sense: she made the rounds and bade the guests to coffee.

The party was, of course, a kaffemik, to which all the people of the settlement were asked in shifts of as many as the house would hold. Its feature was the decorated cake—two cakes, in fact, and big enough to give a piece to everyone. And so beautiful were they with their burning candles, and *Helena* written out on them, and hearts and things, that Salamina was reluctant to start cutting. Yes, they were beautiful. But that, as everyone had been told, was not their greatest virtue; nor was the taste of them. I won't say much for that. Their charm was hidden—it was money. And what followed upon the pieces' being handed round resembled nothing in the world but the Yukon gold rush. Eat it? Yes, later; first they dug. They tore the chunks apart, they crumbled them. Two öre, ten öre, five öre, fifty: that was enough small bait to keep them eager for the prize, the Crown. They loved the game, they lingered on to watch the next shifts play it; the house was packed. The word went round the settlement; no need to send Helena for the guests; they came. They crowded in the passageway, they massed outdoors. At every cutting of the cake excitement grew: the Crown was still to be unearthed. Suddenly there was a piercing scream; old Abelone, two-toothed witch, was screaming loud. And held up in the air in her scrawny hand was the Crown. "*Aja, ajajaja!*" sang Abelone; and everyone was shouting with excitement.

That night there *had* to be a dance. So when the time came round they called at Trolleman's and asked him for the key. "No," said Trolleman.

Now you just can't have all the people of a settlement like that come to your house and dance. Of course the house was bigger than the dance den, and the overflow could wait, as there, outside; it wasn't size. It was somehow the quality of the place, the fact that it was clean and that we kept it clean; and that my things, good things, stood out on shelves. And my work table, and my papers, and my books: they stood exposed to all the dirt that dirty crowd would bring. No, certainly we couldn't have them all; but some. Come, Salamina, let's ask some of them around. So, it being Helena's birthday, and a Saturday night, and there not having been a dance, as it happened, for at least a week, we planned to hold a *little* dance, just ask a few. I think we asked—well, maybe twenty.

And twenty were enough. But no sooner had the strains of

Peter's accordion been wafted to the settlement than lo! the solitude outdoors became a crowd. It massed around the windows and the doorway, it surged around the house like surf around a reef. We drew the curtains, shut the doors, danced on. The smoke and dust and heat grew stifling, unendurable; we gasped for air. We made a break for out of doors. O sweet clean icy wind, O gorgeous night, O moon, O glistening snow and ice, O North—so beautiful! And you, great crowd of friendly folk grinning and bearing it out here! I weakened; took a dozen more indoors with me. *That* made a crowd.

Helena sat back on the sleeping platform, silent and wide-eyed, taking it all in. Tobias, our small chore boy, danced. We got him started, and no power on earth could stop him. He showed a complex for big girls: Marghreta was his style. He stood with her, chin up, just nipple-high; that set us all to laughing. The crowd *was* dense. Who are they all? Good Lord! they've crashed the gate and swept in like a flood.

After our having in a pleasant but firm manner cleared the house of, say, two-thirds of all the uninvited guests, Abraham, as foreman of the community council, harangued them cheerfully about their manners, suggesting to them that on the grounds of its not being their house, nor their party, and especially since there wasn't room inside, they all contentedly stay out. They did; and in order that there might be no misunderstanding, no confusion, no mingling of the dancers and the outcasts, they cut the latchstring. We were prisoners.

I didn't like to smash my carefully made latch; there was no other course. I did it well, and to the sound of splintering wood I catapulted out. The night was thunderous with stampeding feet. One man remained—the catechist. "I didn't do it, no, not I. Not I." Oh, miserable catechist!

XXX. DARKNESS

MY DIARY of 1931 reads: *Saturday, Dec. 19th. Over 200 presents wrapped for Christmas, 45 bags of candy, 22 cornucopias of candy (beauties). And the tree stands made and trimmed. A curtain hung from the ceiling hides the tree. We pretend to Helena that a man is hid there. She won't go near him.* And there is a long entry about Justina, whom I had recently met, and a list of her presents. Then:

Sunday, December 20th. An inadvertent tragedy last night. Salamina sat working at the table. I at the desk. Finishing my work I moved to the table to read. Finding the light bad I exclaimed disgustedly, "Ajorpok" [*No good*] *and moved back to the desk. Read there three-quarters of an hour, with Salamina continuing at her sewing. Now to bed. And Salamina put her work down and stood up.* [It was her nightly job to make my bed up for me.] *Salamina was very quiet. I spoke to her: no answer. I went to her and looked intently at her face, and saw that it was blotched from crying. Oh, what is wrong, Salamina? And at that she burst into bitter reproaches for my having called her* ajorpok!

And now, possibly because it may somehow relate to Salamina's tears, certainly because it is related to my own, and particularly in that it has to do with Greenland life—my Greenland life, and anybody's life away from home—we turn back on the calendar and learn the truth about the real dark time in Greenland. There'd been a parallel between the deepening of the winter twilight and the overshadowing and darkening of my thoughts.

There is a Greenland East Coast legend about an old man who journeyed south and westward with his son in search of better hunting-grounds. They found them in the shadow of the West Coast mountains. Time passed, and, like a sickness, sorrow came to rest on the old man. And it came to be that he had but one thought: it was to see the sun rise from out of the ocean once more before he died. Then, so that this might be, they journeyed toward home again. They turned the cape at last, and reached the eastern coast; they camped. And the next morning the old man rose, and stood and watched the sun come up out of the ocean. For joy of that he died.

What a delight it is to sit at home and let our thoughts go traveling. "Here," we may say, with finger on the map, "here I would like to go. Here I could live." For it seems to us that we have need of no more than that freedom which money could give us to go to almost any fancied spot and live our days out there. Freedom and means, or none, who hasn't thought of better hunting-grounds? Our race has overrun the world in search of them; and found them, settled there. But few among those emigrants from home have not some time fought down nostalgia. Of all that our nostalgia relates us to, of its proportions in our thoughts, the radiance, the warmth, it has for us, there is no better symbol than the sun. I am an old traveler, an old mover-on from place to place: I should know better than to look for sunrise every day.

Not sunrise, maybe, but the glow of it; its light reflected in the clouds; some tidings of the sun, some word that it still was: at any rate I did. And when as fall advanced no tidings came, when schooners with the post brought none for me, when, listening on the air, I caught no whisper of my name, then, let me tell you, darkness settled down.

Salamina was well aware of the importance of my sun to me on my horizon; it stood surrounding me in effigy. I used to tell about it, for Salamina and all our friends delighted in hearing about my world, its ways, who peopled it. My tales extended their horizon; they got to know my friends, my family, my farm, my house, my

This is a kayaker in his full jacket
t looks as if I didn't know the
anatomy of hands : the Greenland mittens have two thumbs .

horses, dogs. They really liked the family album. Confined to such a little sphere, forever seeing but that few of their own race that they had known from childhood, knowing of people and their life abroad through only the remotest channels, it thrilled them hearing of my world at first hand. "If I were rich," I said, "I'd buy a ship and come to take you there to spend a year." Quite long enough to make them long for home.

So Salamina knew my world, my sun. And with that swift, unerring intuition that was hers in everything that much concerned my thoughts she sensed the overclouding of it. As though it were her darkness too, she entered it.

As from the sunlight I look back on those dark days, they're hardly real to me. It now appears as though perversely I had shut my eyes to make the gloom. I know, today, its utter unreality. It was a nightmare: good. And polar nights are—God, how long!

One may speculate—I often do—on what we need, what human beings *need*, to be contented. On whether we need books and art, or work, or leisure, or fresh air, or so many pounds per week of potatoes, oatmeal, meat, or love: what *do* we need? It would be good to know. Yet one is led to think that there is no specific list, that it depends on—what? On temperament? If that is it, discussion ends. We can't have dealings with that nursery pet. Yet it does seem to depend upon the individual, upon—if we dislike temperament—his taste. But that's a cultivated thing; it's merely what he's used to. Are we to be the slaves, through need, of all that we're accustomed to? Here we assert ourselves in self-defense: we're not mere sensualists. Judgment comes in, eliminates; and character enforces it. The residue, however, we *do* need. On that we lean: for happiness, perhaps for life itself.

Within twenty-four hours of the failure of a radio message that was due, I had begun to think. That's dangerous. In forty-eight I wondered. In a week my powers of imagination for both good and evil were at work. In two weeks I had—one does—discarded good and concentrated on the worst. I reviewed all possible dire happenings, dragged in a few impossible horrors, played with the thought of them awhile; and exalted them all to the plane of the highly probable. November found me frantic. To get a message through to the radio station at Godhavn: life seemed to hang on it. But how? Perhaps a winter post would be sent south from Umanak; how cross the fifty miles of sea to meet it? No one would. The best kayaker of the settlement overhauled his gear, borrowed a water-tight jacket—he was a poor man and hadn't one of his own—scanned the weather and the sea for two days from the harbor hill, reported no. Money? I offered plenty. The Greenlander takes small interest in his widow's affluence.

Meanwhile with every day the cold grew more intense; it struggled with the wind to freeze the sea. You *watch* the ocean freeze, *see* it congeal. It gets to have a sluggish, glassy look as though before the freezing moment its fluid had become appreciably thicker. Then suddenly it is ice, strange ice like pancakes on a griddle, run together. Given a calm cold day it quickly forms a sheet. That for a start, you pray for calm's continuance. One, two, three days, a week; still calm. November ice: what luck! Hunters are furbishing their dog harness, working the stiff rawhide to soften it; tightening their sledge lashings. Hourly lookouts on the harbor hill report clear ice as far as eye can reach. Ice! That means release, the opening of a prison gate, the freedom of the world to island prisoners. Freedom to travel, hunt, to work. Release means food again for everyone—and a message to America for me. The ice will stay, say the young hunters; the ice shall stay, say I. And old men shake their heads and murmur their accustomed "*Imaka*," perhaps. "Tomorrow? Umanak?" I ask of David, my sledge man, as he returns from the hilltop. "*Imaka*," he answers. "Or the day after—maybe." Oh, God, when can we start? And what a day tomorrow was! Clear, calm, and bitter cold. Only the crabbed very old now shook their heads; old fools.

The gradual overcasting of the sky which occurred that afternoon would have been more noticeable if the whole region had not on November 14 entered its nine weeks' period of sunless days; it might certainly have caused uneasiness but for the exuberant optimism about the ice which now prevailed in the settlement. Cloudy and dead calm: it might mean only snow. It meant a gale. Throughout the pitch-black hours of the night it raged; it raged next day. And when in the twilight of that noon we gathered on the hill to see its work, we saw, where ice had been, a clear expanse of storm-swept water.

That the sunless days, the twilight, wrought upon my mind and enforced the poignancy of my thoughts, I have no doubt. Yet I welcomed the pitch-darkness of the most clouded nights as offering release from the continual restraint that I was under to conceal my trouble. Then only, in the darkness, could I be alone; and I'd parade the strand for hours to find relief in talking to myself, in tears, in the complete abandonment of self-control. My house at times became unbearable. She understood, she knew, so much. I had no secrets there, and this was mine, my own most personal and secret grief. What if I didn't talk, and grin, and laugh at things. Had I no right to my own thoughts? And Salamina, watching me, would suddenly get up and go outdoors. I knew, of course; couldn't I read it in her reddened eyes? God, but I hate this weeping all the time!

On the twenty-third of December, as we sat in the lamplight at supper, three slips of paper were brought to me by Trolleman's servant, three radio messages. I gave the boy some cigarettes and thanked him. When he had gone I picked up the slips and read them, one after another. I laid them down again, reached for the butter, and began to spread a slice of bread. Suddenly Salamina was at my side. She put her arm over my shoulder and her head down against me, and she sobbed convulsively. She knew *the* message hadn't come.

I've said that this was all a nightmare, that I had shut my eyes and made the darkness. It was at any rate so real to me, such utter gloom, that the single dingy little slip of paper that was brought to me *next* day, on Christmas Eve, was to that midnight like the sun itself. That risen sun shone bright on Christmas Day.

XXXI. CHRISTMAS

THE trunk of the tree was the narwhal tusk, a tapering, twisted shaft of ivory six feet tall. Its branches were of wire, delicately curved. Its heart-shaped cardboard leaves were painted green; they were attached in clusters, and on their slender stems of springy wire they trembled like aspen leaves. It seemed a living tree; it bloomed with many-colored paper flowers. It glittered with pendulous ornaments of tinfoil, and it blazed with candles. It was a lovely tree.

The presents were wrapped in tissue paper saved for months from everywhere. They were tied with strips of colored paper and with red ribbon from cigars. There was a pile of presents.

The dinner—we had been cooking that for two weeks past—was a whole barrel of—what shall we call it?—Beluga stew. Into the making of it had gone dried peas, dried beans, pemmican, bacon, seal meat, matak—of course—and white-whale meat. It tasted good. We had dozens of loaves of bread, and we had brewed two barrels of beer.

Salamina was dressed for Christmas. She wore a pearl-gray anorak of silk, a Roman-striped sash in which red predominated, new breeches with exquisite leather appliqué, new kamiks—vermilion, of course—and red pendants in her ears and a red bead necklace.

Helena was dressed for Christmas in new kamiks and a bright calico frock over her boy's clothes.

I was dressed for Christmas in new kamiks—beauties. They

were of fine black seal hide; a two-inch band of white bordered with embroidery encircled the tops, embroidered stripes ran down the shin of each, and a narrow edging of white marked the line of the turned up-and-over soles. Young bucks go in for style. I wore a cotton anorak of robin's egg blue, had had my hair cut, and had washed my neck.

Everybody had dressed for Christmas; it was a very swell parade that climbed the hill to church. It was a sweet parade of kids that came at noon to our house; they'd been washed.

When the children had all been given presents of candy and other things, and had stared their eyes out at the tree, they all filed out again, bursting into sudden hilarity outdoors as though for the past twenty minutes they had been holding their breath. They are a quiet lot, the Greenland children, and it doesn't contribute to their liveliness in our presence that we outlanders—travelers like me, or the doctor, or the trader—are used behind our backs as bugaboos to frighten children with.

With adults it is different. They may find us of use to frighten children; themselves, they're not abashed. And whatever the relative proportions of the wonder, envy, affection, and contempt with which they view us, they look forward to our hospitality as to a feast, and come prepared with appetites. If by any stretch of the imagination we may believe those relishers of tepid porridge to have taste, then, Salamina and R. K., your food, your drink, your hospitality, was good. They liked it.

It was, as usual, the very old who did the most to make it fun. Whether by inadvertent breaches of modern etiquette that sent the younger generations into fits of laughter, or by their spontaneous hilarity, they whooped things up. "*Aijaja!*" screamed Charlotta, as among her presents she found a plug of tobacco. "*Kuja, kuja kuja!*" She was off, and none could head her. And if that wouldn't enliven a party, nothing would. Give me the very old for guests; or let me have lived when these old derelicts were young. They must have lived well who as they totter to their graves go singing "Thank you!"

From dinner at our house the guests are sent for coffee to Sophia's, a brilliant plan by which we cleared the house each time for the succeeding shift. And if the people chose to hang out there —well, she could handle them. There was, however, enough entertainment—kaffemiks, of course—at various houses to draw them out to new attractions. And as the afternoon advanced, as darkness deepened, the whole settlement became a scene of festival. It may, for all I know, have lasted all the night; next day, at any rate, it flourished on. And you were no sooner home from coffee at one house than an overdressed child appeared to summon you to another. Yet I must record that although the houses had all been scrubbed, and all been decorated with such art as could be had—from plain news print in the poorer homes to colored Christmas cards and lithographs in the homes of the rich—and all more or less hung with homemade paper festoons, and many furnished with homemade wooden Christmas trees, and all illuminated by candles, and all equipped—in turn, I'd guess—with coffee cups and spoons, and almost all dispensing cake and, some, cigars and cigarettes, although, in short, everything had been done to make the parties gay, they weren't. "We're all dressed up," the people seemed to say, "and don't know what to do." That's Greenland now.

XXXII. TO TWELFTH NIGHT

BANG! Bang, bang! You'd think it was the Fourth of July; it is only December 30. They're tuning up for New Year's Eve. Next day it starts in earnest.

Bang! The report is so loud that it might be in the very room. The door bursts open and in rushes old Beate. "A kroner, a kroner! give it to me. I shot it!" And she cackles with laughter, rolling her quaint body around in her delightful way. "I shot it, I shot it. Give it to me."

"You couldn't have shot it, Beate, for there isn't a kroner in the house. Here: maybe you shot these cigarettes." And I give her a handful. And so I saved the bank from such a run as would have broken it. A run? It was a hold-up. All day long there'd keep occurring ear-shattering explosions just outside my door or window, and in would come the marksman claiming something. I saved my lamps, my flute; I saved a lot of valuable things—at a considerable cost in schnapps, tobacco, beer, and condensed milk. Those who didn't shoot my property acquired it by coming to the house to wish me Happy New Year. Singly or in groups, and all dressed up, they'd come, boys mostly. Entering, each would courteously shake my hand, and then just stand there in embarrassed expectation.

And then that evening, New Year's Eve, suddenly, as though all the people were scrambling to get done before the new year came those things they'd left undone, there began to pour in upon me such a stream of rather dreadful, sealskin matchbox-holders, scissor-holders, watch-holders, tobacco-holders, money-holders, as to overwhelm me with almost tearful gratitude. So that I immediately summoned all the donors and their husbands to a feast and dance. We—let me tell you—celebrated New Year's Eve! As a plum pudding that from its fruit-packed rum-soaked richness bursts into flame, so flamed good-fellowship with us. So that at last, no longer able to confine our love of man to us, we armed ourselves with bottles of the milk of human kindness (90 proof) and, going from one end of the settlement to the other, up and down from house to house, rousing the inmates where they slept, we gave them one and all "A Happy New Year."

New Year came in, but Christmas had still five more days to run.

I didn't know what day it was, what hour, or where. I didn't *know* a thing. Just heard as in a dream, dream music, angels singing. A dream? Incredible; I was awake. I opened up my eyes: yes, there was lamplight in the room; and I could feel the stove's warmth on me where I lay. There, too, was Salamina tiptoeing around. And yet the music: voices in harmony, near me but hushed, and wonderfully sweet. "*Venite adoremus*," they were singing. My senses came to me, and I leaped up. I took the lamp and held it at the window so that its light shone out upon the snow. There, dimly through the frosted panes, I saw the people standing. We put a row of lighted candles on the window ledge, and I went out.

Just as the singing ended I came out to them. It was cold, and very still, and dark. The lower atmosphere was veiled as though by falling snow, and in the upper sky a few stars shone. "Thank you, thank you," said everyone for what I brought to them. It was the morning of Twelfth Night.

By the time that the minstrels had completed their tour of the settlement and returned to us we were prepared with the repast of cakes and coffee that I'd asked them to. Coffee and cakes on Twelfth Night with the angels! No sooner had they flown away than many guests arrived; the day was starting well. And on the echo of their footsteps as, well warmed with coffee, they went off again, there was a great hubbub out of doors, the sound of people entering the vestibule, a thundering on the door. The crowd burst in, pushing before it three demoniac beings, black-faced, grimacing hideously, clothed shapelessly in furs, and capering obscenely: the incarnation of libidinous nightmare. Twelfth Night—the dance was on. The very dogs slunk off in terror of what prowled abroad.

XXXIII. ICE

THE new year started as it should—with ice. All through December it had been in that disheartening state: almost, not quite. With every calm the ice would make; with every wind, break up again. And the broken floes drifting here and there on the tide, or driven by the wind, would crash together forming, where their edges met, those escarpments and chevaux-de-frise of ice which are to prove of just such pleasure to the weary traveler as what I've called them do to storming troops. But the power of cold is relentless. Once ice, in those cold days, it stayed ice; and the open areas became at last so small that at the first fair chance they froze and held. So it was that finally, on January 1, David, knowing that my mind was set on sledging to Nugatsiak, pronounced it safe to try.

The Greenland sledge and the Greenland method of harnessing dogs deserve description or, more definite than words, an illustration. Here, then, is shown the Greenland sledge:

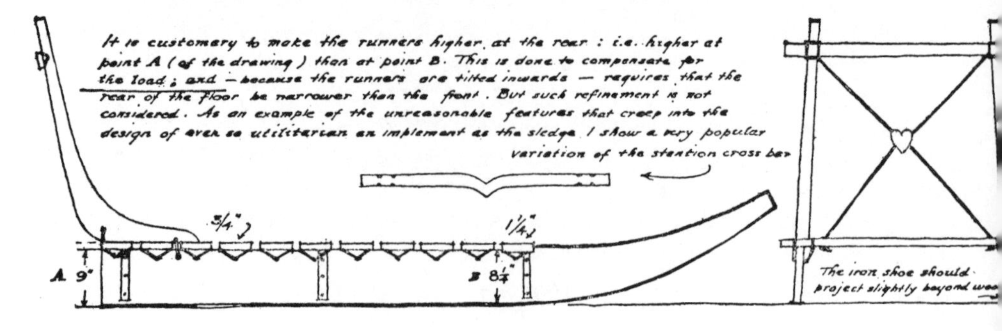

My sledge was nine feet long and three feet wide. The sledges are put together with rawhide lashings; the flexibility that this allows is essential to sledge construction. The dogs are hitched in fan formation.

There would appear to be a loss of power in the tangential pull of the outer dogs so hitched. In theory there is; in fact, the loss is insignificant. The traces are from nine to twelve feet long, and good dogs well driven stay together. It is surprising what a small front is presented by a well-bunched team of even twelve or fourteen dogs. The fan formation has advantages, and sledging conditions in Greenland favor it. There are few obstacles to be met in driving, and no trees. And the snow on the sea ice is generally so well packed by wind as to require no breaking of a trail. The Greenland driver sits at ease, his dogs, at even whiplash length away, in good control. "*Eu! eu!*" He taps his boot. We're off.

There are three of us on my sledge: David, Salamina, I. And Martin accompanies us on his sledge—alone. She won't ride with him. It is half an hour past noon when we drive off; the day is beautiful: calm, cloudless, mild for New Year's Day. The mountains facing south glow pink; ours, back of us, stand dark against a luminous sky. We have at first to cross a mile-wide field of barriers of heaped-up ice; it looked to me, a novice, quite impassable. It is not, however, over such ice that one rides reclining at his ease; it's work, hard work. Lift, shove ahead, hold back, ease down; cast off that trace that's caught around a point of ice; pull up that dog that's fallen in a hole. But Salamina rode; she wanted to, she liked the fun of it. And somehow she came through intact. Once past that pressure field we had good ice, the sledges traveled smoothly on light snow, the dogs kept up an even trot. And by the time that darkness came—and it was dark that night—we had covered three-quarters of the twenty-two miles to Nugatsiak.

But the real darkness that then came upon us suddenly was underfoot. The smooth white plain of snow gave place to dark glare ice, with here and there black areas of still unfrozen sea. All to the eastward, landward from our course, was open water. What lay ahead, that troubled us. Driving up to one of the innumerable bergs which reared themselves out of the frozen plain, we stopped the dogs, and David and Martin climbed to reconnoiter. Bad prospect, they reported. And transferring Salamina to the sledge of Martin, we drove on, bearing off however to the westward, almost at right angles to our proper route.

If I should now, in telling about those hours on the ice, pretend to having had any judgment or knowledge of what we were doing I would rob the adventure of what then gave it zest, my ignorance. If I had happened by some fatality to be alone out there, I would have fled from that glare ice as from sure death. It looked like window glass through which one peered into those depths which are always so terrifying to the imagination. Our minds, our reasoning faculties, don't always work: we'd drown as quickly in six feet as in six hundred, yet hundreds lend a horror to the thought of drowning. And when what intervenes is ice, our minds relate its thickness to the water's depth.

It appeared, presently, to be not only thin to my imagination but to David's knowledge. The dogs were halted while the men explored, testing the ice as they proceeded by driving into it the long chisel-ended pikes they carried, one of which is of the equipment of every sledge. And when we moved ahead, then David led the way on foot.

The dogs' obedience to his spoken word was remarkable, and the commands they heeded were often spoken in so low a voice as to escape my ears. Great quiet reigned; it was as though we needed all our senses to explore the way.

The lights of Nugatsiak had come into clear view, but it became at about the same time apparent that we were separated from our goal by a body of open water some miles in width, and extending out of sight to right and left across what should have been our course. We bore on to the westward, skirting this; and that we did eventually pass around it was due both to the men's good judgment based on long familiarity with ice conditions there, and to David's unflagging energy in leading the whole way on foot.

This is David — walking on
thin ice. He is married to
Karen. He has no fear
of death.

Close to Nugatsiak we encountered firmer ice. David threw himself down beside me on the sledge, the dogs broke into a run. "*Eu! eu!*" The journey's end was near. People came running out across the ice to meet the season's first arrivals from outside, a real event. Then suddenly a dog collapsed. He staggered for a moment, fell. The sledge ran on to him and pinned him down, and dragged him bodily along. We stopped and got him up again, and set him on his feet; he staggered drunken-like, and fell again. Up with him on the sledge, and sit on him, and hold him down; drive on. With the crowd at our side we went crashing up over the barrier and on to land; up the steep slope of the shore, across bare wind-swept ledges straight to Pavia's house. We stopped. A dozen hands unharnessed dogs, unlashed the load. "Come in!" cried Pavia, the ear-ringed buccaneer.

The dog? Oh, he was quite all right, or would be in the morning. Just drunk, just doped on stolen fresh shark meat; he'd gorged himself somewhere. It poisons them.

Pavia's house was a mess, it always was. It was dirty everywhere, but the nucleus of the dirt was the kitchen. That was filthy. How could it help being filthy with its eight foot square of space packed day and night with filthy hangers-on, bums, vagrants, servants, relatives, and friends? It was the club and bunkhouse of Nugatsiak's poor.

From the kitchen you looked into the bedroom; you looked in because the door stood open. Open so that the fetid warmth of the kitchen could pass in, and the family fumes pass out. That room was crowded too. There was one big double bed for all the family. Some were in it, some were on it, some were sitting around on chamber pots. Ane, the buxom wife, was seated in the midst of all of it lending her Holstein breast to an orphan child that they had taken pity on.

"Come!" said Pavia; and I followed him through another door into what, because it wasn't so much used, was doubtless called the living-room. It was a fine big room, warmed by its own stove, and furnished with one of the more elaborate of the mail-order suites in Swedish mahogany. From kitchen into parlor, from what he was to what he would become. But Pavia and Ane were incorrigibly genuine, a good-natured, old-fashioned, free-and-easy Greenland couple, distinguished in their elevation by their heedlessness of it. It gave him only more to give. Come one, come all: that was his way. Come in, sit down, eat, drink, be gay: yes—drink; he loved it. And as you could always count on Pavia's having beer, and plenty of it, you could never count on getting to bed until between you it was finished.

The kitchen crowd—oh, they would still be there; they slept there on the floor—they'd send a girl in to wipe up the floor, it needed it. There Salamina spread our sleeping-bags. "Good night, old Pavia." Thank God, good night!

XXXIV. TO UMANAK: FIRST DAY

ON CHRISTMAS EVE, at the midnight of my self-inflicted torturings of soul, there came, as I have said, a message. I'd had one dominating thought since then: to answer it. To get a message through to Godhavn.

One of the great advantages that Igdlorssuit possessed over most of the settlements of the district was the dependability of its ice. Sooner or later in the early winter's course, unfailingly, the sound would freeze and make the sea a highway to Nugatsiak and the mainland fiords. And it was of little or no concern to hunters what happened to the great expanse of Umanak Fiord, or whether Umanak got ice or didn't. It had become of late years rather the exception than the rule for that fiord to freeze, and the winter post made shift—sometimes by boat and sledge—on the circuitous route of Satut, Uvkusigssat, and the heads of Kangerdluarsuk and Kangerdlugsuak, a long way round, but who should care? Postmen are paid per mile.

Yet in the early days of the January of our narrative the detour was as far from fit for travel as open water in the fiords could make it. Our eyes had taken in that fact on New Year's Day. And the reports of hunters on succeeding days brought no encouragement but that the progress of the ice was slow. Nor did my watching from the hilltop hasten it: the watched pot never boils, nor does it freeze. But David was my oracle. "Tomorrow," David said at last, "we'll start."

It was a most lovely early morning, moonless, but faintly

lighted by the stars and by the immaculate whiteness of the land and the frozen sea. One rather felt than saw the veil of snow mist that hung low over the earth. Sledge packed, dogs caught and harnessed: ready? Good! With a wild rush downhill we're off—downhill, across a level stretch, across the beach, crash bang across the heaped-up shore ice, there! The sledge glides smoothly on the level plain. Out of the darkness on ahead a human form looms up; it is old Thomas looking after his shark lines. "*Inuvdluarna*, Thomas!" "*Ivdludlo*"—"Good-by"—"the same to you." The darkness swallows him, and we're alone. High overhead, behind us in the south, the aurora waves a glowing veil over the snow peaks of our island.

The water route to Umanak is fifty miles; the detour we were traveling tripled it. We planned to do it in three days, sleep two nights on the way. Farther than that one doesn't plan in winter traveling. We left Igdlorssuit at eight.

And now, in apology for the minutiæ of arctic travel which must have recognition in these pages, I may say this: that if there is *any* likeness of this book to life itself it is in that its point is not accomplishment but what occurs along the way. One charm of Greenland is that there they entertain no thought of living for an end. Things just go on. It's good to have no flag to plant, to bear no silly banner with a strange device, to find it good to stop along the road to nowhere, and look back. Aurora's veils above the snow peaks of Igdlorssuit are quite as moving as those stars above the mist that shrouds our course. Follow me then—for you like me are novices in arctic travel—and share with me, if I can bring you to, the pleasures and anxieties, the thrills, the weariness, that the successive miles unfold.

There are two of us, David and I; and seven dogs. It is not usual in Greenland for two men to occupy one sledge. But David had no dogs, and I neither could nor would have traveled alone. And two men are no load for seven dogs when traveling is good. We carried nothing of much weight: some clothes and camping things, my cameras, and rations for ourselves and dogs.

Our course to Kangerdlugsuak was unobstructed by more than an occasional ridge of ice blocks or such isolated chunks of glacier ice as we could easily avoid. The dogs set such a pace that I, who being thinly clad had chosen to run behind the sledge, found myself put to such a pace as tired me in no time; and when, gasping for breath, I at last threw myself down beside David I was soaked with sweat. "You'll catch your death of cold," we'd say to one who sat down wet and hot like that. You somehow don't, up North. You just *get* cold. I did, and soon was on my feet again—to run, and get all hot again, and wet. Hot, cold; hot, cold: all very well to run like that if I so wanted to; though I might have recollected that we had forty-five or fifty miles to go that day before we slept, and that living cooped up in a little island settlement for three months is poor training for a marathon. Caution be damned. Could one sit still with ardent thoughts like mine? With such a message as the one I bore pressing against one's breast? "*LOPUM DUBCU DUBEW DUBME DUBOG*," it read. These burning, magic words: in code? Of course. We'll leave it so.

It was fifteen miles to the entrance of Kangerdlugsuak, and looking backwards as we turned the point we saw the southern sky all bright with day. Hail, day! Farewell. A canyon's gloom confronted us; we entered it. We were at once as though reduced to insect size by the overpowering immensity of the mountain walls. We crawled along, it seemed; we hardly more than crawled in fact. The snow-covered plain had suddenly given place to a floor of ice as level, smooth, and unobstructed as the newly frozen surface of a pond. Its new black ice was barely covered by a rime of white—by snow, I thought; by rime in fact, a salt deposit left, I guessed, by a repulsion of the freezing. The dogs strained to their work; the iron-shod sledge ground over it as though on sandpaper. Now for our legs, the two of us.

Relieved of weight the dogs could trot. Dog trot—we learned the pace that day. Too fast for a man's walk, too slow for his trot, it is one of the most exasperating paces human legs can undertake. Mile after mile we'd stick it out, at last, more from mind weariness than real fatigue, to give it up and ride. Just one of us on board would stop the trot; we'd ride by turns. And stop for nothing. There was still far to go that day, and night; full darkness caught us soon—not more than halfway in. From then on we were guided by no light but what strayed down from the small zenith arc of moonless sky which showed between the mountain walls; that light, and starlit peaks.

We had now been traveling for several hours, mostly on foot and at a trot, on a surface as hard and unyielding as a concrete pavement. We were shod in native footwear, kamiks. And while these are lined with dog fur and their soles stuffed with grass, they yet were insufficient cushions for that pounding that we gave our feet. We both went lame. It hurt—to keep on pounding your sore feet on that hard ice. But when I'd try some sympathy on David he'd just grin. "*Ajungulak*," he'd say; and limp along.

As the darkness ahead of us was impenetrable, so were the hours endless to my thoughts, the hours and the miles, the distances. A huge dark mass showed up ahead of us against the sky. There, David said, we'd camp. But it was hours ago when he said that; the place looked still as far away as ever. *We* looked ahead and lived to reach a goal; achievement counted in *our* thoughts that night. It had to. What could that black monotony surrounding us have been to anyone? If you *must* live for what's to come, then make the present dreary to your thoughts, force it in proper Christian style to be a vale of tears, and live for Paradise. And we may say that the ardor of one's conviction of the blessedness of immortality is the inverted measure of his capacity for having a good time.

I don't know how it happened that at last we got there, that the black mass, a cliff perhaps a thousand feet in height, was at our side; that the rocks that had fallen from it littered the way; that we were thinking: what if a rock should fall down now! We passed the cliff and drove into a little cave behind it. We stopped. "Wait here," said David, and was off into the darkness. I struck a match and read my watch. The time was nine o'clock.

David returned: the cave, a place that hunters used to camp in, he said was wet; not fit to sleep in. That meant we'd pitch the tent.

Now I knew nothing about setting up a tent on ice; I'd never tried it and I'd never read about it. And Greenlanders don't use them. I stalled along, and, watching David tie the dogs, I learned. He took the pike and with it deftly cut a sunken cleat in the ice. Seeing that that was planned to hold seven dogs in check, the problem of the tent was solved. A few such cleats, some stones that lay at hand along the shore, the sledge: in almost no time we had pitched the tent. I spread a ground cloth, laid our reindeer skin on that, brought in our sleeping-bags—no, only mine—where *is* yours, David?—lit the primus, put a pot of snow to melt; and in five minutes we were sitting there so warm that we began to peel our outer garments off. And David didn't know—I hadn't meant he should—that I was not an old hand at the game.

We ate—what does one eat in arctic books?—ate pemmican. Pemmican was originally a food preparation of the American Indians and consisted of dried meat pounded up and mixed with fat. One buys it nowadays in tins. Mine was as good as first-class Danish cooks could make it. I served it in a pot of rice; it filled us to contentment.

"David, where *is* that sleeping-bag of yours?" (I'd questioned him before we'd left. Oh, yes, he had one, he had said.) Now David grinned. "I haven't one," said he.

David had little of anything, so far as I could see: no sleeping-bag, no furs, few clothes. He wore sealskin trousers, but probably nothing under them; he had a sweater and a worn-out cotton anorak; a worsted cap; his boots. That's all. The night was cold. "*Ajungulak*," said David, laughing. I gave him all that I could spare, and then, crawling into my warm reindeer sleeping-bag, blew out the candle.

Poor, freezing, sleepless devil, I lay thinking. "Snrrrrrrr!" went David.

So ended the fourteenth of January.

XXXV. SECOND DAY

IT WAS about nine o'clock when we got started on our way next day. All had gone well with us, both sleep and morning coffee. We broke camp, loaded, hitched the dogs, were off. Now for an uphill climb.

After some beating about to find a proper place to get on land we made it near the outlet of a frozen stream, and started inland up its steep incline. That was queer sledging on that slippery slope. We'd get a start, lose headway by the slipping of the dogs, hold poised a moment while the dogs and we clawed desperately for a foothold, and then go sliding down again to wind up in a snarl of dogs and men. No creepers on our feet, we *couldn't* hold. At last by putting out a towline which one of us, climbing the steep stream bank, put his shoulder to, we gave the dogs that little help they needed for the grade. That past, we came upon a stretch of such thin ice, a hollow shell of ice, that breaking through at every step we waded knee-deep in a rushing subcrustaceous torrent. And the whole way was steep. But all our troubles ended at their source, a lake, a smooth, hard plain of snow. The dogs broke into a run, we jumped aboard. Sledging was sport again.

The land beyond the lake was rough; we followed up a winding gulley to plunge, lift, push, through drifted snow, on side-hill slopes, up, up. Good Lord! was there no top? Up, up; a top at last. "Is this the top?" "Not yet," said David, and he nodded toward our course. Yes, I'd seen that, that emerald glacier cliff. "We're not to climb *that*, are we, David?" "Yes," he said.

It was the spur of a considerable glacier which, streaming down from among the mountains on our right, spread itself across the pass that we were following, blocked it by the ice cliff which confronted us, and then flowed south toward Kangerdluarsuk, to shrivel up and die before it got there. Our way lay on the glacier. And such was my growing awe of the powers of the Greenland dog that until, at the ice cliff itself, we turned aside, I half believed that they'd be called upon to climb that overhanging wall. The place they did climb neared an angle of thirty degrees from the vertical. Its structure, which was hidden from our eyes by snow, revealed its nature to our arms and legs as we climbed up: it was a dump of ice blocks broken from the glacier. Why in the course of the generations through which it has served men in their winter travels it has not become a gentle slope of human bones is due to the amazing powers of the Greenland dog and master. Well—there it stood, its steepest all of sixty feet, a hundred feet in all. We climbed it.

We lay almost face down against that wall and wallowed up; there was no foothold in the snow but blocks of ice. The dogs would strain and move the sledge a foot or two; then slip and flounder helplessly, get tangled up, and fall to fighting. Then came the whip, its pistol shots, its rapier bites. The dogs would separate and fall to work again. We men helped with our feeble strength, not only to force the sledge upwards—carrying it almost upon our heads—but holding it there when the dogs became disorganized. Heartbreaking climb: we made it.

Going was bad along the glacier top. There was little snow, and the gravel embedded in the ice proved a hindrance to the traction of the sledge runners, a torture to our tired feet, and an annoyance to our nerves. Brrrr! that mean grinding of an iron-shod sledge on gravel. No matter: Kangerdluarsuk was in sight; and all downhill to get there. But it took time: slow work on that old gravel-coated crevassed glacier and its long moraine. And when at last we reached the fiord, the afternoon was half an hour on its way.

We made slow progress on the fiord; as on the day before, the surface was like sand. The empty sledge was lead to tired dogs; they walked. That suited us, the pace was well adapted to our lameness. But we had not gone far when darkness settled round us, for the day was overcast. A raw east wind was blowing in the fiord. At six o'clock we stopped to rest the dogs and to refresh ourselves with food. Hot food: that tasted good. In forty minutes we were on our way again.

David, who knew those wastes of ice as we know our front lawns, had been in doubt of how we'd find the ice off Akpatsiait Point, the land we'd turn on leaving the fiord. His doubt was justified. It was new ice, glare ice, and smooth to travel on: we rode. But we could temper our relief at sitting down again with sweet reflections, if inclined that way, on death. The ice was thin. It grew so thin that David, always sanely cautious, soon left the sledge and led the way on foot. The surface yielded with our weight, and every stab of the long pike went through. Two inches? Maybe three? I didn't measure it. But thin enough.

I have spoken of the obedience of Greenland dogs at such a time: it is impressive. David with a low whistle would signal them to stop. They would instantly halt and lie down, watching him placidly as he went ahead in the darkness. At another almost whispered sign they'd jump upon their feet again and set out after him, again to halt at his low sign. There being absolutely nothing for me to do, and with David in charge nothing, I persuaded myself, to worry about, I stretched out on the sledge and soon was dozing. It was a state of almost slumber, a hovering at the very edge of consciousness; so that a succession of delicious dreams came visiting my mind. Those dreams, the glamorous darkness, and the gentle, quiet motion of the sledge over the smooth ice made that a memorable hour. Sometimes, only half awake, I'd watch the shadowy forms of the dogs in two-dimensional silhouette against the luminous darkness. Feeling no forward progress of the sledge, passing no marks to judge of progress by, it was to me as though they stood there in a row and danced for me. But they seemed manikins, not dogs; queer, gnomelike little men. The illusion was so convincing that I had to force my reasonable mind to solve it. Yet even when I'd worked it out, seen that those bobbing heads of little men were tails, those shoulders backs, those arms with hands in pockets the barrels of dogs' ribs, the legs, legs, sure enough, but only hind legs seen; even when I had by mental effort worked this out, I would relapse again to just enjoy the quaint illusion. And overtaking David was as though David like a giant came looming up on us. Yes, I was tired.

But soon we came on firm old ice, and soon the lights of Uvkusigssat showed; the dogs revived and lit out as for home. We rode. We crossed the fiord; the land's arms reached out, took us in. We clatter over shore ice to the land. A crowd swarms round; we're there.

The trader of Uvkusigssat is a Fleischer, cousin and brother-in-law to Salamina. Noblesse oblige: he's not like Pavia. No bursting out in noisy welcome, no bourgeois unrestraint or buccaneer exuberance. No anything, as far as we could see; where was he anyhow? What should we do with all our stuff? Where should we go? But David, taking my welcome at the trader's house for granted, led the way there. And as we entered through the gate the house door opened and the trader welcomed us. Since then I've many times been Fleischer's guest, been welcome always. I've had him visit me, seen lots of him. Yet beyond the *fact* of his hospitality and the assurances of his friends I have no reason to believe that he's a good fellow. And none to think he isn't. A more lifeless, taciturn, and sour-visaged man one rarely meets. A decent, sober man, good husband, all that sort of thing; not brilliant, not exactly competent, but honest, fair and square, I'm told. Well, there he stood, long-faced and glum. I've said he welcomed *us:* I lied. He welcomed me. "Come in," he said. And when David had set his load down in the entry, Fleischer shut the door on him and joined me. Oh, these educated, good-family Greenlanders are as snobbish as the worst of us. We have at least a kitchen door where hired men find welcome. So, for that matter, had Uvkusigssat, lots of them. David by now had passed through one of them and no doubt sat in the kitchen of his choice and told the settlement his news. We were the first arrivals from the north.

And now, despite its being after ten o'clock, there sounds a bustle and a clatter in the trader's house, and smells of good things cooking. And before long we are all seated at a properly set table —Fleischers, man and wife and child or two, and I—eating as though we hadn't had a meal that day. A good cook, Fleischer's wife.

And a thoroughly nice, clean, capable young woman. She'd been well trained; she'd kept her training up. But one would never by her looks have guessed she was a native. She was but half, at that, her father being, as Fleischer with some pride informed me at the earliest opportunity—well, no matter who; that's gossip. *What* a father is, is always to the point; and I can from my own knowledge describe him as a most courteous and friendly gentleman, one generally loved and honored. But when on calling at his house one day in the course of my travels, and sitting with him over coffee, I started to pay such deserved compliments to the wife of the trader of Uvkusigssat as I thought might please a father's ears, he jumped upon his feet and, alleging pressing business, rushed from the room. Funny, I thought. And I may here remark that the persistence with which the many Danish fathers of good Greenland children—the secret of whose parentage all know—keep playing ostrich is one of the curiosities of psychology. Men *will* nurse skeletons, even when the light of all outdoors has bleached their bones—or tanned their faces and put roses in their cheeks. (There's something wrong about my allegory.)

Oh, but it's late! We can't sit gossiping all night. To bed. What! on that couch? That billowy thing? I spread my sleeping-bag on the first mattress that I've touched for months. Good night.

XXXVI. THIRD DAY

WE STARTED out at ten: bad business letting every night steal one more hour from day. But this day was the last. Thank God for that! For we were both now painfully lame and could only hobble ludicrously behind the sledge. The dogs were tired too. We took our time.

A few miles from Uvkusigssat we passed a little settlement whose lights had heartened us the night before: three small turf houses on a rocky point of land. I little guessed what friendliness I'd meet with there one day. We passed, the people stood and watched. We waved good-by, and turned the land.

The day was as uneventful as good sledging days can be. The snow was firm, the sledges glided easily; we rode in turn. And it was still twilight when we sighted Satut, saw the many lights of that thriving place and the great roofs of its store sheds. We were but a mile or two from there when suddenly one dog gave out. He just lay down, or fell, and stayed. The sledge swept on, dragging the dog along with it. Halting the sledge, David now beat the dog with his whip handle, kicked him to his feet again; the dog resumed his place and we drove on. Again the dog lay down, just quit, collapsed. He lay and took the beating David gave him. "Kill me," he seemed to say. "I *can't* get up." We put him on the sledge; there was no need to tie him there. We drove at Satut to the trader's house, unharnessed all the dogs and set them free. The dogs knew home.

Johan Lange, that unprincipled swindler who had mulcted me

of my fifty kroner each for dogs, that hard-boiled, merchant-hearted Greenland Jew, is not only one of the most shrewd and intelligent of the residents of Greenland, *white* or native, but, if he likes you, as genial and generous a host as one may ever meet. He wasn't home; just left an hour before for Umanak. No matter, in we went. Elisabeth, his young—who counts the years?—his girlish, lovely wife *was* home.

And with that ease with which, apparently, she all her life did everything—from bearing children to helping them in time with theirs—her light, good-natured way that kept her looking like an elder sister of her children, she entertained and fed us two. Our weariness evaporated, our lame feet got well. The girls came in, they played the gramophone; we danced. Oh, it was hard to take the road again.

The road was hard: rough ice for all the sixteen miles, coagulated slush, all points and sharp-edged chunks to stub your toes against and sprain your insteps on. Men lame and tired, dogs played out. And dark, pitch-dark. Oh well, why agonize about what's past! At ten o'clock, dogs sprinting, sledge clattering, men putting on a lot of side, we made the settlement, tore in. Wake up! dead Umanak, the first sledge from the north has come.

"What on earth is the matter with your hair?" said my Danish host, staring at it as we came into the light, and laughing. My hair? What could be wrong? Salamina had cut it for me the night before we left. "Make me so beautiful," I had said, "that the girls in Umanak will fall in love with me at sight." "My hair?" I answered now. "Why, I don't know. I haven't looked at it." "Look now."

Ye gods! Locusts or brown-tailed moths, it seemed, had been at work on it, and quit before they'd finished. Great woman, Salamina; a capable, shrewd manager of what belonged to her.

Next morning saw me at the office. "When does the post go south?" I asked. "Most any day now, soon," they answered me. I gave my message in. And in that peace of mind that only comes to one on having done his best, and finished it, I put my feet up and lay back. We stayed four days at Umanak.

XXXVII. THE HUSKY

ALERT, intelligent, in type related to the chow or samoyed. And as for being bred of wolves, as some assert, there's either not a trace of it—or wolves are chows. But is such misbegotten offspring fertile? I don't know. However that may be, whatever may have been the dog's remoter ancestry, they're Greenland dogs of centuries of unmixed blood today; and centuries are many generations in the lives of dogs. There are, nevertheless, certain variations of type to be observed, such as a rangier build, and longer and more pointed muzzle. In color they will vary from pure white to black, or fox-red or dark brown. They may be patterned white on black or brown, or the reverse. Of my dogs, six were white and one was brindle.

Every day, at Igdlorssuit, as I sit working at my window, my attention is drawn from time to time by my neighbor Hendrik's bitch letting herself into his house. The outer door of that house is hung to open outwards and its latch, or whatever keeps it shut, is controlled from without by a string of rawhide. Whenever the bitch wants to enter—which is whenever they have put her out—she raises herself on her hind legs, places her forelegs against the door, takes the latchstring in her teeth, and, holding it tight, drops down and away from the door. The door is now ajar. She drops the string, opens the door wide with her nose, goes in. She doesn't shut the door behind her. All of Hendrik's dogs can do the trick, but not as deftly.

It is hard to say whether or not the Greenland dog has any

special aptitude for learning to work in harness and draw loads. He grows up doing it; it is one of the conditions of his life to which with good grace he adapts himself. If he has not as a puppy been put in harness, and whipped and driven by barbarous small boys, he is at any rate soon put to work in earnest with a practiced team. And if he lacks incentive to go ahead regardless of what may be tied to him, it is generously furnished by the whiplash. He fears the whip; he has good reason to.

Let us now, in writing of so fine a creature as the Greenland dog, accord his whole life that consideration which is allowed to men by their biographers. Birth, parentage, the early years, the early influences: these are factors in a dog's life as they are in man's, and in the lives of both must be accountable for adult traits. We have in mind one trait of which our hero stands accused, convicted, even, in the public mind: his savagery. I am defending him from that. We'll take a dog—take two. Let them be Hendrik's, for I watch his as I write.

Two dogs of Hendrik's, puppies five weeks old: I often see them playing with their mother, that same bitch that opens doors. I saw one of them a little while ago catch hold of the mother's tail just as she was mounting the steps. She was caught off balance, and came rolling down. Now, however, she is in the house; they're humane people and they tolerate her there. And one of the puppies is sitting on the top step looking around. The door opens, and out comes Hendrik's boy. (If it were the boy and not the puppy we were writing of we'd have to qualify that parentage. But let it go.) He's a fine-looking, sturdy boy of eight, and wears gold earrings like Hendrik's. A manly little fellow; he'll grow up to be a good hunter, a good husband, a good father. Well, he comes out. He sees the puppy. Nonchalantly, hands in pockets, he gives the puppy a swift kick that sends it spinning down four steps. Not that the puppy shouldn't have been there, nor that it was in the way; it wasn't. Hendrik's boy just felt like kicking it. But the puppy hasn't minded it much; he picks himself up, and a minute later he's frisking about. He frisks up to Hendrik's boy, who has just come sauntering down the steps. Out goes the boy's foot, catches the puppy in the nose, knocks him six feet or so. That hurts; he kiyis and goes running off. "Oh—ho!" yawns Hendrik's boy; now what to do?

The catechist's young son comes over; he is aged ten or twelve. They are great playmates, these two boys. But what to do? Let's play with dogs! Where are the puppies?—there they are, in under the steps. Here, take this stick and poke them out. A few good pokes and out they come. You will, will you! And the catechist's boy lambastes one puppy with his stick. And now each boy has got a puppy by the tail. They're swinging them in circles, round, round, round. They set them down; the puppies try to walk, and can't. They're dizzy, drunk. Great fun. Now, swinging the puppies around in great circles, they make them collide. Plunk! they go. That's fun, do that again. They try swinging them, and bumping them, by one leg. They try swinging them and letting them fly off at a tangent on to the ground. Let's see, they say, who can chuck his the farthest. That's no more fun: let's try them on the roof.

Hendrik's is a sloping wooden roof. Its eaves toward my house are about five feet from the ground. Taking the puppies each by one leg, the boys throw them up as far as they can. The puppies land, and then come rolling down again. They flop off on to the ground. Try it again. Once more. Again. The puppies are quite groggy now.

Hendrik's boy has an idea! He gets some string, two pieces: one for each. They loop the string behind the puppies' jaws, and swing them that way. You can get a bigger swing with cord. Oh! try this: try holding them up by the cord; see how long they can stand it. They stand it long enough; too long. The boys are bored. Dropping the dogs, each gives his groggy dog a good hard kick; and boys and little dogs go off in different ways.

Sometimes they try drowning them in the drain ditch—well, not really drowning them; just holding them under, pushing them down into the mud with sticks. Or, I'll tell you what's fun!

Getting puppies in a corner where they can't get out, and lashing them with a whip. It's good practice.

Puppies, in spite of boys, grow up. And they grow up much faster than boys do. They get to be so big that boys don't like to monkey with them. Boys leave big dogs alone. And dogs, I don't know why, leave boys alone. Once in a while a child does some such unexpected thing as stumbling over one, or slipping and falling down in the midst of them. He may get bitten; sometimes they've been killed. Grown dogs are best avoided, though if one walks straight at them with a manly stride they'll generally slink away. The dogs are cowed: that's what's the matter with them. Among both dogs and men only the cowards bite.

Dogs take their disposition from their master. They fear him always, and have reason to. But they get more than blows from him, they get their food. The sight of him makes the saliva run; they flock around. He feels their loins to judge of their condition; that's a caress to them. He plucks their fur, plucks out the matted last year's hair; that titillates their nerves; they like it. And the degree and extent of such attentions is reflected in the bearing of the dogs. Dogs like their masters and they don't too much hate man.

Men like their dogs, but dogs must know their place; that place is neither at the hearth, nor on the lap, nor in the heart. They don't *love* dogs. That is perhaps a blessing to the Greenland dog and an expression of men's common sense.

It is the generous custom of the Director General of Greenland to give the people of Umanak a kaffemik on each occasion of his annual visits of inspection. He thus commemorates his happy memory of the golden days of Umanak when he was local manager. The scene of these parties is the level open space, or plaza, which, surrounded as it is by the spick and span buildings of the administration, dominated by the peak of Umanak, and smiled upon—as on the day I write about it was—by August's sun, is as impressively beautiful a spot for drinking coffee as the world can offer. There in the center of that place was set a great table; and on it many of those things to eat, and one of those to drink, which most delight the native taste. And at the appointed time the people all came flocking there, to make the plaza flower with the red, white, blue, green, yellow, orange, pink, and purple of their costumes. Now on this day there happened to be present many distinguished European and American visitors who, as passengers aboard the steamer then in port, were touring Greenland. It was a treat for them to see this festival. And so the Greenlanders, to do their part, all stood together when the feasting was concluded and sang to them. It *is* affecting when these people sing. They love it, to begin with, and they have so good a sense of time and pitch and harmony that despite their raw and untrained voices their choral singing comes to have real quality. This was a Sunday and their songs were hymns. The solemn music was in keeping with the scene, the day, their thankful mood, the mood—one might suppose—of everyone. It *made* the mood, for such is music's power.

Now the withdrawal of the singers into a compacter group had left an open space of ground between them and their audience; and hardly had the music started when some puppies frisked in and began to play about. "Oh, *see* those darling puppies!" cried a lady. And so it happened that during the entire course of the concert the guests were occupied with winning puppies' love with honeyed baby talk and lumps of sugar. It drives the moral home to tell that all the eyes of all the little children there pursued those lumps from paper bag to ladies' fingers into puppies' mouths. They wanted them.

The Greenland hunter does not humanize a dog; the hunter's wife has children. No man in looking at a dog will say, or think, "And was he daddy's little darling." The men are realists, and dogs are brutes. They're useful brutes: for that they're kept and fed. Or kept and fed a while, then killed and eaten, in a time of need, as we would kill and eat a cow. Yet if the Greenlander's treatment of dogs is unhuman, it is far from being canine. And we can spare our tender hearts much suffering from such spectacles as Hendrik's boy affords, by thinking of how *dogs* treat dogs. Those puppies of Hendrik's are alive five weeks from birth because of the indefatigable vigilance of the mother in protecting them against their father and their uncles. Having survived that peril, they have yet to face in those incestuous fangs that disciplining which all dogs must undergo from all their clan to learn respect for elders. It scars and toughens them. Theirs is a dog's life among dogs. And for one dog wantonly *injured* by a child or man, dogs must have slaughtered thousands.

Since the Greenland dog is not maintained as a luxury, and under the conditions couldn't be, all treatment of him must be judged by its effect upon his usefulness. If they were pets, would they be better dogs? That's hard to say. They lend themselves to kindness avidly; give them an inch of it, they'll want the ell. And let one get his nose in at the door, he'll push on in and eat your dinner up. Besides, you don't let Greenland dogs indoors. There is a reason.

One does sometimes see wanton cruelty to dogs: it's rare. The good dog-driver, like the good horseman, is he who gets the best and longest service from his animals. The whip is, like the spur, used best when used the least. And this is so well understood in Greenland that nonchalance and seeming effortlessness in driving are established as good form.

Dog-owners get one savage thrill a day: at feeding-time. That ravening, snarling, yelping, howling, screaming pack that leaps and surges round him as with tub of meat held high above his head he wades out to the feeding-pen is as superb a spectacle of animal ferocity as man may ever see. Then dogs are dogs, hyenas, wolves, most any savage thing you like; not pets. There might is right, and flashing swift and fierce in its self-maintenance. Don't say what dogs are till you've fed a pack. Who's who, in dogs? Pitch out that meat to them, and learn. Watch them; not once, but time on time. Theirs is no random savagery, those snarling leaps and lightning fang-thrusts. Observe how from the momentary chaos of a guzzling free-for-all there has emerged an absolutely ordered state, where preëstablished might determines precedence, and precedence means food. All that had had the look of dog annihilating dog was no more than the reassertion by fierce show of an authority already established beyond serious dispute. Look at the leader with his pile of meat chunks to himself, devouring them at leisure, while the rest, long finished but not satisfied, just let him. Observe his unconcern, his utter nonchalance in power; he is the state. How? Why?

It has been the honor of America to be the first among the foreign nations of the world to send a minister of state to Greenland; it is our greater honor to have had one who would want to go. Ruth Bryan Owen, Minister to Denmark, went, and let her light so shine in every colony from south to north that Greenlanders would want, we trust, if they weren't subjects of the Danish king to be Americans. Now as the official party was strolling about in one of the colonies they came upon a group of dogs among whom stood one of such striking nobility of mien that all the people cried at once, "Oh, look! the leader." Then they discussed the very question that we've asked above. "But who appoints the leader?" asked a lady. "Does the King—or, I would say, the dog's owner?" Now Mrs. Bryan Owen is her father's daughter and a democrat. "No," said Mrs. Owen, "he is not appointed. He is chosen."

"Democracy," says Nietzsche, "which is rule by force." So then, by rule of force, by counting at the polls the man power of opposing armies in America, by testing out dog power in the dog democracies of Greenland, are leaders chosen. A dog having once established himself in the control of his democracy is accorded the almost unquestioning respect of all the rest. (That ought to interest *us*.) Their loyalty to him is such that they will support him and maintain him in authority against an even more powerful newcomer to the pack. Such undisputed leadership will last for years. The end, I'm told, may be a tragic one, a duel to the death: a dog election. (Not a bad idea!)

However violent at times, authority among the dogs is well-intentioned. The leader keeps good order in the pack; he tolerates no family rows. The lion's share of food he makes his own: it is the leader's perquisite. Dog leaders qualify by resourcefulness, alertness, energy, and strength, by canine virtue. By what, one sometimes wonders, do our leaders qualify?

Dog's social life is intricate and marked by rigid rules of precedence and etiquette. In many ways it differs from our own. But in the involuntary, and as it were instinctive, nature of their conforming to established social law they differ from us little, if at all. We're both behaviorists. And if we *must* find likeness between dogs and us let's put it there: We're not much different from dogs.

My dogs: I got to own sixteen at last, two good-sized teams. The nucleus of the pack were Johan Lange's; their leader stayed Grand Sachem of the pack. I went in heavily for dogs; I learned a lot. I had a lot to learn. I made a start at Umanak; we left with ten dogs pulling us.

We left, and drove straight home; the whole of Umanak Fiord had frozen hard. And as at noon we looked behind at Umanak, we saw its peak glow red like heated iron. The sun had risen.

XXXVIII. THE GARDEN OF EDEN

SUNLIGHT to see by, ice to travel on, and work to do. The work was painting. It was for that that I had come to Greenland; by that, and maybe for that, that I lived and found it *almost* good most anywhere, alone. "If a man," said Socrates, "sees a thing when he is alone, he goes about straightway seeking until he finds someone to whom he may show his discoveries, and who may confirm him in them." So does the artist then seek solitude that, seeing when he is alone, he shall be constrained to such utterance as may endure to seek and find his friends. They will confirm him.

"Discoveries"—are we discoverers then, we writers, poets, sculptors, picture-painters? It is all anyone at most can be. Leif Ericsson, Magellan, Cook, the architect of the first pyramid, the builder of the first arch, Homer, Shakespeare, Euclid, Newton, Einstein: all are discoverers, revealers, of what was and is, of continents, of natural law, of the human soul. God, let us say, made Adam. It was for Michelangelo to discover, as though for the first time, how beautiful God's Adam was. And it remains for all of us, forever, to discover as though for the first time how beautiful the sunrise is, and the moon, and night, and plain and mountain, land and sea, and man and woman; how *beautiful* life is. And whether we pursue discovery in the environment at home which is familiar to us all, or abroad in the remoter and less-known regions of the earth, we'll find the field still unexplored and rich in undiscovered beauty.

I'm one who travels around; and in Alaska, years ago, I found an island that I liked, fixed up a place to live in, and settled down to work. Now about twenty miles from the island there happened to have been built, for no ostensible reason, a small town, which, being in Alaska, was populated by men who had come to look for gold and hadn't found it, by men who had found and spent it, prospectors, and by such camp followers of gold as tradesmen, hotel-keepers, brothel-keepers, brothel-kept, et cetera, all of whom were reduced to that last extremity of hope, the owning of building-lots. So they of course got together and formed a Chamber of Commerce, got out "literature," got a slogan—"The New York of the Pacific"—and, there being nothing left to do, put on the rags and tatters of their hopes and squatted on their tails to watch for suckers. It hurt when I passed up a 25′ x 100′ piece of swamp on "Le Grand Boulevard" and settled on an island. Did I think there was gold out there? Art?—what was that? I was at worst, they figured out, a German spy; at best a poor damned fool. I didn't get much of the talk out there: I worked. Short of a year, I finished up. I packed what I'd panned out, came into town, and waited for the steamer. Down in the freight house stood my box of "dust," a big box, all my work. I'd written its insurance value big across the lid: "Value: $10,000." Yes, stare at that, you bankrupt realtors; there's gold on earth where you would never dream of it. They stared.

Men have divining-rods for buried wealth, for water, oil—I'm told; for gold—for all I know. I don't think that they work. They don't in art; I mean the rules, the formulae that men work out to tell you whether things are beautiful or not, or show you how to make them so. The best of them are sort of like the old witch-hazel rod that found you water where you *and* the rod manipulator felt quite sure that water was. Maybe with beauty things are just reversed; maybe we don't find God, but God, divining us, reveals Himself. At least He did one February night up North.

It was just bedtime, and I'd laid my book aside and gone outdoors. It was a moonless, starlit, cold, clear night, a dark night except for a faint illumination low in the southeastern sky as though from lights behind the hill. Even as I looked at this, the glow became converging shafts that, reaching upward, touched into incandescent light a gently waving veil that hung in folds across from east to south. It might have been a glorified Isolde's veil; and where the breath of her desire touched it, it grew hot and bright. Her breath swept over it; it pulsed and surged. It was her cry, almost: He comes! Ah, God, he comes! It burst in flame and kindled heaven.

The beauty of those Northern winter days is more remote and passionless, more nearly absolute, than any other beauty that I know. Blue sky, white world, and the golden light of the sun to tune the whiteness to the sun-illumined blue. If we personify the sun and feel for it in its incessant toil of making varicolored things to harmonize—red barns fit summer landscapes, wild roses go with buttercups, of making harmony where purposeful disharmony prevails—what vast delight we must believe it to experience in shining down on snow. "I who am nothing," whispers that prone whiteness, "partake of you, dear sun, and of the blue heaven in which you shine, and become beautiful." In Greenland one discovers, "as though for the first time," what beauty is. God must forgive me that I tried to paint it.

I did, incessantly. I would attach a large canvas to the stanchions of my sledge as upon an easel; I'd hang my bag of paints and brushes from the crossbar, lay my palette on the sledge. I'd catch my dogs, and harness them. And then, after the mad stampede downhill and over the shore ice which was the inescapable prelude to a trip, I'd recline upon my reindeer skin with the indolence of a sultan and drive off to my rendezvous. Arrived, I'd halt my dogs, swing the sledge into precisely the position that I wanted it, lay out my paints and brushes, get to work. To keep my brush hand warm I used a down-stuffed thumbless mitten through a hole in which I would insert the brush, and hold it in my warm bare fingers. I found it sometimes cold work, painting; my blood seemed not to circulate. That, thought I, is because we use our brains; our blood is occupied up there. It was a flattering thought. When I would finish work I'd merely get my dogs upon their feet—they, all the time, had lain motionless—swing them around with a "*Eu, eu!*" ("left") or "*Ille, ille!*" ("right"), bunch them prettily with a smell of the lash to bring the stragglers in, tap on my boot for speed, and race for home. They'd take me to my door. Traveling like this, one mile, or ten, or twenty-five—what difference?

Except that on the long trips I would take supplies along and plan to spend some days. The long trips, for convenience, necessitated a base. I'd make my base Nugatsiak. The fiords near there, for grandeur, quite surpassed belief.

On a certain one of these trips, intending to confine myself to Nugatsiak, I took along David, promising him the use of my sledge and dogs for hunting during the days that I would be occupied on shore at my work. Now about five miles from Nugatsiak is the island of Karrat, which, though one of the smaller islands of that archipelago, is an imposing landmark by reason of its comparative isolation and the noble architecture of its mountain mass. With towers and buttressed walls reared high upon a steep escarpment, it has the dignity of a great citadel standing to guard the gateway to the glamorous region of Umiamako. I'd thought of some day camping there, to paint. So that when, having arrived at Nugatsiak on this trip with David, it came to my ears that there stood an untenanted house on the western end of Karrat I had at once but one idea: to look it over with a view to staying there. I promptly called upon the owner, a Nugatsiak man, crawled in to him, bowed low to him and stood with bended head in deference to his ceiling and my head, sat with him and his numerous family in one of the smallest, lowliest, dirtiest, and most friendly houses I'd had cause to enter, and got at once his glad consent to use his Karrat house. "You'll need the key," he said. "It is standing in the lock."

That I went next day to Karrat with supplies for only overnight was sheer stupidity; for no sooner had I seen the cove where stood the house, and had one glimpse of its stupendous views, than it was settled in my mind to stay my time out there. "You'll leave me here," I said to David, "go straight back to Nugatsiak for the night, bring me more canvases and food tomorrow, and then go hunting where you please; and stay—five days."

The cove, three sides surrounded by the steep hillsides and ledges of the foreland, lay beautifully sheltered from most winds. Its background was the donjon keep of Karrat; it faced the mountainous environs of the mouth of Kangerdlugsuak. One would breathe deep and fast who lived in such a place.

The house I might not readily have found had I been there alone, so dwarfed were man-sized things. David, who knew the place, drove straight in to the head of the cove, whipped the dogs up the steep and high embankment of a knoll, and stopped. An edge of turf across a mound of snow: that was the house.

It took us but a minute or two to clear away the drifted snow from around the low doorway, to turn the key (the owner had been right, the house was locked), pass through the low turf passageway, and enter. We found ourselves inside a sort of ice cave, dimly and glamorously illuminated by the cold daylight which filtered through the snowbank at the window and through a snowed-up stovepipe hole in the roof. Where, through this hole, and through innumerable leaks in the flat roof, water had trickled there hung great glittering ice stalactites that were at variance with my intentions there. And directly under the stovepipe hole—there was no stove—was an accumulated mound of ice a foot thick at its crest. Walls, ceiling, floor; ice, ice: it wasn't as you'd picture home. No matter; it would do. We brought my things indoors, I set the primus up and lighted it and put on snow to melt; in twenty minutes we were drinking coffee. The sound of dripping water filled the house.

And now, with David waiting to depart, I took pencil and paper and drew up a list of those things of which I'd have need in the days to follow. It was a problem to express my wants in such a way as Pavia would understand: I supplemented pigeon Eskimo by art. Rice, oatmeal, coffee, a Greenland halibut—that's all. Oh, no! a postscript just for fun, to make old Pavia laugh. "And,"—"*ama*," I wrote, "*niviassak pinakak*." And I drew a picture of the thing: a pretty girl. Then, instructing David to bring me from my own supplies a quantity of canvases, I sent him on his way.

XXXIX. ADAM AND EVE

WHO hasn't, over and over again in the course of his life, fixed up places to live in? Houses out of chairs and shawls, houses in trees, houses of snow, caves, lairs in impenetrable thickets, tents, log houses, lofts, abandoned houses, sheds, boats, homes: the thrill of making them is never lost. I looked my ice cave kindly in the face; it wept encouragement. Enough. And with an ardor worthy of the task I set to knocking the stalactites from its hoary brow, scraping the ice from its incrusted cheeks, digging the ice up from—we'll have to drop our physiognomy—the floor, and melting it, as much as my small pocket primus would, from everywhere. And at bedtime I had the deep satisfaction of having converted a dry cold ice cave into an ice-cold sump. Such, we may say, is progress. I crawled into my sleeping-bag and slept.

Just as a painter doesn't *have* to have a duplex studio, north light, and inside balcony with silk brocades draped over it, so does he not have to have an easel. Outdoors they're such a nuisance that I never use them. A stick to prop the canvas with and stones to hold it down: that's good most any time of year. But in *deep* snow, a couch; I found one in my Karrat house. It was a rather elegant affair, homemade, of course, just wood, but shapely, with a sort of arm or back at one end of it. With this couch planted to its belly in the snow, my canvas propped up at the arm-embellished end, my palette flat in front of it, I sat next morning on the hill and worked. My theme was mountains, and its foreground, snow, the snow plain of the frozen fiord. So hours passed. It must have been near noon when, looking up, I saw that there had crept into my foreground plane a minute sledge propelled by insect dogs. They *did* look small in that immense environment. I left my work and went to meet them at the house.

David had brought my things, I made that out as he drew near. But what a lot of stuff! My canvases, they bulked up large; but it was hard to see just what he had, against the sun's glare on the snow. The hill now hid both sledge and dogs. I heard the whip's report, the shrill yap of a dog; "*Eu, eu!*" the voice of David. Heads down, tails up, the dogs appear, the dogs, the sledge, the driver—David, and—by God—the girl. My postscript in the flesh.

"So you brought everything," said I to David as we unpacked.

"Yes," said he, "I think so."

"Then come indoors; we'll all have coffee."

"Five days. Remember, David, and come back."

"I will," said David, and drove off.

Pauline—that was her name—and I watched from the hilltop till he turned the point. We waved good-by.

She was a pleasant, quiet-wayed, mature young woman of twenty. She was dumpy, round-cheeked, good-looking only if one fancied Greenland looks. She was a normal, healthy Greenland Eve. But for the respect that I had formed for Spartan Greenland womanhood I would have felt misgivings about the Eden that I had brought her to. She let me put such thoughts away. And whether, during the days that followed, she was occupied with chipping ice from the ceiling, or with digging out the rotting bones and filth from the frozen bog which was the floor, or shivering in idleness, or wading in the snowdrifts to keep warm, she was absolutely, peacefully, content and happy. Entering that dripping house I'd shudder and, by way of cheer, ask, "*Ajorpa?*"—Are things too bad?" She'd look up from her work and, smiling, say, "*Ajungulak*"—"It's good." We praise the lark for singing under summer skies; Pauline would stand there singing by the hour in that cave.

We hadn't much to eat; I hadn't figured on two mouths to feed. For lunch I cooked a mess of rice and pemmican or fish, for supper, oatmeal porridge—eaten plain. We had no dishes, so we ate by turns out of the pot; we had no tableware, so I whittled a wooden spoon from a piece of board. "*Mamapok*," said Pauline, tasting the porridge. That means "Delicious."

It never got warm in the house, the primus was too small. And I couldn't burn it continuously, for I had little petroleum. Within an hour of putting out the stove the floor and lower walls would freeze again. Pauline had little on. "Where are your clothes, Pauline?" I asked. "There," she answered, pointing to a pair of kamiks and an anorak.

There was no way for us to sleep but in my sleeping-bag. If out of gallantry I'd given it to her, I would out of misery during the night have crawled into it beside her. And if I hadn't, no one would believe it. We both got in the bag. We tried to get in with our clothes on, and we couldn't. Then we took them off. Two fingers in one finger of a glove: that tight, we managed it. The nights were hell. We shared the privilege by turns of working out an arm and leaving it outside to cool and almost freeze. That was our one relief. She slept a little, but she didn't sing.

I could have sent Pauline back home the day she came: not for the world would I have sent her back. I'd written for a girl: well, here she was. And whether Pavia was to be credited with a rare sense of humor or with incredible efficiency as a storekeeper is beside the point. *Sent home!* Pauline could never have lived down the ignominy. She knew that well; and stayed.

By day she'd clean the house, and wash the pot and spoon, and stroll around and sing. And then at night, following the example of my intentioned shamelessness, she'd strip her pauper's garments off and slither into the warm reindeer bag beside me. Poor little shivering, ice-cold, uncomplaining Eskimo: how almost numb with cold she was! Then warmth would come and with it, sometimes, sleep.

The days were uneventful; they were mild and fair. Over our

Pauline, the Arctic lark, the Eve of Karrat — just a little bit idealized.

heads the dark deep vault of blue, before our eyes huge snow-incrusted mountain walls and one restricted vista far across the snow-covered plain of the sea to the distant peaks and ranges of Nugssuak. The peak of Karrat towered over us; its dark-red rocks were gold against the zenith sky. We seldom walked far, for the snow was deep and heavy, but from the summit of the foreland what a view there was! One saw, near by, the marvelously corrugated mountain sides of Kekertarssuak, and then the whole broad tossing panorama of the northern ranges. Pale gold of sun-illumined snow, and blue; with here and there a patch of bare black mountain side to prove the blinding pitch of all the rest. Snow-blind: perhaps our eyes are stricken to preserve our souls.

We rose at earliest daylight, and turned in at dark; almost all day I worked. We had two visitors. The first, a hunter coming out of Kangerdlugsuak, saw me at work and came to pay a call. He was a most unhappy man. He told me that his wife had died, and how his house stood empty now. So good a house, glass in the windows, and a stove. Yes, there it stood in Nugatsiak, no one in it. He sat a long time in silence. "There were once many houses on Karrat," he continued. "One house stood there, another there. Yes, there were many houses here one time. Now, only one. The houses, people—gone." I thought he'd weep. He used, he said, to catch a lot of seals; now he caught none. Hard days, hard times. And he had nothing now to eat. Would I lend him twenty-five öre? If he got a seal, he would pay me; if he got none, he wouldn't. He told me that his name was Jakob.

Our second visitor was named Abraham. He brought me a letter from Salamina. And he brought me two ptarmigan; of these we made a feast.

Two visitors and a brace of ptarmigan: these were the events of five days in the life of Pauline. The routine of her island days, and those events, might be the type of what her life would be for forty years. A house, a man to do his work, whatever it might be, apart from her, the household chores, long idle hours at the window or outdoors, a little food, a little warmth: these make the pattern of a Greenland woman's life. And children as a by-product. Yes, Pauline in the course of years as she'd stand idly gazing from the window and singing softly to herself would rock her body soothingly to lull her child to sleep. There'd be that difference.

I wonder what it would be like, that island and Pauline, for life. I wonder whether a white man would have sense enough to let things be, just let the days and the relationship run on and not go prying into her exotic soul, nor even thinking that she had a soul, nor caring. The silly fool would doubtless fall in love with her and spoil it all; display, to her astonishment, the strange behavior of romantic love; insist on finding in her placid face some revelation of unfathomed pagan depths; get staring at her disconcertingly, annoying her. If at such antics Pauline didn't get, at last, the poor oaf's measure, size up what he *was* good for in cash expressed in clothes and beads, in *Danish* clothes, in leisure for herself and servants to support it, if she didn't contrive that her fatuous adorer should leave the island and move with her into the great city of Umanak, she'd be a fool—or a philosopher. Pauline, I think, was neither. And if a romantic white man lured by the visionary primitive did fall in love with her, she'd serve him in her own behalf as other "primitives" have served such men.

Therefore, when on the fifth day David came we packed our household goods and art, and drove away. The people of Nugatsiak crowded around us as we came to land. "How did you like the pretty girl?" asked Pavia. "The pretty girl," I answered him, "was swell."

XL. OLD HOME WEEK

AT LAST, after weeks of talking about it, the goodwill visit to Nugatsiak was to start. All kinds of things had interfered: this man or that would be absent on an expedition, I had a picture to finish, the post from the north arrived; then we had snow. It lay so deep and loose and dry that dogs went in it to their backs and sledges sank in almost out of sight. Deep, beautiful, soft snow; and the very devil to travel on. Then, suddenly, there came a thaw, a thoroughgoing day and night spring thaw in February. The water settled through the snow down to the firm ice underneath, forming on top of it a layer of slush which still supported what remained of the blanket of the last snow. It looked all right, but try it to your sorrow. Then on the twenty-ninth it froze. The start was ordered for next morning, ten o'clock.

It was a fine fair day, just made for such a holiday, and as the hour for the start approached the settlement became alive with preparations. At ten o'clock like starting at a gun the sledges left the land. Leaving from many points along the shore, they all converged toward the beaten track and strung out there in single file, a long procession of twelve sledges winding northwards. I saw it all; all ready on the dot to start. I now stood stamping on the shore and watched them go. As we'd come tearing out across the flat, a fellow called to us, "Stop! Wait. Beate's coming." Like a bewildered hen the old girl had been running back and forth all morning. First she would go, then wouldn't. Yes, she would; no, she wouldn't. Her final word was no; too bad, we wanted her. And now she *was* coming after all: of course I'd wait. And there far off across the snow the sledges crept away. Damn women anyhow.

Beate came at last, a funny-looking object running down the hill. She brought her feather bed: it almost covered her. Below it there appeared her nimble little crablike legs; above it, her big head, a kerchief tied around it and her twisted scalp lock bobbing as she ran. Her sawed-off pipe of course was in her mouth. "All right, sit down, Beate, there's the dear. Let Salamina tuck you in."

We'd started with a rush, I, all of us. We quick enough slowed down. Good going? It was vile; the snow was almost slush. And that for the first few miles we held a moderate pace was due to the strength and the exuberant spirits of the dogs. Hard work: they loved it. We overtook and passed sledge after sledge and were finally trailing the leaders. These, giving us a trial to qualify, had mercy on my dogs at last and stopped to wait for us. Martin was one of them; he was again alone. I gave him old Beate for a girl. We leaders kept together from then on, the vanguard of the great invasion of Nugatsiak.

We had been hours on our way, and still were hours from port, when darkness fell. The going got continually worse. The dogs could hardly draw the laden sledges through the slush; and when we went afoot we sank at each step to our knees in it. No trouble sinking in; it was the pulling out again that wore us out. At times our pace could have been no more than a mile or a mile and a half an hour. Yet even at that snail's pace, when I once lagged to recover a mitten I had dropped, it was only by desperate effort that I overtook the sledge again—twelve feet ahead. If a strong man, I thought, were to be set down in the midst of that sea of slush, alone and without sledge, he'd never get beyond a mile.

I had brought with me, on my sledge, a contrivance of footwear that had excited the curiosity of the Greenlanders and, possibly, provoked their mirth: snowshoes. Strangely, they are quite unknown in Greenland. I put mine on, while all the drivers stopped to watch the demonstration. It was a snowshoe triumph. The snow that at a snail's pace they could hardly struggle through, I ran upon with ease. They were *too* good; I had to lend them round and round in turn, till Salamina ended that by running off in them. In no time she had left us far behind, to then, confound her, stride off at a tangent to our course; as if she couldn't see the lights across the snow ahead of us. She either couldn't hear us as we called, or wouldn't. And only when it became quite clear that we were not following her did she come back to us, explaining, for excuse, that in January the Nugatsiak people had had shark lines over there, and that there'd be a trail. All laughed.

As we drew near Nugatsiak a man named Eskias came out on skis to meet us. "You should have come that way," he said, pointing to the way that Salamina had taken.

The settlement, of course, turned out to meet us, and lead us to the several houses of our destination. On entering Pavia's I looked at my watch: it was seven-thirty. Nine hours and a half for twenty-two miles; the distance has been done in two. And the rear guard of the caravan would still be hours on the way.

The invasion of Nugatsiak was of the nature of an Old Home Week reversed: the parent settlement went out to meet its off-sprung friends and kindred. Pleasant as it would be to represent such wholesale visiting as an established ancient custom of the people, I must admit its origin to have been no older than the current year, and no more of the folk than I was. The Greenland settlements are stagnant pools; this was a plan to stir them. Living as Greenland people do, in separate little groups on isolated islands in a wilderness, they ought, it seems, to have some social life outside of watching at funereal kaffemiks and dancing with, and sleeping with, and marrying first cousins. We may *call* the culture of Greenland today a transitional culture, call what we see there progress; yet the improvidence of the people, their too common sloth, their appalling general inertia, mark many of them today as lower in the societal scale than animals and bugs. *We* call it Progress; the young Greenlander whom I have quoted called it decline; and it probably *is* degeneracy. I've watched the chipmunks reap the tender pine cones when they were ripe for food, and harvest them when they were cured, and store them in the ground for winter use; and I can't, for common human pride, admit that men who can't or won't provide against inevitable need are not degenerate. To point the statement that improvidence and sloth are symptoms of subnormality I drag in, fondly, by the heels, my son, a normal boy of fourteen, here in Greenland with me as I write. He has been six months in the country. In two weeks he learned to use the kayak fairly well, well enough to stay out far away from land for hours, gunning for birds; in two months—since we've had ice—he has trained a team of miscellaneous, young, hitherto undriven dogs and made himself a good dog-driver (a more *intelligent* driver, I may say, than many young Greenlanders). He makes his own seal nets, sets them himself on the sea ice many miles distant from the settlement, drives out to tend them by himself, spending eight to ten hours of at least every other day out on the ice. He has four seal nets and has caught seven seals. The value of one seal pays for all the nets. He would be *now* a substantial contributor to the support of a Greenland family; in a year he might, by being provident in season, be the mainstay of one. All the boys of the settlement can drive dogs, all could set nets—get twine on credit, and quickly pay for it. None do. I don't think that there's a youth under eighteen who catches seals. Most of them do nothing. They can, they need to; and they don't.

Of the degeneracy of the Greenlanders their pathetic social life is as sure a symptom as, of their inertia, it is an expression. This damned thing, Progress, has to come. The Bible, education, all such pretty things aside, its gospel word is Trade. And so intent are Greenland traders on their little perquisite of a percentage on the fat and skins, and so intent—inevitably so—the well-inclined administration on the measurement of Greenland progress by the kroner scale, that the former too often discourage social dissipation, and the latter can't think of it.

So Trolleman refused the dance-den key self-righteously: they ought to work. Less righteously he'd kept the cooper of the settlement at work two years without a weekday off, and now refused him leave to go with us. That was hard lines on Rudolf and Marghreta, and too bad for us. (But it was all set right, in time, and will be told of in its place.)

The festivities of the two nights and a day that were our Week were various and many. There were of course the kaffemiks, and lots of them; but what a difference! What life it gave them to have visitors! The people found their tongues; they talked and laughed. You didn't just go in, sit down, gulp down your saucerful of drink, count off the minutes of propriety, get up, go out. You stayed. And before you were ready to leave one party, someone was urging you to the next.

Second to Pavia's house in prestige was the house of Benjamin, the catechist. The traders' houses have prestige per se; the catechists' have not. And that little jumping jack, Benjamin, had no importance in the eyes of anyone but him. His house his mother dignified; she reigned there like a queen. And all that any of them were, derived from her. She was a swell: sixty perhaps, hardly a wrinkle in her face, sound teeth, and what a smile! She was immaculately dressed, and wore her hair in the old-fashioned topknot. A black silk scarf worn turbanlike around her head enforced both the oriental cast of her features and the queenly dignity of her manner.

There was the house of Eskias, of Eskias and Debora. Eskias was in all respects a man of parts. A catechist in the far south of Greenland, he had been, it is said, so loved by women, and himself loved women so, that the church at last would have none of him. No wonder that the church ends up by having few that anybody loves. But Debora, it proved, was wiser than the church. Between them, and despite a lot of children, they are among the most prosperous families of the region. Eskias retains his hunter's skill despite his education, his education without pride, and Debora despite the women. And Debora, despite her looks and charm, has brains. Theirs was the house I liked the best; and there I gave *my* kaffemik.

We've had the houses of the rich; now take the poor: the house, the cave, the den, the miserable lair, of Morton. Morton was a short man of powerful build, presentable in feature though a trifle soft, with melting eyes, and lips that sought to drool. Morton was dirty; the tatters of his garments only bound the fabric of their grease. Morton had a way about him. "My name is Morton," he would say in passable Danish, accosting a stranger, "What is your name?" Then he would shake your hand. "I am an expedition man," he would continue. "I have been with Lauge Koch. People say you are a fine man. I am a fine man. You shall take me as your man." But you don't. Morton is fatuous; you don't quite trust him. And then you learn about him. He has the most evil name in all the region. Greenlanders don't tell you all they know, inclining to conceal from strangers those occasional dark deeds that might reflect discredit on their race. They have that solidarity: they don't tell on themselves. And your best friend among them may leave you to discover for yourself the well-known worthlessness of someone you've employed. Someone once breathed to me that Morton had killed his wife. I pushed inquiry and encountered silence. But many say that he is bad; *that* bad he is. A drunken Greenlander, I'm told, will fight. Not many, my informant added, not like the Europeans. Fist fighting is taboo in Greenland. But I've seen Morton, sober, do that grizzly thing: plant his hard-knuckled fist in another's face. It happened in Nugatsiak, once when Pavia was away, and Pavia's kifak tapped his master's beer and drank a skinful; he got reeling drunk. He reeled outside, and entertained the crowd. I don't know just what happened; I stood some distance off. Morton was in the crowd and may have taunted him; and the boy—for he was hardly more than that—have answered back. At any rate Morton went at him, hit him a hard blow in the face and sent him sprawling. The boy got to his feet and went at Morton; and Morton knocked him down again. It was so pitifully easy. Back came the boy for more, and Morton gave it to him, terribly. The boy quit coming back; he went into the house. All over now, I thought. It had all been so swift in its recurrent starts and finishes that I'd stood as though petrified. The crowd had moved away; the fighting frightened them. Now, as they stood, they gave a start and moved to scatter; out burst the boy, a rifle in his hands. Morton began to back away toward me; the boy, to follow. He stopped and raised the gun, aimed long; then threw the gun away. Of course, as I thought about it afterwards, the gun, lying about in the house, wasn't loaded. The drunken boy would not have thought of that. I'll get a gun, he'd thought, and kill him. Aiming, he doubtless pulled the trigger, pulled it persistently, then realized the fact. He threw the gun away and picked up stones and hurled them after Morton. Morton turned back at him, but I had got my senses and came running up. "Come out of it!" I yelled at him. "Get out of this, get home." Morton obeyed. The boy, still hurling stones, came on. And he was shouting—not his love, I'd guess. I couldn't understand the words; I got their tone. It matched his bloody, rage-distorted face. I'd never heard such *cadenced* speech before; it was as though his labored breathing and his pounding pulse imposed their rhythm on his words: heroic stuff, as art. Even his talk to me, as at his coming up I halted him, was like a litany of rage. Leave him reciting it and follow Morton.

His den is hardly five feet high, and six by eight, not more, around the walls. The walls are turf. The floor was turf; its composition now eludes analysis. The roof is turf, with poles as beams to hold it up. More than half of the floor space is occupied by the sleeping-platform; sitting on that are two women and four children. Bedding as filthy as the women's clothes is stuffed against the wall behind them. There is what was once a small drum stove; it is patched with old tin cans and bound around with wire. There is no door to it, and the ashes flow out and lie in a heap around it. There is a filthy pot in the ashes, and some filthy meat in a corner of the floor. Phew! the place stinks. Come out. There are few houses worse than Morton's in the district.

But Morton wasn't stupid. When he came back from Copenhagen he had a medal, from the King, he said, to him. He sold the medal for five crowns. The medal wasn't worth five crowns; its value was two crowns. It was a Danish brass two-kroner piece.

XLI. FOG

THE great event of Old Home Week was staged the night we got there. They had prepared for it at Pavia's house as long as it takes days to make and ripen beer. Beer *makes* a festival in Greenland; and Pavia made the beer. There was enough. There is enough when every man forgets his troubles and himself; when all men love their neighbors and display it; when those who can't sing, sing, and those who can don't mind; when everybody laughs at anything; when they all want the moment to be always and the ocean to be full of beer; when they think that the bucket standing on the floor is full of it, and one says, "Watch me drain it at one go"; then when he picks it up it should be empty: that is enough. It was, and so was every bottle, jug, pail, keg, and barrel. A darned good thing the ocean *wasn't* beer; they would have tapped it through the ice and either drunk it dry or drowned.

It was an old folks' night again; they were in fine form with their stuff. Six of them danced: three from Igdlorssuit, and an aged local trio of grotesque accomplishments. This local three performed together, one in the circle dancing with the drum and two accompanying his song and dance with loud and rhythmic grunting: "*Huh, ha! Huh, huh, huh!*" The crowd joined in and swelled it to a pulsing roar. Beate danced and won all hearts by her fantastic grace; Emanuel lent the popular erotic touch; Peter Sokiassen by his consummate artistry excelled them all.

Then the accordion struck up and swept the past away; foot beats for heartbeats, but lots of them, and loud. The time was furious. In the one, two, three, four, of a quick walk the young men got in sixteen steps—eight to a second, as I counted them. Not heel and toe beats; every one a free, resounding stamp of the whole foot. A dozen doing it at once, it has the volume and low resonance of distant thunder. The whirl that alternates with this is dizzying. In all there is inviolate precision; the whirling couples on a crowded floor no more collide than do the prancing horses of a merry-go-round. We drank beer, danced; beer, dance, beer, dance; and sweat. Whew! but that place got hot.

Next day it stormed, a heavy snowfall and a gale of wind. Between the kaffemiks we worked at making skis to fit the runners of our sledges, for the snowfall promised bad conditions on the homeward trip. That night there was a general dance held on the ample floor space of a storehouse. We were a dance-starved lot, we visitors. For all I know the dance went on all night. So closed the great festivities of Old Home Week.

Cold, wind, and heavy fog; deep snow. We could have managed it without our skis; some did. But for two-thirds of the way they helped. We started out at ten; by noon the wind had died, and fog hung round us low and thick; we had no sight of land; and only by the faintest brightness in one quarter could we surmise, with that as south, where our course lay. The newly fallen snow, of course, was trackless.

Primitive man is sometimes credited with special faculties which serve him in the problems of the wilderness of his environment. *Direction* he is said to know instinctively. But on this day, out on a trackless snow plain in dense fog, there came to be enough divergence of opinion as to course among the six or eight drivers of our party to dispel all confidence that anybody *knew*. Their guesses ranged an arc of ninety degrees, and no one guessed with confidence; no one till Salamina spoke. "There," she said, speaking in the abrupt way she had when to her mind her words, take them or leave them, admitted no discussion, "there is Igdlorssuit, and there is Ingia." She pointed. Abraham had always respected Salamina; he now agreed with her, and led the way toward where she'd indicated Ingia to be.

I had incessant trouble with my dogs. There were but five of Johan Lange's left; the rest I'd picked up here and there. They didn't like each other's company, and kept up an incessant weaving in and out of place as though in search of their lost teammates. I'd traded off one absolute irreconcilable to Eskias and brought along a beauty in his place. But he had temperament; he balked right at the start. I dragged him to his place and got him started with the whip; within a hundred yards he quit again. Just turned and bolted back; and when the harness brought him up, lay down and let himself be dragged. He pulled that trick repeatedly the whole way home. It took some days to break him. Eventually, however, he took his place among the five aristocrats, the only outside dog that they accepted. He was pure white and matched them well in size and type. Perhaps looks count, to dogs. And when at last I parted with him to a German moving-picture troupe and he was put aboard a skiff and rowed out to the motorboat, the other five with one accord entered the water and swam out. That fall the six were reunited. Taken to Switzerland and featured there in an abominable travesty of Greenland adventure, they flickered for a night or so on Broadway and, victims of the well-earned fate of their associates, went out.

We plowed along, keeping our course straight by the track we left. We were headed for a *point* of land, a needle in a fog; five hundred yards would be enough to hide it. Our next point, if we passed it on the right, would be some point on Baffin Land. But land loomed up at last: the land was Ingia. Salamina never claimed to know things; if one praised her for her almost occult sense, she honestly, in much embarrassment, disclaimed it. Yet she appeared to be gifted with extraordinarily keen senses which were so finely coördinated as to give her in a flash a clear, full round perception of a fact that seemed not yet to have betrayed itself. That her perceptions were as though of her subconscious mind, made them authentic.

Our route now lay along the shore; the dogs, aware of home, braced up. Five-thirty saw us at the settlement.

"Marghreta, did a message come for me? No message?" God!

This is Beate — whose love I once
declined. How she could dance!

XLII. THE CALENDAR

THE calendar was graven on my mind. For the past month I'd searched it every day as though it were an oracle. All prophecies I'd read in it had failed. No message came. "Tomorrow," they had said in Umanak, "the post will start, tomorrow, or the first good day." That was the twenty-first—of January. From Umanak to Godhavn took five days with ice and weather good: allow three more. My message to America, the answer back and broadcasted to Igdlorssuit; three days. Eleven days at most, so I would get my answer on the first of February. The man's a fool who figures dates in Greenland; I didn't know it then.

Spring is a solemn time; the year begins with spring. Its promises are not as real as the fact of things undone and hopes unrealized on which the page then closes. On February 29 I wrote: "*The past two days have been true spring. A warm south wind is blowing; the snow has melted from the houses. The deep, loose snow is now all slush below the surface. On the ice it has settled so that the sledge tracks stand up like causeways. Everyone is out of doors: women hanging out their wash and bedding, young girls carrying babies on their backs, boys everywhere. Last evening I walked on snowshoes to the harbor hill to have a look toward Umanak. The bay was full of ice, but there were big patches of open water. I was so hot when I got back that I moved a chair out of doors and sat there smoking.*" That night it froze; but spring—I knew it in my heart—had come.

XLIII. OLD MEMORIES

IT MUST be good to be so old as to remain untroubled at the turning of the page to spring; to let the past be past and relish it for what it was. Old people do, in Greenland; and in the winter nights they gather around the little warmth and glamorous light of soapstone lamps, far older, maybe, than their memories, and reinvoke the past by ancient tales; they read from memory their race's Ancient Testament. That these old tales are memorized and told today shows an enduring sympathy with their pagan atmosphere, if not an actual belief in the reality of their events and characters. Surely our Testament is little read but by believers; and we, believing not at all in the superstitions of Eskimo legend, find little in the tales to interest us. Another evidence that the Christian Greenlanders of today believe the stories of their past is the fidelity with which many of the tales have been transmitted down through countless generations. A people ignorant of art have reverence only for the truth. To Greenlanders their tales are history.

To old Emanuel, that lusty grandson of an angakok, his tales were family recollections; their setting was this region where he lived, their characters his ancestors. Their period was of the past yet close to now. They show the background of today. Let's have Emanuel:

In the year 1869 [he writes—continuing a bit like Mr. Mulliner] *I noticed for the first time that I had an old grandmother. As was the Greenland custom, I slept with her. Thus I came to be with her all the time until she died, in 1876.*

While she was alive I used to ask her to tell me about her forefathers, when in the evening I lay down with her to sleep. Thereupon she began, and her stories were these: (1) What she herself had seen and experienced. (2) What she had heard.

This person (my grandmother) was originally unchristened. (But she was christened when she was grown up.) Therefore, according to heathen custom, she was called Arnape. At christening she got the name of Karen. Her husband was a heathen by the name of Ersakilo.

She used to tell of how she had seen her father killed by other men—a sight she could never forget. And thus she began her tale:

"Once, immediately upon a trading ship's arrival in Umanak, my father prepared himself to go to the colony—that is, from Kekertat to Umanak—with another hunter as companion. Each was to drive his own sledge and I was to accompany my father, being, at the time, unmarried. My father's name was Nernak; his companion's name was Aje."

As they were leaving, Nernak's wife warned them against going, for it was rumored that those living farther in the fiord were thinking of killing Nernak. But Nernak said, "I cannot well avoid them." Then they left. Arriving at Umanak, they did their trading and then set off upon their return to the north.

They passed on their way an inhabited island named Agpat, and the people, seeing the travelers, asked them to stop and come up to the house. When Nernak—so the story goes—entered the house he saw that there were no women there but only men. Then it was that he realized that it was planned to kill him. They gave him first some meat to eat, and he ate of it until he was satisfied. Thereupon he and his companion left the house to continue on their journey.

As soon as he reached his sledge he got his dogs ready and, without hindrance, started. But now one of the islanders, called Ertagssiak, ran after him, and overtaking the sledge caught hold of the stanchions and upset it. When Ertagssiak had done this all the other people came running and took hold of Nernak. And Ertagssiak had a long knife which he was going to use in the killing. The story goes that Ertagssiak tried to push the knife into Nernak's heart, but that Nernak caught it by the blade. Then as the killer pulled the knife away all the sinews of Nernak's hand were cut. When there were no more sinews in his hand they killed him instantly.

Having killed him they dissected the body, as was then the custom among heathens. And at this a woman who had been watching at a window of the house cried out, "Oh, now they are dragging him along!" One of the other women, named Matila, pulled her away from the window.

While the murderers were dissecting the body one of them said, "A minute ago he ate a lot, so that his stomach ought now to be full." So another man, who was carving, quickly opened the stomach; he found, however, absolutely nothing in it. "Oh! what has happened to what the man ate!"

What the First Greenlanders Did When They Murdered

When the old Greenlanders murdered anyone, the murderer would eat a mouthful of the dead man's liver. This was now done by the murderers of Nernak. (But, they say, if you didn't want to eat of the liver you might drink of his blood.) When they had dissected Nernak's body they threw it into a crevice in the cliff. And now the companion of the dead man, Aje, leaving his dead partner behind, continued unmolested on his way up north. Before leaving, he had tried to take along his dead partner's goods which had been gotten in trade. But those bundles which seemed to contain the most the murderers took and kept. They proved, however, to contain only salt.

Meanwhile Nernak's family was longing for his return. Those who so awaited him were two brothers, Nernak's sons. Their names were Kiviulik and Atate. Watching for him, they at last saw two sledges approaching; they passed behind an iceberg, and when they appeared again there was but one. Upon the arrival of this sledge, Aje told how his companion had been killed by the people on the island, and that he had only brought his own packages.

This story Arnape related with great sorrow: how those at home had hoped in vain to get their father's packages—because he had been killed.

[What Emanuel's grandmother was doing during all these goings on I know no more than how a ship could be at Umanak in the sledging season.]

How Nernak's Descendants Avenged His Death

Many years had passed since then, and Nernak's sons, Kiviulik and Atate, were growing up and developing. In secrecy they tried their strength.

One spring one of the people from the island came to visit Kekertat, and his sledge was the one that Nernak had used long ago when he went to the colony to trade. When it came night, they all lay down to sleep. And when the visitor awoke his sledge was gone. Maybe Nernak's eldest daughter, Unasalen, had recognized her father's sledge and at night, when everybody was asleep, had hidden it in a crevasse in the ice.

Several years after this had happened two young men came to visit Nernak's widow. They told her that at their settlement there lived a female relative of her husband's murderer. To get revenge she should kill this woman, and they would help her with the killing.

At last Nernak's widow determined to act. It was spring; the sun was warm and people left their houses and set up their tents. The tent roofs were of sealskin and the sides of seal guts. So one day Nernak's widow saw the woman whom she was to kill standing at the opening of her tent picking lice off her kamik socks, which she had turned inside out. She had her face turned toward the sun. And Nernak's widow stole up from behind; the woman didn't notice her, she was so intent on killing lice.

When Nernak's widow came up close she seized the woman's shoulders from behind. The young men who of their own accord had offered to lend aid stood near. Nernak's widow tried in vain to catch their eye; they did not come to help her.

Thereupon she put her knee between the shoulders of her enemy and pulled the shoulders back, and so blood came out of her mouth, and all was red.

[It was the custom to remove to other places in the tenting season. Nernak's widow could thus have found herself in the vicinity of her enemy.]

As Nernak's sons, Kiviulik and Atate, grew up it came to be that they could do anything, even while they still lived at Karrat. When they had become big hunters they left Kekertat and went to Sarkak and settled there. They were then already christened.

When they came to Sarkak there was ice, and in the spring the ice was right up near their house. So they went white-whale and narwhal hunting at the edge of the ice. When the sun brought its heat they put up their tent, and went to live in it. In a tent farther inland there lived a man called Etarkutok.

One day, while the hunters were at the edge of the ice hunting narwhal, they heard a voice crying, "A ship!" It proved to be the English whaling ships. The Kiviulik people were very pleased to see them, as they made a lot by selling the women's trifling little embroideries on the ships. The things that Kiviulik's people used to get in exchange for the women's embroideries were as follows: different little bits of iron, sewing needles, and different old clothes.

They say that in olden times there were many whales in the fiords near Igdlorssuit. The English ships had been told of this by the people from Kiviulik's, and they used to catch a lot there. Now when the English ships had left something happened.

A white dog from Karnussak had been visiting the houses in Sarkak, and when the dog wanted to return home the Kiviulik people tied a kerchief which they had got from the English around the dog's head, and let him return with it to the Etarkutok settlement. The dog, as it happened, belonged to the daughter of the oldest man at Karnussak; she, being the youngest of the children, was much loved. When, therefore, the dog returned with the kerchief around its head the father killed it, and told his wife to skin the dog and dry the skin as quickly as possible.

Kiviulik and his younger brother had by this time lost their mother and had now only their elder sister Unaralak to keep to.

When the dogskin had dried, the mother of the dog-owner—with her husband watching her—cut it into such strips as are used with the embroidery of women's breeches. They then took them to Unaralak. Unaralak made the present up into breeches, and when these were done she put them on. No sooner had she done this than her legs became paralyzed; she couldn't urinate; and she began to shake all over. Since Karnussak's oldest inhabitant had many evil ways and powers, Unaralak wearing the new breeches' embroideries now began to walk on all fours like a dog.

When Etarkutok, the oldest man of Karnussak, had made her like this, he sent some of the dogskin strips to Nakerdlok as a present to Eserajuk, the eldest unmarried daughter of Kassiak, who lived there with her father.

But Kassiak had already heard how Unaralak after receiving strips from the same skin had been paralyzed in her legs. He, therefore, before she even saw the strips, took them and conveyed them up above Nakerdlok, returning empty-handed. Even then he said nothing about the matter. At night when they were going to bed he said, "I walked around the house with them, and then threw them away."

Later they heard that all the people of Karnussak had had their legs paralyzed, so that their evil plans had been turned against themselves.

Kunak and Evi

At the beginning of this story we told of two men who went to the colony to trade, and of how one, named Nernak, was killed. Nernak's wife had two brothers, Kunak and Evi. Evi took a wife and got a son. When the little son started to walk, Evi put beads on his kamik strings, as is the heathen custom. As he developed, you could tell that he would be a very fast walker. When others showed surprise at his quickness in running, and praised him, his father used to say, "When a bead starts rolling, it does not stop so easily." (For it happened that the father had put the beads on the kamik strings as an amulet.)

Evi was a fast sledge-driver because his dogs were fast; and he had taught them to be fast by making them run after a ball. When the son was big enough he would go with his father when he went sledging.

Sometimes, when out driving, the father would get cold; he would then get up from the sledge in order to get warm, and he would hold on to the stanchions while the son sat in front of him on the sledge, with both arms pulled into his fur sleeves. When he felt like it he would get off the sledge on the left side and run in front of the dogs, waving his fur sleeves like wings. His father would then compare him to a falcon that flies swiftly and near the ice. They were then living at Kekertat.

The son eventually got a kayak and went out with his father. In those days there were lots of reindeer around Kekertat; and when the father and his son were out in their kayaks together and saw reindeer on the land, the father would make his son go on land and drive the reindeer into the water. Even though there were many, the boy would hit them all on the back and drive them into the water; and there his father would kill them with his spear. And when the father came home he would tell of the wonderful lot of reindeer he had seen swimming; and of how he had killed some of them. In that way he kept his son's ability to run so fast a secret from his neighbors. For he didn't doubt for a moment that if they knew that it was his son who drove the reindeer into the water they would get jealous and, as was their evil habit, kill him. While Evi was in this way concealing his son's ability, the son one day ran after a fox, kicked it, and killed it. He also chased a rabbit, but he was a little longer catching that.

When the ice came father and son would go out on the ice to hunt. In the old days one always went seal-hunting at an opening in the ice, and killed the seal with a harpoon. One day when they were thus hunting at a hole, the son, the fast runner, fell into the water.

Now at this very moment Evi's brother, who was at home, was particularly happy. He sat on the bed platform and sang without stopping.

When the fast runner had got out of the water he ran as fast as he could toward land; but as it was very cold his clothes soon froze to the ice so that he couldn't move. His father then took hold of him and dragged him toward the land. To start with all went well, but before he reached the land his strength failed him; he could pull him no more. Surprised at this, he looked around; there was his elder brother, he who had all the time been singing on the bed, pulling in the opposite direction. Evi made him go away, and started dragging again.

Presently he could again drag him no farther, for his elder brother had again caught hold and was pulling against him. Again he made him go away, but the father had at last to give it up, for someone was constantly pulling back. The fast runner having now lost consciousness, the father, leaving his elder brother behind, ran to the house to fetch a sledge. When he entered the house he saw his brother there, still sitting as he had been at the end of the sleeping-platform, undressed. As but a minute before he had seen him holding back the son whom he was trying to save, he could not help saying some angry words to him. But the elder brother had not been outside the house at all. This just proves what terrific powers of magic Evi's brother had.

The son whom they had left behind they fetched with a sledge, but of course he was dead by now. When they had brought the body on land they buried it behind a little hill. People now call it the grave of the big one who was drowned.

After this Evi left Kekertat forever.

One winter, after the ice had come, a lot of people from different settlements went to Kekertat to play ball. Every time a sledge arrived Evi's elder brother would ask, "Who came then?" because all the arrivals had to be treated to some frozen meat. After a while Evi also arrived to take part in the ball game at his brother's place. It was the first time he had been to Kekertat since the death of his son.

At his arrival the elder brother inquired, as usual, who had come. When people told him that it was Evi, he said, "I wonder why he has come." Maybe he was afraid, because he, aided by his magic powers, had caused the death of the fast runner.

When all had come, they prepared for the game; and all the sledges were placed so that their dogs faced the settlements from which they had come. It was the custom in playing ball to use the skin of a fiord seal, filled with sand to make a ball of it.

Now they went out on to the ice, and all of them, men and women, started lifting the ball. Also Evi and his elder brother joined them in the game. Suddenly one of the players caught the ball and ran with it toward his sledge, which stood there all prepared. But one of the pursuers caught the runner and pushed him so that he fell, and now the game was really going.

While they were playing it was noticed that Evi's elder brother had caught hold of Evi and was struggling with him to throw him down; and it was seen that the elder brother, as was like him, had hidden an iron rod up his sleeve, and was trying with this, in vain, to kill Evi. So all the ball-players ran toward them and, seizing the elder brother, took the iron rod away from him and gave it to Evi. Evi took the iron rod and hit his brother on the head with it several times, and killed him.

Thereupon he started wailing over him, and said, "You, that I used to listen to, oh!"

Evi said this because when his brother was alive he used to listen to his songs.

Then the people turned around to the ball; and they were all very keen on the game. You chase the one who has the ball, push him over, and, taking the ball, try to reach your sledge so that you may take the ball back with you to your settlement. He who reaches his settlement with the ball will run with the ball toward his house, and despite its enormous weight throw it into the house through a broken window. If he succeeds all of the people of the settlement will be very proud that one of their people had won.

The ball was not always filled with sand alone. Sometimes the Greenlanders would put things into it, which in the old days was much appreciated, things such as follows: the meat off the muscles of the narwhal, just cut through; or reindeer skin for fat; or several other things. So they were all very keen to get the ball. In the old days, when reindeer were scarce in the north of Greenland, borders of reindeer skin for women's hoods were very expensive.

When the winner of the ball game came home with the ball and all the different things in it, he would invite all the people of the settlement to his house for a song festival. As a rule a lot of people from the other settlements would also come, and the house would be full of people; they would all enjoy themselves immensely. Then when the people started to settle down to go to sleep, the women would go out to meet the men from the song festival; they used, therefore, not to bring the children, but would leave them behind in the care of an invalid.

After they had played ball at Kekertat, and the winner had returned to his house with the ball, he arranged a song festival. Some of the guests left their children at home, as was the custom, in the charge of a weak person. Upon a certain one of these children beginning to cry the person in charge was persuaded by one of the other children to make an ajagok *out of the shoulder blades of a dog. Then they all played with the* ajagok.

In this game, when a child missed hitting one of the holes in the ajagok *it was passed to the next child; and so, in turn, it reached the youngest child. He never missed. While this was going on the children noticed that the bed platform they were on was moving, and that the skin window was bulging in. Then one of the children threw the* ajagok *at the window. It was very windy, and at that all the lamps were blown out. So the children fled into the foot of the bed, while the biggest child went to another house to fetch fire to relight the lamps. When that was done they started playing again, and, as before, when the youngest got the* ajagok *he couldn't miss it. Whereupon again the bed started to move; and there now appeared down at the end of the passage a large person wearing an* amaut [the fur garment in the hood of which small children are carried]. *Facing out toward the sea and keeping her back turned to the children, she approached. When she at last turned and showed her face the children fled. Then the woman in charge of the children took her* "ulo" *and struck the ghost in the face with it, and kicked the ghost, and made it go out.*

When the guests returned from the song festival, the old ones said, "Ajasisarput."

This is the end of the story about Nernak and his family, told by Nernak's daughter, Arnape.

[There is reason to believe, from the following and concluding part of Emanuel's "reminiscences," that the angakok, his grandfather, was—if he ever lived—his great-great-grandfather. The story clears that point, but it confuses us again with dates. His dates are queer. It is all very well for Emanuel to tell us that "*in the year 1869 I noticed for the first time that I had an old grandmother"*; but the records show that not until the twenty-eighth of March in 1871—or, to give her credit for eight months' foreknowledge, August in 1870—did Emanuel's mother notice that she had Emanuel. But what do these old people know about dates? And what do they care? On the birthday of Emanuel's sister, Beate, I said to her, "What age are you today, Beate? Thirty-two?" "I don't know," she answered, "maybe." "Or maybe thirty-three," I added. "*Yes*," she said, and beamed. And yet these stupid records show, *Beate Elisabeth Katrina* (*Samuelson*) *Lövstrom b. June 13, 1878*. At any rate, if Emanuel's great progenitor could not have been born, as Emanuel says, in 1700, he could still in the eighteenth century, or possibly later, have been a heathen angakok in the remoter parts of North Greenland. Let figures lie, but not Emanuel.—Silence! Emanuel speaks:]

The Story of Arnape's Husband

The one who told me this started this way: "Now I will tell you about my grandfather. He was born around the year 1700, and he was a great angakok, and his wife was also an angakok. As she was a greater angakok than her husband, her eyes were protruding, caused by a great fight she had had for her helping spirits." The couple lived north of Igdlorssuit near the coast, at Erkutane, which they never left. They had only sons, and the wife longed to have some daughters. When, at last, she could stand it no longer she borrowed another man so as to become pregnant and get a daughter. And when it was born, sure enough it was a girl. It was her last and youngest child; she was so happy that she hardly ever left it.

One day, when the child had gotten fat, the mother was sitting on the bed holding the child on her lap. Suddenly she felt as though intoxicated, and she became senseless. Being an angakok, she could keep nothing secret about her bad life. She threw her precious daughter to the end of the passage—where, luckily, it landed safely and unhurt on top of the dogs—and then in her senselessness told her mother all about the intercourse that she had had with another man. Thereupon, one of the other women took charge of the child and called her Arnaluak. She was not christened until she was very old.

One year there was an epidemic of an illness brought by some English whalers; and nearly all the people of the settlement died. This happened in the summer while they lived in tents. Whereas all the people got ill and died without her being able to do anything for them, Arnaluak's mother made charms over her children before they caught the illness. She did as follows:

One morning, very early, she took all her children down to the beach with her, placing herself in the midst of them, dressed only in trousers, and without kamiks. When she reached the shore she let all the children, one after another, fall into the water; then she sprayed them with the salt water. When this had been done to them all she walked back with them, placing them in line in the order of their age, the eldest being in front and the youngest last. Not until all had touched the hidden tooth of a white whale caught by a moon-man might they enter the tent again.

When all the children had reëntered the tent she placed herself first in one corner of the room and then in another, continuing thus all day. In this way she cast her angakok charm and prevented her children from getting ill. Not one of them died, despite the death of all the others in the settlement.

As the children grew up they would watch their father practicing Tornak magic. When the father prepared himself for Tornak magic the children hid under the sleeping-platform. They would light the lamps there, being careful to cover up all the chinks. They lit the lamps because in those days it was difficult to get fire, and they dared not light the lamps in the room where the angakok was doing magic.

They used to put the angakok on the floor, and tie him up in such a way that he could not loosen the cords; and they laid down a fur for him to sit on. Then the angakok would sing the angakok song, "akiut," *and the people inside the house would sing with him. While this was going on the angakok would loosen his cords, stand up, and call one of his helping spirits,* Mitatdlussokune. *Sometimes when it arrived it could only say,* "Putukuto, putukuto." *They say that spirits spoke like that only when people were about to suffer from need; people were always very sorry when they heard that. But sometimes the spirit on entering said,* "Kajak, kajak": *people then were happy, for it meant abundance.*

When the helping spirit had left the angakok would call in his Kavdlunakune, *and this never said anything but, "Isn't it true—Tornarsuk is bad?" When the angakok admitted this it could suddenly speak Danish: this the angakok would translate. When this one had left he would call in his* Arnakune [*his female spirit*]*; and when the big woman arrived all the people in the house fled. When she came near the men, the bottom opening of her breeches would make a terrific noise; there would be "bang!" after "bang!" as, without help, her clothes fell off. Therefore the men were very much afraid of her. Even the angakok was afraid, and he would cling to the beams that carried the roof of the house, for spirits were afraid of that.*

When she, at last, has left he calls his Atdlernakune [*underground spirit*], *but this one is not frightening in any way.*

Amongst the angakok's helping spirits there was a big kayak, consisting really of only the front part of a kayak. This was to be used in case any of the angakok's sons were out in their kayaks in a storm, and needed help.

There was also an iceberg among his helping spirits.

If he wanted his spirit, Mitatdlussokune, *to come into the house he would bang a lot of skins at the back of his house, and he would put out the lights. Then it would suddenly get lighter, and the meat on the skins would begin to rattle. He used to show this helping spirit the wing of a falcon that had grown gray with age.*

The angakok's only daughter was Arnaluak; she used to tell of her father's big woman spirit, Arnakussuane; *how it would be let in while the children were under the bed, and the grown-ups were nearly dying of fear.*

It was terrible.

This is an old girl promenading.
If she didn't hold on to her pants
they'd come off. Modest old girl.

XLIV. OLD FAITH AND NEW

ONE stormy night in the darkest time of winter the little group that was sitting around my table in the lamplight fell somehow to talking about angakoks. Oh—I think I had been fooling with a coin; yes, that was it. And I had done some simple little trick; just done it once and, for a wonder, well; and had the sense to stop. And everyone was mystified. So it was that we fell to talking about angakoks, for they were the magicians of their race. "You maybe are an angakok," said one. "Maybe," I said, and smiled significantly.

"My grandfather," I continued, for there was decided interest, "was an angakok among the Indians of America. Tornarsuk, though he is known by another name, is their God. And although I have never practiced as an angakok, Tornarsuk has given me a *tornak* [a guardian spirit], and by my grandfather I was given an *arnauk*. My grandfather also instructed me in the mysteries." "You have an arnauk? Let us see it then," cried all the women. They were three: Marghreta, Salamina, and by some chance, Regina. It is significant in view of what follows that two of them were exceptionally enlightened women and women of superior natural intelligence, and that Regina had had ample time, since Trolleman's magic had loosed her girdle, to penetrate the mysteries of one white angakok. As for the men, Rudolf and Abraham, they either laughed with me, or doubted me, or thought it might be true, but what of it. At any rate we hung together and they enjoyed with me a thoroughly unprincipled experiment with women's faith. Scratch a Greenlander, it seems, and find a pagan; for after persisting for a few minutes with proper dramatic earnestness in my pagan rôle, I had them staring at me with the most flattering looks of awe and fear, and ready, had it been my pleasure, to go off into screaming paroxysms of terror. The effect on them of the little that I did and said was real; and as they sat close-huddled, watching me, I had only to release a wild-eyed look to send them back in a recoil of fear. They were afraid, and fascinated. My arnauk, or amulet, which I had told them was hidden on my person, they implored me to show to them; and, far from doubting, they revealed a childlike eagerness to look upon a wonder. Regina begged: Would I not *sometime* show it to her and teach her how to practice magic? (God knows what she'd have turned her husband into!) "I will," I answered her, "but be prepared for consequences. I have known of those who just on looking at an arnauk such as mine have lost their hair. One woman had her left arm paralyzed." Regina shuddered. "Maybe," she said self-consciously, "if I had already been to Denmark I would risk it. But I can't go there with no hair."

The upshot of the evening was that for some days I had a frightened woman on my hands; and a lot of petty, extra things to do—like going into the cellar whenever anything was wanted from there, or accompanying Salamina on every errand to the dark outdoors. She was afraid—not, I may say, of me, for I had tried at once to rid myself of my embarrassing grandfather, but—of a supernatural world in which despite her education under the iconoclastic Uncle Jens, and her shrewd common sense, she still believed. I had just stirred the past. That past is living to most Greenlanders.

Tornarsuk, ruler of their ancient spirit world on whose abode men tread, the superdemon—they believe in him. They believe in *kivigtoks*, men who having fled the settlements maintain themselves in a demonic state among the hills; in the *igaligdlit*, wild inland ghouls who as they go about devour their foul carrion; in the *erkigdlit*, half man, half dog. In terror of them Salamina clung to me one night in camp at Umiamiako. These erkigdlit had once been men, an incestuous clan descended of a murderer who with his wife had fled from vengeance to that ice-infested region. Either as something of the nature of kivigtoks, or as erkigdlit, or as at any rate a wild man-hating tribe, these mystic denizens of Umiamako were real enough to people's minds to have caused an airplane survey of the region in the year of our Lord 1932. Sledge tracks, arrows, footprints: if people *will* believe, they'll find the evidence. Greenlanders believe in the *atdlit*, noseless male loreleis who lure the kayaker to death. They believe in witches and in the power of their curse. Rudolf in sport once pinched the cheek of little Ane. Boleta, an old crone said to be a witch, saw the act and, misconstruing it, cursed Rudolf's hand. Soon after, sure enough, that hand got lame. It troubled him for months. "Maybe it wasn't because of Boleta," said Rudolf, "I don't know." Greenland mothers scare their children into good behavior by threatening the visits of Tornarsuk's crowd. Many grown girls of the enlightened younger generation of today won't go outdoors alone when it is dark.

But what of it? What if they do believe in demons, trolls, hobgoblins, witches, in the whole infernal outfit of their pagan faith? We did in our most Christian days. Such beliefs are no more inconsistent with Christian theology than, as we know, riches are with its ethics. And no one knew that better than Hans Egede, the first apostle of the Faith to Greenland. What they believed in he confirmed. Tornarsuk and his crew were made to order for the Christian faith: they were its Powers of Darkness. He taught the natives that, taught them to loathe, hate, shun their ancient demon gods, but not to disbelieve. Believing in them now, the people fear them as they fear the storm and violence and death. The very mildness of the Christian God makes Him not feared, and hence not thought about. Then, too, God hasn't been too kind to Greenlanders; and people living on a treeless barren rocky fringe of land around a continent of ice might search the Scriptures in vain for any mention of material blessings given *them* by God. God's *presence* isn't felt; that makes the Gospel just a bit unreal; God is perhaps nonresident. The early Christians had good cause to deify and worship Him who preached the Sermon on the Mount. Downtrodden masses of a cruel autocracy, they learned there to respect their poverty, and find in poverty and unresistingness the key to joys in Heaven that their lot on earth withheld. So might *that* Gospel have struck home in Greenland. It might have said to them: "You *are* God's children by your way of life. You live in charity; have only faith in God, and hope will animate your lives and bring you happiness." But the apostle, Hans, was eighteenth-century, and merchant-subsidized. He came, a testament in either hand: the old and new; the old—the Sermon on the Mount; the new—the Ledger. One held out promises; the other, cash. One said, Give no thought to the morrow, bestow your riches on the poor, *be* poor. The other said, Live carefully, work hard, save money, and get rich. The church and trade were well united in apostle Hans. They still do business hand in hand today: it makes the Gospel just a bit unreal. But they are Christians, and they go to church.

When of a Sunday morning Jörn Möller, the town half-wit, tugs for the third go at the knotted, worn-out fishline which hangs down from the little church bell, and clatters out the last call to service, they come; the people flock from all the houses, dressed all spick and span, and file into the church. The little wooden church is hardly big enough to hold the crowd; they pack it to the doors. On one side sit the men and boys, across the center aisle from them, the women and the little children. There are large windows on both sides, but all the people look to the left, for out there are the sea and the distant mountains and the blue sky. And fresh air too, for it is foul inside. And everyone is coughing.

Things beautifully done are as though done by God; they share His attribute, perfection. Bad carpentry, bad handicraft, bad art, must be offensive in the eyes of God; in church they're blasphemy. And if one sought evidence of the decline of Christian faith he'd find none better than the fake construction, fake design, and fake adornment of the churches of today. How *can* they worship God who like bad art? Are the chancel rail and altar of this Greenland chapel wrought with ivory-tenoned joints and inlaid with the ivory images of seals and whales, those only blessings God in His great mercy gave these people for their food and warmth and light? Is here a loving tribute of the best that they for love of God could make for Him from whom all beauty emanates? Cheap Danish back-stair balusters support a plain plank rail; the altar is a clumsy box with bastard Gothic arches nailed across the front. Crude workmanship is hidden by cheap paint. What sort of love of God is cheap pretentiousness the shrine of?

The ancient angakoks were usually the men of greatest distinction in their communities; they were leaders, men of proven manhood, men who worked. A Danish trader, writing in the year 1750, said of a certain angakok: "He visits me every day; he likes to be informed about God and His divine works, which he never fails to admire; but there the matter rests, and in other respects he maintains his own principles intact. On the whole his life is exemplary, and I must grant that I have acquired my stock of experience of Greenland from conversing with this eminent man."

Samuel, the catechist—we have returned to church—now rises. Of Sunday are his black alpaca anorak and celluloid collar; of every day, his pinch-eyed look, his sallow and unwholesome skin, the little cultivated poodle tuft below his lower lip. His manner now is unctuous and, toward God, more ingratiating, one would say, than reverent. He is inclined to posture: he minces with his feet, he elevates his chin, and, raising his elbows, he grips fingers by reversing one hand on the other. After a short, benevolent scrutiny of his flock, Samuel turns to a blackboard and writes the numbers of the hymns in chalk. It is a little tedious, this pantomime, but it no doubt has a value in his mind. When the hymns have been written down, Samuel crosses over to the melodeon and seats himself. He opens up the hymn book, finds his place; he rubs his hands, for it is cold in church. And now the pedals squeak, the bellows wheeze, the keys rattle, the melodeon speaks, and Samuel sings.

I once knew an itinerant preacher—a tremendous fellow, used to be a brakeman on the B. and M.—who would roar out between the verses of a hymn, "I can't sing, but I can make a joyful noise unto the Lord." So it was with Samuel. His noise was as the sound of brass; it blared his joy to God. If the Lord really likes that kind of thing He most liked Samuel's middle tones: they were by far the joyfullest. No one else could compare with him; and it was only when Samuel's notes were placed very low—bass was his part—or very high, that one could hear the melody at all, as the clear soprano voices of Sophia and the rest carried it on. So, with much singing, one hymn often following right upon the echoes of another, the service went on; and presently there was Samuel at the reading-desk. The sermon was about to start.

It concerned John the Baptist, and it was a long sermon. It began moderately, accumulating pace and volume as it went. It caught its maker up at last, exalted him. Eyes on the far-away of a blue wall, he soared; he lost all contact with the earth, and people there. They let him go. And, as though during a long interlude of his absence, there came to be a hubbub of snuffling, sniffling, sneezing, coughing, creaking of seats, scuffling of kamiks, whispering, whining, whimpering, babbling, talking, and baby crying. Some stolid people dozed, some outright slept, two mothers fed their babies at the breast, and all the rest were restless and looked bored.

One night—oh, we have left the church; the sermon stopped, the service petered out; we filed out and went home—one night there was a dinner party at my house to which, for some special reason that I've forgotten, Samuel and his old witch of a wife had been asked. Things were going splendidly; we had finished dinner and were sitting about the table talking and drinking beer, when suddenly Samuel began an unprovoked attack on the local council, two of whose members, including their foreman Abraham, were present. His object seemed to be less the belittling of them than the glorification of himself, but after telling us what a magnificent fellow God and himself had made him be, he sought to enforce it by pointing out the contemptible ignorance and incapability of the three members of the council and of the cooper, Rudolf. His theme delighted him, he warmed to it, and, standing up, he poured out words as he would do on Sundays from his pulpit. Invective, it appeared to be; he raged. They bore it patiently. Then, just as it began to appear that it would never end, Knud and the silent Hendrik rose, walked quietly to Samuel—I've never seen a comparable thing more smoothly done—took Samuel by his shoulders and his pants' seat, lifted him, kicking, gesticulating upward like a martyr on Ascension Day, and, raving on, bore him out through the entry, and pitched him out into the night. He sat there on the hillside for a while and wept, then quietly went home.

XLV. THE BREAKING-POINT

IT WAS now March—and no word yet. Could I have known that the post was still in Umanak? As if I wouldn't long ago—if I had guessed at such procrastination there—have traveled there again, and picked the message up, and carried it, no matter what the obstacles, to Godhavn. You live and learn, but often at what cost in senseless agony of mind!

My trips across the sound were stern self-discipline. Go off, my private doctor said, and stay—two days, four, five; have David leave you there. Get off where you'll at least count days instead of hours and seconds. Good theory, and a dismal practice that only led to the compounding of my hopes to a compound fracture.

It always seemed that I'd be better off alone; I wanted solitude. And there I lived in that one room cooped up with Salamina and her child. *Always* at home, forever puttering about and doing things, sewing, or rattling pots and pans, or clattering dishes. And that she did her work with stealth, and tiptoed in the house, somehow just made it more infuriating. It said, I have my mind on you. She had. It hung upon me like a weight. "Stop tiptoeing round!" I wanted to scream out. "Don't sit there with your eyes on me." That's what she'd do; I felt them on me when my back was turned to her. Those long dead silences with just the faintest little sounds from her: I knew what that meant. She was crying. Then I'd go out.

Before I'd paced the full length of the strand three times she'd be there at my heels. She was as one demented; so was I. Not that

I'd raved or wept; I'd said no overt thing—how could she know my state? She didn't: that alone demented her. Poor soul! She who was so sensitive to every shade of mood would look at the cast-iron shell of me aghast. Not knowing what ailed me, she laid it to herself. "Is Salamina bad?" she'd ask. "No," I would answer her, "you are good." Words, words! She'd turn away and cry. At night, long after we had gone to bed, when everything was still and dark, I'd hear her smothered sobs. Once she got up; her bare feet pattered on the boards, then she was kneeling on the floor beside me. She spoke my name, softly; I feigned sleep. For a long time she knelt there in the cold, and wept.

What is so provoking as the inscrutable? It is a Bluebeard chamber to the mind; no matter what the consequences, we *will* pry. And if its lock defeats us, we'll use dynamite, destroy ourselves and everything, but *look*. So Salamina, desperate, laid her train. One night she touched the match to it. We were sitting at home, I reading, Salamina stitching, and all had been as usual. Then presently she laid her work down, faced me, spoke. "You are continually giving money to people," she said, "money for which they have done nothing. I came to work for you in August. It is time now that you paid my wages." "Your wages! What?" I heard her well enough; it merely staggered me. And she was right. I *hadn't* paid her wages.

In fact, Salamina, at the time of my employing her, had not mentioned them; and I, impressed by her apparent confidence in me to do the right thing by her, and further impressed, as I came to know her, by her stanch loyalty to my interests, had decided to far exceed the meager stipend of ten crowns a month which Danish housewives pay. So, beginning by putting my money box unreservedly in her hands, I instructed her to take from it for everything that she and her children would need; and although I met with strong remonstrances from her I finally, I think, prevailed. Nor would I ever let her give me an accounting of the money spent—either for herself or for our household expenses—nor heed her when on starting for the store she'd say, "I'm taking a five-crown note to change," nor even look at the change when she put it under my nose to count. "Take from the box," I said, "and when it's empty I will fill it up again." And God knows, she played fair. But as to salary—well, I made her gifts, in cash. She'd banked, by then, the wages of three kifaks.

But there she sat. "I want my pay," she said, and looked at me with a hard face.

A face like that is hard to talk to. I tried to explain matters, to tell her what I'd meant to do, and done, and how she'd profited. "Yes, *presents!*" she replied with vast contempt. "I want my pay. As for the children, I haven't touched your money in the box. I've paid for them myself." No doubt, since she asserted it, she had. I had caught her once drawing money from her savings-bank account to buy herself material for a coat. I'd stopped that steal. But it was hard for her to accept the irregularity of such provision for them all as I intended. And now she only sat defiantly demanding pay. I hated her.

"Good, then," I said. "Tomorrow you'll receive one hundred and twenty crowns, for eight months, fifteen crowns a month. The Danes pay ten."

"*Ajungulak*," she said. "And now I go. Tomorrow I shall take my things. I return to Ikerasak by the next post to Umanak." And with that, Salamina got up, removed her bedding from the sleeping-platform, laid out my blankets there, and went.

"Thank God for that!" I breathed.

The echo of the alarm clock seemed to be still ringing in my sleep-befuddled brain as I turned out next day. How dark it was, and cold! Not like those mornings when I'd get up to the warmth, the lamplight, and the purring kettle. I lit a candle, slipped a wrapper on, cleared the range of ashes, laid the kindlings, lighted them. I went outdoors. It was starlight, and the air was crystal clear; there were no lights in the houses, and no one was about. Alone in the whole world, it seemed, and that was good. A disembodied soul, I thought, would have no need of any beauty but the stark esthetics of the universe. I felt the ecstasy of that; then shivered and went in.

I sat drinking my coffee when suddenly the alarm clock went off. I'd just imagined it before.

Salamina came early to the house. I wasn't sure that she had come to ask for the money, but I gave it to her, wrote a check. She took it and went off.

In about half an hour Salamina was back; her eyes were red from tears. "I understand things now," she said. "I'm sorry." She stood there waiting. "May I come back?" asked Salamina.

"No," I said, "I'm not a business man, and I won't have a business woman in my house."

"I won't go to Ikerasak," said Salamina. "The ice may be unsafe, and it will be too cold to travel so far. I'll be ashamed to go to Ikerasak."

"Tell them I cheated you, tell them I beat you, tell them anything you like: you don't have to be ashamed. But you can't come back."

"I won't go to Ikerasak," she said.

We argued it, and fought. I threatened to leave the house to her and move to Nugatsiak. She wept. Her face all blotched and red, she returned to Marghreta's.

That day was Marghreta's birthday; I had promised her a party. Salamina returned, and asked if she might cook the dinner. I let her. That dinner was too salt—from tears. Just before dinner Salamina put on a fine silk anorak that I had given her at Christmas. "I wear this tonight," she said, "for it may be the last time that we shall ever have dinner together." The party was a solemn one, for all loved Salamina. From time to time her thoughts brought on fresh tears; she'd go outside to weep alone.

The next day Salamina moved her things. She looked as though she hadn't slept, as though she'd cried all night. She packed her things and cleaned the house; a girl came up to help her carry down her trunk. While she had worked at cleaning she had continually begged to be allowed to work for me again. "Let me come in the morning and light your fire; it is cold then. You will be so cold! Let me do your kamiks for you, wash your anoraks. Let me cook for you, wash your dishes, clean your house. I want to work for you. I want to give the money back. I want no pay for anything."

"No."

And then at last she was to go. She stood before me to say good-by, her face streaming with tears. "Thank you," she said, "for everything. For the presents and the money that you gave me, for the food, for the house. Thank you for being good to me. Thank you, thank you." For a long time after the door had closed upon her she stood outside; then with her tears unchecked she went off down the hill.

Salamina had left her bedding; she came at bedtime to fetch it. She begged to make my bed for me. "Oh, you will be cold," she sobbed. "Please let me come to make the fire in the morning."

"No."

I couldn't let her go alone; I walked down with her to Marghreta's house. I couldn't leave her till the door had closed on her.

She came at seven in the morning. "All night," she said, "I called out 'Kinte, Kinte, Kinte, you are cold.' Oh, Kinte is cold, and there is no one to do things for him. And in the morning he must get up in that cold house, and make the fire, and make breakfast, do all that work himself. And how can I be idle when one I love must work? Please, please let Salamina work for you. Oh, please! I want no money; let me work."

I called at Marghreta's. There lay an anorak of mine that Salamina had stolen away to wash for me. Salamina took it in her hands. "Kinte's anorak!" said Marghreta dolefully. And then both wept.

On looking out of my window I would see Salamina standing out of doors down at Marghreta's. She would stand there looking toward my house, hugging herself with folded arms, for it was cold. Only for a few moments would she go into the house, only to get warm, then again she'd stand and look. Sometimes she'd pace about, disconsolate, with folded arms and hanging head.

She would find a pretext to come to my house. "Oh, Kinte, Kinte," she'd weep, "Salamina doesn't eat, she doesn't sleep. All night she lies and thinks: maybe Kinte is cold, or wants for something. Oh, it would be better if Salamina were dead." And how the tears would flow!

Once she took up a big hunting-knife that I had, and brought it to me. "Kill Salamina," she said. "Kill her, kill her."

Stopping in at Marghreta's one day, I found Marghreta there alone. "Maybe," she said, "Kinte won't come much to our house any more." And she began wiping the tears from her eyes.

This couldn't go on long; of course it didn't. Salamina was reinstated, though she was to continue living at Marghreta's. It was quite true that I had needed solitude; the privilege of the house alone at night relieved the strain. I think that Salamina too was more contented, though I had constantly to defend the freedom I had won against the persistent encroachments of her insatiable possessiveness. Possibly in no respect was she shown to be more truly a daughter of her race. Referring to a certain well-known amusingly extreme case of the sort, in which the poor, decent, soft-hearted fellow had lost all rights over his own body, heart, and soul, I used to say: "Look here, Salamina, I am not Andersen, and you are not Sophia, so we'll have no more of this nonsense." She would laugh.

March days crept up as though in fear of me, each moment trembling as it neared, then halting in its tracks. And having passed, they'd leap away to lose themselves in the abyss of yesterdays. That first of February was as years ago, a date before my lifetime; tomorrow was a lifetime off.

March: it is near the equinox, when the days' invasion of the nights begins. It is springtime to the senses, but winter in cold fact. The ice is thickest now, the snow lies deep; it is the time for traveling. So one day into the capital, Godhavn, there come two sledges from the north: the winter post has come.

That next day is a busy day at the Manager's office, sorting out mail and sending local letters around to the people's houses; they're busy days up at the radio station on the hill where Holton-Möller is getting off a pile of messages as fast as air can swallow them. All for one place, as far as he's concerned, all south to Julianehaab. And all for one place, Denmark, out of there—no, one! America. That's via Louisburg. "*LOPUM DUBCU DUBEW DUBMEDUBOG*," the operator clicks. And Louisburg, picking it up, relays it to New York, or Boston; sends it on.

In a little telegraph office in an Adirondack hamlet sits a patient and devoted operator, Mrs. Coventry—whom, for all she is to all she serves, may the Lord bless and the Western Union Company reward. She got the message, and with the last click of her instrument was reaching for the telephone. Maybe there was snow piled up on that telephone wire; March snow is thick and soft, it sticks. If there was snow, it melted at the words. What I had whispered to myself in January had at last, in March, been heard.

The answer came. Of course it came—damn fool that I had been—so quick it might have been an echo of the call. It came by Enoch, Trolleman's chore boy; just a slip of paper.

"Salamina," I said casually, "I'm starting south in a few days, to meet the first *Disko* at Holstensborg."

So *that's* it! Salamina beamed. Bad times, she knew, had passed for all of us.

XLVI. THE START

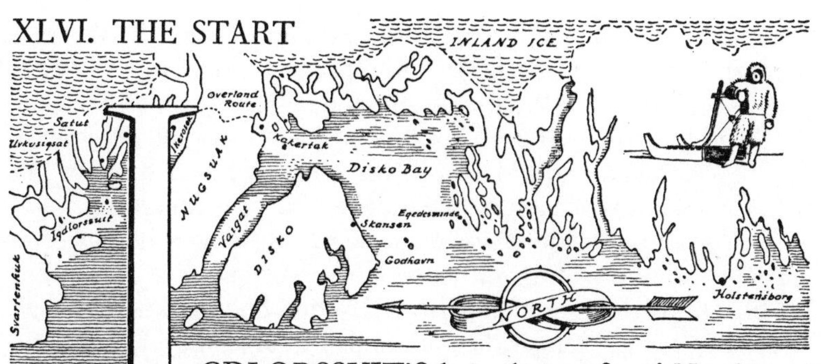

IGDLORSSUIT'S latitude is 71° 15′ North; and Holstensborg's, due south, is 66° 55′. There are, therefore, two hundred and sixty miles between them. But dog-sledge travel is uncertain and it may be devious; for it depends on that variable and unpredictable element, the weather in its all-embracing, thermometric, barometric, sense. Bodies of water such as Umanak Fiord, the Vaigat between Disko Island and the mainland, and Disko Bay may one year be ice and the next continuously open water. There may be firm ice somewhere for a week, and not again that year. Ice during the period of its formation is so entirely dependent upon an exact combination of all the factors in the weather that one sometimes wonders how it ever gets a chance to form. Your route, however, may at best be devious, for those land masses which, as you plot it on the map, obtrude between your starting-point and your objective are either quite impassable or only to be crossed by here and there some doubtless steep and winding pass that men have found. Igdlorssuit to Umanak, straight line, was fifty miles; by sledge, most part or all of every winter, three times that. My goal was Holstensborg: I couldn't hope to sledge there. One might by skirting Disko Bay reach Egedesminde, from there go south by boat. But it was all conjectural; I only *willed* to be in Holstensborg on April 20. I left Igdlorssuit the thirtieth of March.

The solicitude that Greenlanders show for us is far from flattering. It is their fixed idea that we are weaklings. That nonsense of

Salamina's about my suffering from cold, her weeping, as she used to, at my sleeping on the floor. "You're not a Greenlander," she'd say, "you'll freeze." What white men have they learned it from? The night before I started south I had company at my house: Rudolf, Abraham, and Martin. Over a map we talked about my trip. One thing was certain: We'd have to go by Kangerdluarsuk again, for Umanak Fiord was open water. Moreover there was no ice at the mouth of Kangerdluarsuk, no reaching Uvkusigssat but by boat. But that I'd planned for: David should take his kayak over the pass to Kangerdluarsuk and, leaving me in camp there with the dogs, proceed to Uvkusigssat and send back a boat for me. "What! leave you with the dogs, alone? We can't do that." The remonstrances were concerted and emphatic. The upshot was that Martin, volunteering for the trip, unpaid, should come and camp with me, and bring the kayak back. There was some sense to that, the kayak part of it; it was the offer of an act of friendship: I accepted it. But the thought behind it was that alone I'd somehow perish.

And with Salamina, the thought that I would freeze was an obsession. She was forever trying to bundle me up; and when I wouldn't have it, appealing to Marghreta and the rest. All right for Greenlanders, she'd say, but not for me. And mufflers! If there's anything I—yes, dear Aunt and Mother, I may as well confess—if there's anything I loathe it's having my long neck bound round with scarfs and things. And Salamina loved them. The morning of my start she came with hers. "Now, put this on, you must." "No," said I. Whereupon she lassoed me with it. "Thank you," I said and took it off again. But I did have a cold, a nasty one, my first in Greenland.

March 30. New snow has fallen overnight—a foot of it. The day is clouded. It is nine o'clock: the sledge is packed, the dogs are straining to get off. "Good by, Marghreta, Salamina; we'll be back in May." And unhooking the corner of the sledge from the post that held it, we're off downhill in a whirl of snow, me hanging to the stanchions, heels dug in, to brake it. Then, right in the

is is a hunter – winter style :
ndeer above , dog skin below ,
ttens of seal .

middle of the hill, there's Salamina at my back winding that muffler round my neck.

David and I, one sledge well packed with dog food, man food, cameras, sleeping-bags, a tent, and clothes—and fourteen dogs; Martin, a kayak on his sledge—nine dogs: that was our party. It was my hope to buy more dogs and another sledge at Satut from Johan Lange, who having trimmed me in my innocence would maybe, now that I had lost it, give me a fair deal. I needed more dogs; I began by losing them. We hadn't gone five miles before a dog I'd bought the day before convinced us of his worthlessness. We set him free, turned him toward home, and gave him with the whip good cause to go there. A little farther on a splendid dog I'd bought from Pavia went lame from injuries inflicted by his loving teammates. He couldn't work; he barely kept the pace.

That afternoon at four we met two travelers who had come from Uvkusigssat. They brought good news: the party that had brought them lay with their boat in camp in Kangerdluarsuk; they would remain all night. If we pushed through we'd find them there and save the kayak trip to Uvkusigssat. No sooner heard than settled in our minds. So, as a sort of girding of our loins for it, I got my primus out, and all of us had coffee. It was the only food we took that day except a little hardtack as we drove along.

At the head of the fiord we delayed a few minutes to gossip with some campers from Nugatsiak. They were inhabiting a sort of cave under an overhanging ledge of rock, a jolly crowd. To them we gave the dog that had been Pavia's.

Crossing the land, we reached the crest of the divide just as pitch-darkness settled down. The crevassed glacier, the rough moraine, were hard to travel in the darkness. A strong, cold wind had risen in our faces; it soon began to snow. We reached the fiord and plodded on, following the windings of the dimly seen near shore. I tell you it was cold—that wind and driving snow! Heads down, just endlessly putting one foot down before the other, seeing nothing, hearing nothing but the rustle of the drifting snow, we plodded on. And then we stopped. "They're here," said David.

There was a boat drawn up on shore; there were two kayaks; no people were about, nor any sign of where they were. We chained the dogs and pitched the little tent. I lit a candle in the tent, and read my watch. It was just two o'clock; we'd traveled seventeen hours. I lit the primus and made coffee; *that* was good! I went to bed.

Did David, and did Martin? No. They sat about. In two hours dawn would come, at dawn come seals. They'd stroll around till then. I woke when they came back, at five. No luck, no seals. We all had coffee. By the gray light of the dawn we discovered the dwelling-place of our fellow tenants of the spot: a little hollow in the hillside, banked round with snow, and roofed with a patch of canvas and some creepers. It was a cozy lair, so cozy that despite our somewhat noisy presence there its inmates slept on undisturbed for hours more; then four men crept out blinking at the day. Martin set out at noon for his long journey home. I've tried to think of other acts of friendship in my life to equal his. I can't remember one.

Meanwhile the wind had shifted and the day had cleared, but every hour the wind increased in violence. Our tent was on the land just where the fiord ice ended. That day a mile of ice drove out to sea. Good thing we had a boat, the dogs were useless now. We spent the day in idleness, and I humored my cold, which had gotten worse, by staying most of the time in my sleeping-bag, where between alternating chills and fever I could indulge my fancy with thoughts of dying of pneumonia in that miserable place.

David was up again next day at five, and off for seal. Again no luck. But we had luck in weather: it was fair and calm. We broke up camp, knocked down the sledge, launched the boat off the ice shelf, loaded it, threw in the dogs, and rowed away: six men, twelve dogs, a pile of goods and gear, and two kayaks in tow. Toward evening it grew overcast and cold, a storm came up. We hoisted sail and used the wind. Careening to a squall we drove in through the broken ice and made our port—in time. Whew, but it blew that night!

Next day was warm, but it was blowing half a gale. It cleared the harbor of the ice, but held us wind-bound there.

The following morning was not propitious for a start. The day was dark, the clouds hung low and threatening. But the wind had moderated; we embarked. We had three miles to go to turn the point of Akuliarusak, then maybe one mile more to reach the ice. But as we neared the point we looked out from its lee at such a driving, seething, steaming gale at sea as sent a shiver to the heart. We made for land. I've spoken of the little settlement that nestled on that rocky point, and how I would one day find shelter there: this was the day. The people, seeing us, came out and welcomed us. We drew the boat on shore and carried all our goods into the houses. And within ten minutes of landing I found myself established as the guest of as delightful an old Greenland couple as I had known. They were Pavia Amossen and his wife.

They were more than delightful. Their devotion to each other, their mutual dependence—he, like a child that needed her and looked upon her as omnipotent; she, lovingly amused by him, by his old ways, his constant coffee-drinking, his endless talk—this was to remain in my thoughts as a moving instance of matured conjugal happiness. "I can't understand these things," said he as I was showing him the works of my moving-picture camera. "Show it to her, for she understands everything." And at bedtime—we three alone slept there, David and the rest being accommodated in an untenanted house near by—at bedtime when he had undressed and lain down, and when she, having put his thermos bottle of coffee within reach, and matches, and a pot to spit into after his coughing spells, got into bed beside him, they lay facing each other, and each rested an arm about the other; so they slept. Old Pavia has died since then; the wonder is that she lives on.

The gale that day surpassed belief. Now and again we'd venture out of doors, leaning against the gale to watch its work. The fiord was raging, and the wind, shearing the wave crests, shivered them to spray and drenched the air with brine. Five miles of ice drove out of Itivdliarsuk Fiord—the ice we would have landed on. All day it raged. At dark two men arrived from Uvkusigssat; they had come on foot along the mountain side. People, they said, observing that the storm had risen shortly after we had left, had looked for our return. That failing, they had grown concerned. So Ditlief and Carl Willumsen had come to see if we were safe on land. They wouldn't stay the night; they'd told the people at the settlement that they'd return if we were safe. It is for such acts that one becomes indebted in Greenland. We pay for them with what? A little tobacco, a cigar or two, a glass of schnapps—and think we're splendid fellows.

The uncle of Carl Willumsen, an old enfeebled hunter of Uvkusigssat, had two sons, Rasmus and—oh, I forget his name. Reared safely through the perils of childhood, they at young manhood were become the prop of his old days. They were good props, good men. Then came, in 1930, the great Wegener expedition for the investigation, among other matters, of the phenomena of the inland ice. It established itself at the head of a fiord not many miles from Uvkusigssat. The world has read of the tragic end of the expedition's leader, Alfred Wegener: how, after establishing a winter station in the center of the inland ice, two hundred and fifty miles from the sea, he with two others made a last trip there to carry in supplies to the courageous pair that were to winter in that place. They got there, Wegener and his two companions, one with a frozen foot; then Wegener and one man set out on their return to camp. They never got there. The body of Alfred Wegener was found next spring; crossed skis had been set up to mark its resting-place. In the pockets of his clothes were his watch and a large sum of money, but the scientific notebooks which he'd always carried—they were gone. That at the approach of death he had entrusted them to his surviving comrade there can be no doubt. That was perhaps bad judgment, for there was no one to mark the place where *he* at last, perhaps not far from home, lay down and died. His name was Rasmus Willumsen. The loss of Rasmus left old Willumsen one son. That very summer, '31, that son was drowned out kayaking.

This is the dear old wife of Pavia Amossen, bringing water to make coffee for him.

It stormed two days. Then on the third, the day calm, sunlit, cold, we started on. With us, conveyed along beside us in a clumsy old boat manned by his wife and a crew of grandchildren, and then driving along with us on a diminutive sledge drawn by five dogs, came Pavia. He was going to Satut for a visit. Every few miles Pavia would halt his dogs and turn to me and say, "How about a little coffee?" And he'd produce a thermos bottle. There seemed to be no limit to them.

We stopped for twenty minutes once while David stalked—and missed—a seal, drank coffee as we watched. Near Satut we encountered broken ice; I got one leg wet as the only mishap. We fetched up on a little island and could drive no farther. Island: a piece of land surrounded by water: such that day was Satut. But we'd been seen, so people came for us and ferried us across.

Johan Lange at Satut, fifteen miles from Umanak, was in a position to be informed about many things of current consequence. My motorboat for one thing, he informed me, had been fixed, was in the water now, had been at Satut just the week before. The ice? Well, that was bad; no going on to anywhere from Satut now. "But what of that?" he said. "You're welcome here. Just make yourself at home, and stay." We had arrived at three; at five, David in a borrowed kayak set out for Umanak. Four hours at most to Umanak; my boat would be at Satut in the morning.

The evening was immaculate: not a cloud was in the sky, and not a breath of wind to ripple the surface of the water. The calm, the brilliant sunlight, made it seem to have the warmth of spring. It hadn't; it was bitter cold. One realized it when the darkness came. The myriad glittering stars *looked* cold. "Come in," said Lange, "he is there by now. It's cold, it's ten o'clock. Come in." He poured out schnapps. "*Skaal*, David!"

There is a noise in the entry: opening and shutting doors, scuffling feet, men's voices. Johan, listening, jumps up, throws the door wide open: there stands David. Some men are holding him as though he might collapse. We lead him in and seat him by the stove. David looks up and smiles, exactly—it occurs to me—as he had smiled on that October day when they had saved his life at sea. He'd saved his own life now. This is what had happened: An hour and a half from Satut the glassy surface of the fiord began to freeze. That, for a kayaker, is a solemn threat, and David heeded it. He turned and made with all his might for Satut; it was a race with death if there was ever one. The arctic sea in early spring is freezing cold; it hardly needs cold air to freeze it. Given a calm, it quickly turns to ice. It had, that day, the calm; the cold came with the sun's decline. And almost in the instant that the air permitted it that broad expanse of water turned to ice; once ice, it thickened with the minutes. But not only had David to break his way through an unyielding element; he had to propel that constantly accumulating weight of ice that formed on the kayak, and wield with iced-up mittened hands an ice-incrusted paddle. It was a race with time, and distance was against the man. But David won. David was not one of the more powerful Greenlanders. He was slight of build and narrow-shouldered. He had endurance and great skill, sheer strength he lacked. Could then a stronger man have run a longer course? Not much. I went next day and looked the kayak over. The water line was marked by a clean half-inch chafe, half of the thickness of the hide in depth. Death's bow has many strings.

Let us not, in this account of going to meet a steamer in Greenland, lose track of days elapsed. Just as the belated commuter hurrying to make his morning train keeps taking out his watch to count the minutes and the seconds left, so I each night took out my calendar and checked the days. We were at Satut on the sixth day out: six days; and only—if we'd had good ice—one good day's trip from home. Right at the very start we're days behind.

A little worry is your best alarm clock: I was up and out of doors at dawn. "Good morning, David, out all night?" "The ice is bad," said David. "Come and see." Climbing the hill, we stood and looked toward Umanak. The fiord that yesterday had been a summer sea, that last night got a shell of ice, was now choked up for miles with ice floes that the tide had carried out of the fiords.

We were marooned, imprisoned, square in the middle of a slowly moving field of broken pan ice; and not a chance of getting off, a pessimist might say, till June. It did look bad, not hopeless; or we wouldn't have spent the day as, on and off, we did climbing that hill to look and speculate. So passed the seventh day; by night I had a plan: start with a boat and crew and make my way across and through that ice to Umanak. Then if the pack consolidated David would follow with the dogs; and if the ice dispersed I'd motor back in style and fetch him.

It seems that Heaven smiled on us, so fair and beautiful a day was given for the start. I took one last survey of the ice field from the hilltop, said farewell to my host, and, adding my shoulder to those of five husky Greenlanders, shoved on the boat, and off we went across the ice. Five hours, exactly, saw us back; we'd been four miles.

What happened? Nothing; everything. It was just a matter of shoving a heavy boat along on the ice; not smooth ice, by any means, but jammed-up pans, small pressure ridges everywhere. At last you come to water; not real water, it's thin ice. You can't walk on it and your boat crunches through. Neither can you row in it, until you've smashed it up around the boat and on ahead. You're glad when you're on solid ice once more. But then to get there you have had to haul the boat up; that's hard work. And then you push across that tumbled ice. You're glad to come where you can launch the boat again. Yes, there are many and recurrent reasons to be glad; but you're extremely sorry in between. Just two miles out from Satut lay a little island; we went ashore on it to reconnoiter from a rise of ground. And what we saw, combined with what we'd done—and the two hours and a half that we'd been doing it—decided us. With wind and weather what they are you don't go spending nights at sea on ice like that if you can help it. We went home.

So ended the eighth day, and hope.

XLVII. THE FINISH

NINTH DAY: calm, cold; ice forming everywhere. "Come, take it easy," said Johan. "You'll not get out of here for days."

Tenth day: calm, cold; ice somewhat broken overnight but freezing still. "No good," said our good host. "Come in again, sit down." But I didn't. I just kept going up on to the hill and looking.

Now there lived in Satut an old expedition's man named Carl Mattiesen. He met me wandering about and asked me to his house. "If you want to get out of here and go to Ikerasak," he said to me over coffee, "you can maybe go tomorrow." Did I! Ikerasak was straight upon our road. They'd told us that we *couldn't* go that way. "There is a land pass up near the head of this fiord," said Carl. "If it stays cold tonight you can get off tomorrow."

"Yes," said Johan, when I told him we would leave, "if you want to go *that* way." As if we cared what way we went!

All night was cold and calm; in the morning it was bitter cold, with a raw head wind to face. The ice would hold, but it was thin; how thin I only guessed. David, with the guide I'd taken for the route, went cautiously ahead on foot; I followed with our sledge but only two dogs hitched to it; ten dogs ran free. The guide's dogs followed driverless, in line. Two dogs of mine in harness, ten others following; twelve dogs of mine in all. I'd had no luck in Satut buying dogs.

Scattered over the broad surface of the new ice were many men and dogs, for access to the fiord sent men to work again. Nor were we among the first: an hour later we passed some fishermen at work, jigging their lines through holes in the ice, to bring up every now and then a Greenland halibut. It was a bitter day; each fisherman had stood his sledge on end to break the piercing wind.

Itivdliarsuk Fiord: the name denotes a pass, a crossing-place from fiord to fiord. If I'd known Eskimo, or David had had brains, we would have gone straight there from Uvkusigssat. Once we had gained the fiord we found old ice the whole way in. It was rough ice, the last half-mile, ice smashed and stood on end and piled in heaps from the aborted calving of a near-by glacier. It was hard traveling, that last half-mile before we took the land. One dog got hurt.

The pass itself was nothing: an easy climb, a pretty little stretch across a lake, a short steep slide or two, and we were down again on a small floor of sea ice—just twenty-two miles more to reach Ikerasak. The scenery of our route that day is as impressive as any in all Greenland. Seeing it as we that day did, reclining at our ease on reindeer skins behind a team that raced of its free will, looking off skyward at the passing pageant of huge headlands and sheer mountain sides, one would have had the hours almost be days. Too soon—at four—we reached Ikerasak.

It is a pleasure, in this story of which the "villain," Trolleman, has been a Dane, to record the meeting with another Dane, a trader too, who was as good a man as one would meet with anywhere, and no bit better maybe than a lot of other outpost traders on the Greenland coast. They're workingmen, the outpost traders, most of them, and men who work. And Thompson of Ikerasak produced as a side line to his trader's job an air-cured Greenland halibut that you would search the Greenland world to match. But what affects the traveler is the hospitality he meets, the warm and generous welcome everywhere. That is a frontier specialty. Its roots are in our need of it; we need it most where men live far apart. And near the wilderness it grows luxuriant. It bloomed at Thompson's.

Or started to. He'd hardly welcomed me when, inadvertently, he handed me my hat. "*Disko* has sailed," said Thompson over drinks. "Oh, by the way: there was a message for you on the air two days ago. You have a friend on board." We left Ikerasak at seven the next day.

We had driven into Ikerasak with twelve dogs; we left with ten. The dog that hurt himself the day before was badly lamed; one other was so far from lame that he ran off. We wouldn't even wait to hunt for him. We had a long day's trip ahead: across and up the fiord, then overland to Kekertak. We took a guide along, for in the trackless snow of the mountains of Nugsuak we might easily have gone astray.

The crossing of the land began with the ascent of a long steep stretch of frozen stream. Parts of it were glare ice on which the dogs and men could hardly keep their feet, and through which now and then we'd break with risk of falling through into a torrent three feet down. On land the snow lay deep; deep snow uphill. We went afoot until at two o'clock we reached the summit of the pass. There, on the top, we stopped for rest and food, and from a height of near, I'd guess, three thousand feet, looked down on snow-clad slopes almost to where the pass emerged near Kekertak.

The descent was not as easy as it had looked to be. It was a southern slope, and, lying to the sun all day, was wet and heavy. Toward sundown dark clouds overspread the sky; a storm was brewing; it began to snow. We reached the fiord at dark. Yet we were seen, or heard, a long way from the settlement; even before its lights appeared, a crowd came running out along the track to meet us. At just nine-thirty we drove up to the house of the trader, Niels Dorph. There, finally, well fed and warm, and in my sleeping-bag, and fast asleep, I ended the twelfth day of the trip.

What we learned at Kekertak about ice conditions disposed of all the hopes we'd entertained of following the shore of Disko Bay. There was no ice. The nearest we could get to Holstensborg by sledge was Godhavn; and the prospects of getting a motorboat there to continue south in were excellent. The route to Godhavn presented no difficulties beyond the water crossing of the Vaigat, for the sledge track was on land and in almost its entire extent lay along the shore of the low foreland. The only problem was a boat to cross in; but Kekertak, lying in the path of travel, was supplied with just the craft for just that use. I hired it. Or, rather, I entered upon negotiations and transactions that were not to be concluded to the satisfaction of the piratical crew for days to come. Meantime, and by their means, we got to Disko. But there at Kekertak, the storm that raged next day did much to soothe the exasperation that I felt at the delays of bargaining.

The difficulty that is encountered in all money dealings with Greenlanders is their unwillingness to put a price on their commodity, whether it be goods or labor. Many have viewed this trait of theirs as a naïve and innocent unworldliness. Perhaps! At any rate, the naïve and innocent children of nature who confronted me in Kekertak were prompt enough in rejecting my first offer of the established tariff rate for their services, as that was furnished me by the trader. The rate was based on time, and, thus providing compensation for delays, might have been held applicable to all seasons. But that, they said, was not enough. What *would* I pay? I raised the offer, and threw in a bonus. They accepted it. *But* (I'd made my price per man) they wanted eight men for the trip. That staggered me: a lot of men. Well, I agreed. And with the morrow, if it cleared, set for the start, they all expressed their satisfaction and went off. There was a dance that night, a good one; fine lot of girls in Kekertak, and an old church to dance in. But right in the midst of it I'm sent for, wanted at the trader's house. There, in a group outside, was all my crew. "What's up?" I asked. "They want more money," said Niels Dorph. Niels was a Greenlander, an honest, friendly, generous fellow. He'd learned arithmetic in school and picked up pleasant white men's ways in Denmark. He was a gentle soul, with no backbone. "What shall I do?" I asked of him. "Well, if they want more," said my advocate, "I think they ought to have it." This time they named their price, a flat sum for the trip. "All right," I said, "I'll pay it. And tomorrow," —it was clearing now—"at six o'clock, we start."

At six o'clock—the day was calm and clear—as David and I are loading the sledge and putting our fifteen dogs in harness (I had bought five dogs of Niels), up comes the leader of my crew. "Five men," he says, "don't want to go." Good Lord! then let them stay. Get more, get anyone, let's start. He finds two more, he knows another some miles down the shore who'll go. We start, three sledges packed with men.

Crossing to the mainland of Nugsuak—for Kekertak, as its name denotes, is an island—we drive on land along the shore four miles; there, high on land and filled with, buried under, all the season's snow, reclines the boat. We get to work and somehow dig it out. The sea off there is choked with broken ice; no place to launch a boat. We rig a strap around it, hitch on the fifteen dogs, and off we go up hill and down for half a mile. There from a high ice shelf—the tide is low—we lower down the boat, we launch it on the ice; we load it there. And with the dogs running eagerly alongside, push it across the land-fast ice and launch it in the water. In with the dogs now, all aboard! We pole through floe ice to an open lead; a light fair breeze has risen, we hoist sail. A few miles down the shore we stop to get a man; with him on board, we bear away for Disko.

Our crew, with the exception of their leader, the steersman—who looked like an evil-eyed and sullen Dante—was a convivial crowd. They idled pleasantly, and let the wind to its last dying gasp that afternoon do all the work. They talked and laughed, and smoked my cigarettes; they ate my food which I shared out to them—and, having finished that, produced each man his own, and ate it sharing none. They liked my things and wanted all I owned —my pipe, my watch, my primus stove. The steersman asked for nothing, laughed at nothing, smiled at nothing, spoke to no one, scowled. His pale green eyes glowed evilly in his dark face.

Our plan had been to land conveniently on Disko, and sledge

along its level shore to the settlement at Skansen, and there spend the night. But when we neared the land, all, with what seemed an eager interest in our welfare, deplored our chancing it. The snow was deep, they said, the drifts in spots impassable; we'd never get to Skansen—not that night. Why not keep on by boat, they said; they'd take us there. Like fools we fell for it: David—I watched him waver, be convinced. We haggled over terms, agreed. We changed our course, and on a summer sea rowed on for Skansen.

It wasn't summer, though; our plans had not been changed for pleasure's sake, to let us barge along like Pharaohs on the Nile and bask in idleness. We sat there as the sun sank low quite miserable with cold, the cheerful crew but now and then yielding a chance for one of us to warm up at the oars. David, of course with next to nothing on, at last lay down among the dogs, and pulled dogs up on top of him. Cold in late afternoon, and worse at night: that everlasting sitting still, your feet in icy slush just when you needed a hot-water bag. No, we were not at sea for fun; it merely promised speed—or, if not speed, at least the certainty of getting there. We did get there at last, but it was well past midnight. We made the land on a stretch of gravelly shore below low bluffs. Landing, we pushed the sledge up through a cut, a portion of the crew assisting us, and reached a level plain where scattered around were the dark masses of the houses of the settlement and, some way off, the larger building of the trader's residence. That was my goal.

The house as we came up to it stood dark and silent and unwelcoming. I hesitated what to do. "Call him," the crew urged, throwing open the door. "Call him, go in." So in we tramped, the lot of us; I shouting for our host. A man's voice presently replied; and with the opening of an inner door there loomed the tall and ghostlike figure of a very kindly man in underwear. One felt his kindness; one heard it in his quiet deep-toned speech. He lit a candle and renewed his welcome; then drawing on his socks and shoes —conversing all the while most cheerfully—he went to superintend the bestowal of my goods, while his wife, who had meanwhile entered, got busy with the kitchen stove and, despite my polite and insincere remonstrances, with laying out the table for a meal. These two—Moses and his wife, both Greenlanders—are, I am sure from just one overnight at their house, among the best and kindest people in all that country. She, of the pair, had brains; he had the sense to know it. She was culturally a superior woman, and showed it in the not bad taste and the unusual neatness of her house, in the excellence of her bread, in her interests, which appeared in conversation, and in the whole manner of her hospitality. And when after an hour or more I sought that spot allotted for my head, I was shown by Moses up to a comfortable loft bedroom—for he had meanwhile made a fire there—and to as soft a bed as tired man could pray for.

My boat crew called at breakfast time. They wanted money. Part of their pay they were to get on their return to Kekertak: that was arranged with trader Niels and them. But no, they wanted to be paid in full right now. Fed up with them, I paid. Could I have known that they'd collect again from Niels? They did. And no sooner had David and I gotten started again than we realized that their long tale about bad snow was all a whole-cloth lie. Beware, O traveler, of Kekertak.

The pirates paid, a sledge purchased, we turned to hunting dogs: the five from Kekertak had strayed. Fortunately the snow was recent and we soon picked up their trail among the near-by hills. It led us everywhere, up hill and down and round in circles, and brought us, finally, in sight of all five dogs just coming home. We harnessed and set off. It was high noon.

We had as guide a man I've told about far back, the man who trained his wife by beating her, a first-rate man, and the best dog-driver in that settlement of the best dog-drivers, it is said, in Greenland. The Skansen men are miners. In summer time they work the outcroppings of coal, back in the hills; in winter time they haul their product down and to the market, Godhavn: hard sledging up and down the Disko hillsides.

Our track that day was smooth and hard; we followed it in line: guide first, I next, and David last. He had his little troubles with a miscellaneous team. The day was beautiful: I lay back in the sun and dozed. And I woke up just in time to see our guide at the stanchions of his sledge disappearing down a precipitous bank, and not in time to get upon my feet. We disappeared down too, but upside down. The cold snow finished waking me. There was one very steep descent. The dogs at such a place are brought behind the sledge, their traces passing under it. You take the stanchions, dig your heels in, tilt up the sledge until you're almost sitting in the snow, and take the leap. You won't go faster than the dogs can run.

The track to Godhavn followed the shore for two-thirds of the way; then, where a mountain spur that ended in sheer cliffs confronted it, it turned inland to cross a high divide: a long and wearisome ascent; and, from the top, a long sweet slide to Godhavn.

On the outskirts of Godhavn as the track approaches the settlement is a level plain; there, backing the hillside and facing seaward out across the plain, stands a solitary wooden building, the largest dwelling-house in Greenland. It is the Danish Arctic Station, maintained for the convenience of all students of Greenland phenomena; for their instruction in its library, for their experiments and research in its laboratory, for their sleep in its beds, for their sustenance at its generous board, and for their general mental and spiritual profit through the counsels of its director, Dr. Porsild. I went there seeking food and shelter; I left there more than two weeks later richer to the extent of my capacity in all it had to give. There ought to be more hostelries like that about the world.

It was twilight as we emerged upon the plain and headed at a fast run for the Station. Two Danes were promenading there: they stared. Certain that their admiring eyes were fixed on me, I sat back with that studied nonchalance which is the mark of expert driving. Next day I met these Danes—the Manager, Herr Schultz, and wife. "So that was *you!*" they both exclaimed, and laughed. "We didn't even look at you. It was the dogs. Such dogs, we said, don't come from hereabouts."

XLVIII. THE CAPITAL

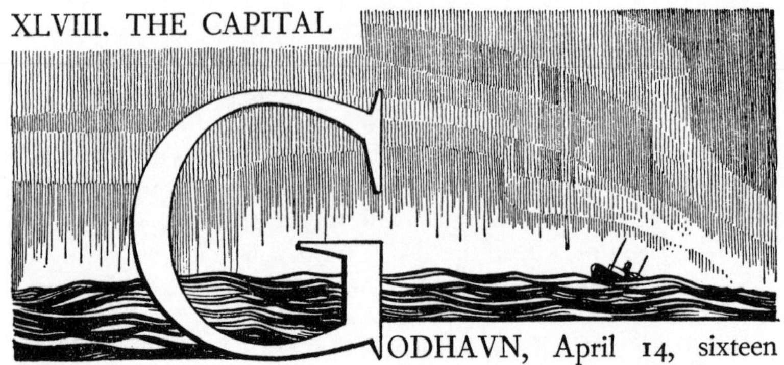

GODHAVN, April 14, sixteen days from home: one week to get to Holstensborg by boat, a three days' trip.

In Godhavn were four motorboats: the Chief Magistrate's, the Arctic Station's, the *Krabbe*—late of the Wegener expedition, and the *Avangnamiok*. All were on land. The Chief Magistrate's was, properly, reserved for high official use; the Arctic Station's couldn't at that time be launched; the *Krabbe* and the *Avangnamiok* might, it appeared, be let and launched.

Greenland, a government monopoly, is closed to casual tourists and to outside enterprise: the traveler there is strangely placed. In theory he should come supplied with everything: a house to shelter him—a tent; a boat to carry him around—and private fuel stations for his needs; and food. In theory, the man of means could starve there in the midst of plenty. He can't *demand* a thing, for Government, which owns the houses, boats, and stores, is government not of but for a people of whom the white-faced traveler is not a part. And while probably no trader but Trolleman has ever refused to sell supplies to an outsider, I would not question his right to. In Umanak one begs to be allowed to purchase goods. "May I, dear sir, so far encroach upon your valuable time as to ask you the favor of your unlocking the storehouse and letting me kindly have a pound of nails." And to the occasional persistent neglect of written requests for some necessity, one may never venture to oppose demand. All government control is apt to be like that; the institution is at fault. And in a monopoly like Greenland it is only saved by the almost invariable courtesy of the officials.

So it was that with no right whatever to demand a boat, I waited upon the Chief Magistrate and begged one as a favor. I was received with the most friendly courtesy; and over a little eye-opener of port wine and bitters I displayed my hopes, and ventured my request. I found a friend at once, and one who in his position of authority was aware of the many difficulties, obstacles, hindrances, and contingencies which in my rashness I had not considered.—Oh, for such counsel in our youth!—and just a little strychnine, arsenic, or piece of twine to act upon it with.—But he would give the matter thought, and meanwhile cause the boats to be inspected and a report prepared on their condition. Life was too good: I walked away on clouds. Five days—no, seven! The ship, I'd learned, was two days late. To have come the distance that I had, and be on time; to *be* there on the wharf at Holstensborg as I had said I would! Such small things count tremendously; it was as though I lived to make that promise good. I hurried to the radio station, sent this message off: "Will be there."

I was, of course, too early at the Magistrate's next day. "Not yet," said he, and smiled. "We can't rush things like that. I'll take the matter up this afternoon." "Of course!" I cried, "I'm sorry, sir." You see, knocking about the world on your own, and doing things pretty much for yourself, you don't realize that plans can't be thought of one minute and carried out the next. I felt a bit ashamed.

I called at noon next day: the Magistrate received me charmingly. He had good news: he'd sent instructions that the boats be looked at. "Now we shall see," said he. That's great, I thought as I walked off; for I had meanwhile learned from the Greenlanders that while the *Avangnamiok* was in poor shape, the *Krabbe* had been absolutely all right when she'd been hauled up for the winter; and was, presumably, in good condition now. So, foolishly, I called that evening at the Magistrate's: he was, I think a bit provoked, though with his courtesy he hid it well. "The report," he said, "has been received. I am having a translation made; that will be ready in due time."

"Come in," said the Magistrate kindly, when I called next day. "Come in, sit down. We'll talk about it." Oh, I could smell bad news; so kind, the Magistrate, and sort of sorrowful. He poured us out some port. "Sit down," he said. He gave a gentle, hesitating cough, and presently began: "I have read the report, Mr. Kent, and I regret to say"—he coughed—"that it is unfavorable. You see, Mr. Kent, there is work to be done on the *Krabbe's* motor. I am afraid it is in very bad condition. Yes—it is unfortunate."

"Well, then," cried I, jumping up like a fool, "why not get started fixing it? Let's get some men right at it."

"No, no," said the Magistrate, a trifle shocked, "we can't do that. You see the man who fixes motors, the blacksmith, is away on the schooner after walrus. No, Mr. Kent, there is no other man to do the work." I left there, wild.

In grousing round the settlement that day I learned of two men who could fix a motor. My hopes revived, I called next morning with the news. "No, Mr. Kent," he said, "those men, I know them, they won't do." No use; the nineteenth gone. "Am desperate, no boat," I radioed.

That night a great thought dawned: Christophersen, a Dane, the Arctic Station's man, expert mechanic, motorman; the best by long odds in the place. "Of course," said Dr. Porsild, "he can start tomorrow." Still time! I rushed off at the crack of office time, burst in, poured out my news. "Hem!" coughed the Magistrate. "Yes, he would do." "Now can he start? Right now," I cried. "No, Mr. Kent, we don't do things like that. No—let me see: no, I should like a letter first, a letter from Dr. Porsild stating his kind offer of Christophersen's services. We need it for our records, you see." Of *course* they would! It seemed I'd never learn to do things right. So back I went upon the run.

"The Magistrate," said I, "is most appreciative of Dr. Porsild's kind offer; and he would like it—if you will be so kind—in writing. For his records, you see. They have to . . ."

"Nonsense!" snorted the Doctor, picking up his pen; he dashed the letter off. I held it in the wind to dry as I ran to the Magistrate's. "Here is the letter, sir," I gasped, and gave it to him.

The good Magistrate read the letter twice.—"Sit down, Mr. Kent, I must consider this"—read it, folded it, returned it to its envelope, and laid it on a precise spot at one side. "Yes; that is satisfactory," said he. "And now about paying him."

"Oh, that's all fixed," I said eagerly. "I'm to pay Dr. Porsild for Christophersen's time."

The Magistrate smiled. "No, Mr. Kent," he said, "these things must all be put through in the regular way. We have to keep our records straight. No; Dr. Porsild shall bill the administration for the man's time, and we'll pay Dr. Porsild. Then we can charge you for it in the bill for the boat. That will be transmitted to the office in Copenhagen and recorded there. You'll settle it on your arrival there on leaving Greenland."

"Yes, sir. And now, sir, may he start to work?"

"Why, no, Mr. Kent"—it seems as though I'd never learn!—"No, I shall have an order prepared, and send it by messenger to Dr. Porsild. On the receipt of that, Dr. Porsild may instruct his man to report."

Elated by success, I ran on to the hill and radioed the good news on: "All fixed at last. Will come." Then, having allowed time for the Magistrate's messenger to deliver the order, I returned to the Arctic Station. But I had been too quick: the order hadn't come yet. It was now about ten o'clock; two hours to noon. Christophersen was waiting around for word to start. At twelve he left for lunch. The messenger, I thought, has stopped for lunch. At one he hadn't come; Christophersen came back to wait. At half-past two or three he went away; had things to do at home, he said. I'd find him there. Four, five: no order yet. At six a man came walking down the path: a letter for Dr. Porsild. The Doctor opened it; it was the order.

"Tomorrow he can start?" I asked.

"No," said the Doctor dryly. "Tomorrow is a holiday."

That night a message came for me: The *Disko* was in Holstensborg.

XLIX. SUNRISE

HOLSTENSBORG, the most southern colony of the district of North Greenland, is a busy place. It has a shipyard and a cannery, and in summer the little harbor is crowded with the motorboats of the halibut fishermen. It is the center of that industry. Men *work* in Holstensborg: you somehow feel it in the place; you see in the decent well-built wooden houses of the people the reward of industry. Ship captains like the port: as stevedores, the men and women work a ship in half the time of any other port in Greenland. If the traveler in Greenland were not constantly reminded by the hospitality he meets that many virtues are consonant with sloth and fatness, he'd pass harsh judgment on the Danes. Incompetence and sloth: these stare you in the face all over Danish Greenland. Yet so delightful is the play-village atmosphere of the colonies with the brightly painted Old World buildings of their administration groups, the tiny native houses, the "simple," "childlike," pretty-costumed people strolling round to animate the scene, the kindly Manager, the warmth of hospitality—so touching to the heart is all of this that judgment is seduced. You wake up with a jolt at Holstensborg. There, at the stroke of the seven o'clock bell that sends the crews to work, out steps the Manager, sharp-eyed, alert; his working-day starts them. His quick steps take him everywhere; things move in pace with him. He is an example to Greenlanders of that energy by which our race has risen; and since the whole avowed intention of the Greenland colonies is to induce the native through hard work to elevate himself, why isn't Greenland filled with men like this? Well, there at Holstensborg in '32 was Rasmussen; and while in Godhavn people were considering, discussing, inspecting, reporting, transcribing, writing notes and orders, and filing everything—in triplicate—in archives, he, getting wind of a couple of radio messages, said to himself: "It's plain they'll need a boat"—and launched one. And there it lay, crew ready, fuel on board, all set to start when the *Disko* dropped her anchor.

There is a vast difference between *getting* ready for things and *being* ready. They are less relative stages in a process than quantitative opposites: *not* being and *being*. They are incommensurates like 0 and ∞, and no amount of adding to the one or subtracting from the other will bring them any closer together. Not, at least, the kinds of mind they represent: you can't make Hamlet into Don Quixote. (And Hamlet, by the way, was Prince of Denmark.) The *ready* mind is what the term denotes: "prompt, quick, with resolution nerved." Annihilating time, it perceives as at a flash all facts, all sides; perceives, sorts, weighs, eliminates, concludes, and *acts*. If there were not such minds there'd have been one less passenger on that March sailing of the liner Frederick IV, New York to Copenhagen; one day would have been deemed too little for connection with the Greenland boat; the time too short, the sea too rough, the North too cold, the enterprise too hazardous; the game not worth the candle. The light, we'd better say, not worth the tallow. We have it now: tallow—or light; fatheads—or living souls. That was a living soul that came to Greenland then!

NEITHER SNOW NOR RAIN
NOR ICE NOR HEAT NOR GLOOM OF NIGHT
STAYS THESE COURIERS
FROM THE SWIFT COMPLETION OF THEIR
APPOINTED ROUNDS.

Storm couldn't stop; it did delay that courier—one day, at Holstensborg. Next day it cleared; they sailed. The storm came on again: they made an anchorage in a small cave of that forbidding shore and lay up overnight. The bare, unheated cabin of a Greenland fishing boat, three Greenlanders the crew. April—but winter time; damp, freezing cold on board. Bad weather on the coast, rough seas: chug, chug, chug on.

April the twenty-seventh in Godhavn is as fair a day as ever dawned upon the Northern world. The sun shines from a cloudless sky so bright and warm that one feels spring has come at last, to stay. Just breeze enough is on the sea to make its blue most beautiful. Give us clear vision and clear days and sharp horizon lines, that we may know what's coming to us. Leaving the hilltop for the shore, I find that they have almost finished with the boat. They have taken the motor apart, and they have put it all together again; they have polished up its brass and steel and painted all the rest aluminum or red. It runs. It always did, but maybe it runs better now. Christophersen has written a report; that, with the orders, correspondence, bills, etcetera, will have its docket in the files. Everything will be on record in the files except what all the things on record were intended for: the trip to Holstensborg. But anyhow, they'll get it launched today—in time, perhaps, to run me out to meet the boat. I take my station on the hill again to watch.

Out on that calm blue plain as I sit scanning it a minute speck appears. Eyes on it constantly, I see it neither move nor grow; yet presently, incredible as its first being there, it has become more real and near. Just like the hour hand of my watch: that stood at three; and now it stands at four. Just like my life as I look back on it: one day I merely found myself to be; then I was six; then twelve; so on. Not *growing* but becoming. It is like a swift reliving of my life to watch that boat. With its appearance I am born again; the hours of the afternoon are scores of years approaching to the moment of today. I am perhaps *not* living as I watch the boat: let time go on, I've stopped. Having outrun my life I wait for it to overtake me. Interminably slow, my life; unbearable to sit and wait. Maybe they've launched the boat! I go to see.

Half of the harbor is a floor of ice. Against the edge of it is moored the Godhavn schooner, home from the walrus hunt; they are unloading heads and hides. Over against the land where the *Krabbe* had lain, men have cut a channel through to open water. Just passing out of this channel is the *Krabbe*, under power. I run out on the ice and shout and wave, but no one heeds. They sail away to greet the boat from Holstensborg.

That boat did come at last. It shot around the harbor point and headed in so swiftly I could hardly breathe. She was on deck. Next instant, so was I.

PART II

Our "Heroine between the lines" does as one does in Rome.

I. BACKGROUND

GODHAVN: the library of the Danish Arctic Station might instruct one that volumes quite enough had already been written upon the first discovery and settlement of Greenland. Yet in this chronicle of days we may perhaps occupy the day of rest that followed on the coming of the boat from Holstensborg in browsing through those histories, to send us north again with modern Greenland's background in our minds.

In the year 985 Eric the Red, an exile—first from Norway, then from the free republic of Iceland—sailed west from Iceland to a not far distant, not quite unknown land, skirted its ice-bound shore, rounded its southern point, sailed north again, and where the ice permitted came to land. The land looked good to him; it looked like home. He was a shrewd, resourceful, energetic man, a true explorer. He sailed the fiords and scanned their prospects; he staked his claim, the finest farm site in all Greenland. And giving to the new country the name that it bears today, he returned to Iceland, made atonement there, and spread the tidings of the free land in the west. Thus, almost eight centuries before our Declaration of Independence, was established the first republic of the Western world. The population came in time to number thousands. It had its parliament, its churches; a cathedral. Its bishops were appointed by the Pope at Rome. It had a literature; and we must remember that the first century of the republic of Greenland was contemporary with the great period of the literature of its mother country, Iceland, a golden age of a small state which has been compared to Periclean Athens.

Greenland resembled Iceland. It promised farm lands to the landless Iceland farmer. So farmers settled there to live and work in Greenland almost as at home. That was to be at last the death of them. Depending upon trade with Iceland and Norway for such commodities as grain and timber, submitting finally perforce to Norwegian sovereignty and to the trade monopoly that that imposed, they perished when it failed. In Norway no one cared; in Norway no one knew. For Greenland was forgotten.

Early in the eighteenth century a young Norwegian Lutheran priest, Hans Egede, interested himself, and finally the merchants and the Danish-Norwegian king, in a project for reclaiming to the fold of the church the lost and, presumably, straying Christian colonists of Greenland. A dual testament in hand he sailed; and landing in Greenland he established there in 1721, as we've already told, the beginning of the modern colonies: Trade and the Word of God: they'd do for natives, since the whites were dead.

Hans Egede was militant; he had the missionary's fervor, the trader's shrewdness, and the conqueror's tenacity. He got a foothold and he stayed. The merchants quit; the Crown got sick of it; failure tried hard to kill the enterprise, and failed. And despite the hardships of the early years and recurrent financial discouragements, the administration of modern Greenland is the lineal descendant through unbroken continuity of the spirit and the acts of the apostle Hans. It is the heir today of eighteenth-century Lutheran virtues.

Those virtues were extraordinary in their day. In an age when the great colonizing nations of the world were enslaving or exterminating the aborigines, the backers of the Greenland enterprise respected the benevolent intention of their missionary priest and worked through him to save the lives and souls and the liberty of Greenland savages. They made those savages their wards. The Greenlanders are Denmark's wards today.

Whether or not the natives had better have been left to their own primitive devices and spared the virtues of enlightenment is a purely academic question. Since white men had to come, thank God, O Greenland, for Hans Egede. His followers have weaned you kindly from your ancient ways; they've nurtured you and taught you modern life; they've reared you, set you on your feet. They've held your hand. Thank God for all of it. They hold your hand today: pray God they'll let you go. They mean so well, and cost you all so much!

The Greenland trade upon which at the inception of the missionary enterprise great hopes were reared never became consistently profitable. The entirely altruistic nature of the administration today seems to have been born of the conclusion that there was little profit to be made in Greenland anyhow, and persisted in, one may suspect, because of the good employment and substantial wages that it furnishes to an army of three hundred Danes. And while the insufficient profits on the trade today are supplemented by the generous appropriation to Greenland uses of the profits of the Greenland cryolite mine, it only swells a total the greater part of which is absorbed by Danes.

West Greenland, for purposes of administration, has been divided into two main districts: North and South; and, for missionary work and trade, into subdistricts, each with an administration center designated "Colony." The more populous of the outlying district settlements have been made trading-posts, equipped with buildings for the requirements of trade, and put under the commercial supervision of a trader. Such an outpost is Igdlorssuit. Almost all the natives are now permanently established either at Colonies or trading-posts. They have become dependent on the trade. And in the remoter waters where the hunters of the past pursued their game, the seals in droves disport themselves in unmolested freedom. The seals, at least, have profited by Progress.

Allowing for the proverbial laziness of civil servants and for the ponderous methods of conservative government routine, the Danes in Greenland are perhaps not one too many for the work entailed. But Danes, *all* whites, live well. They want good houses and good white man's food; good *pay*—for Danes don't come to Greenland for their health. Good pay, good food and homes—they get them here. And Greenland pays for it.

As one enters the harbor of Umanak one is at once impressed by the settlement's substantial, well-groomed buildings: these are the storehouses, the shops, and the residences of the Danes. There are a few native houses built of wood with gabled roofs: these are the houses of the native administration employees. There are many little turf houses, squalid enough as one draws near to them: these are the houses of the hunters. The Greenland hunter pays for all the rest. The doctor's house in Umanak is the largest residence there, an eight-room house with spacious loft, with fenced-in yards and outbuildings for stores. It faces out across an open plot of land and commands a view of the imposing distant mass of Storoen. Behind the doctor's house, just across the back yard, backed up against a cliff and facing as its view the doctor's roof and back-house, is a small, ramshackle, one-story outbuilding. This is the hospital for all the sick of all the district of Umanak.

But the outposts are the production centers of the district; their hunters bear the burden for the rest. An outpost trader's yearly earnings are not large: he gets his house, his fuel, a servant, and a salary and perquisites that total ten to twelve times the earning power of the best hunter of the settlement. The hunters pay for him, his house, his coal, his servant. They've built the house, the store, the storehouses. They pay their share of the enormous deficit of Umanak; of the North Greenland capital, Godhavn; of motorboats and schooners, and steamships; of the administration everywhere. They get for it the right to buy things at the store at nearly cost, and a school where their children learn the A B C of Greenlandish, learn to read and write, and learn about Denmark and Palestine. What use is learning to the Greenland hunter? It may be said of him as has been said of Hercules: "Rude, unrefined, only for great things good."

We shook the snow of Godhavn from our feet, and sailed for Kekertak in—*Krabbe!*

II. POOR WRETCH

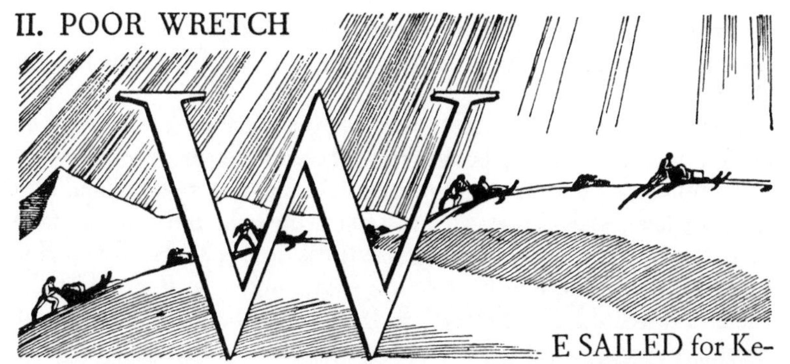

WE SAILED for Kekertak—and didn't get there. It was a mild, calm day; the sun was veiled. That afternoon a strong east wind came up; the day turned dark. Halfway across the bay we met a heavy chop; the wind and sea increased; the sky grew threatening black. We made for Ritenbenk and anchored in pitch-darkness and a gale. Thorsen was trader there: good man! He died last year. I like to read in my diary that "he welcomed us with such magnificent hospitality as we shall never forget." I can recall his wonderfully kindly way; and that, remonstrate as we would, he made us take his room.

We sailed for Kekertak again, at noon next day, and what a day! The snow was melting and running in rivulets over the naked hillsides. It was like June—that April 30; the hot sun shone down from a cloudless sky. The sea was glassy calm. Approaching Kekertak, ice blocked the way. We shoved along a mile or so; then with still seven miles to go we made up to the ice shelf and disembarked. There were four houses at the place and many people; the people flocked around and helped unload. I hired one more man and sledge to help us on to Kekertak; he hired two. I paid for all of them.

The track was not too smooth. It ran up hill and down, over bare ledges, over tumbled sea ice; and it once led us over a sheer four-foot drop off the ice shelf. I pretended that I was a good driver and Frances pretended that she wasn't afraid: thus neither upset the other. And so without mishap we came to Kekertak.

That was at six at night; at seven, in the kind Dorph's living-room, door closed, the house on tiptoe, Frances slept. She missed the dance.

She didn't miss the feast; the table-setting woke her. So at eleven we sat down and banqueted. We were to start at twelve.

Right here, at midnight, poised with loaded sledges and the dogs in harness to cross, in crossing Nugsuak, the threshold to our North, I turn, as one forgetful until now, to introduce—my wife. The introduction had to come—and yet, as writer of a book, I feared it; feared it and put it off. If this were fiction I'd be unembarrassed, I could tell the truth. If it were fiction I could let her be the heroine she was, paint her from life; she'd *be* the lines of text, not just between them. Yet now, only because we do not write about what matters most, I may only lead you out to where the sledges stand and in the almost darkness point to one. "See there, wrapped up in reindeer skins and tucked in warm? That is a young woman who has never been North like this before, who was, in fact, born and reared in Virginia, and who is quite without experience in roughing it. I only wonder what she thinks of it." She hears us; we can see the shine of her teeth as she laughs. Well—let's be off. "*Eu, eu!*" The dogs jump up, the traces strain, away we glide. "Good-by!"

We were five people on four sledges: why such a caravan I didn't know—unless Niels Dorph who'd managed it and drove one sledge had little stomach for the homeward trip alone, or didn't like to carry much; but this was Kekertak. We didn't need a guide; we did need help in carrying all our stuff. The two we hired shared a one-team load—and made hard work of it at that. Soon we were toiling up the slopes that two weeks earlier we'd coasted down. Slow work uphill, and yet the way seemed short; and daylight found us far advanced. We'd planned to be; the midnight start was made to beat the May 1 sun on Nugsuak's southern flanks. One of my dogs went lame; I turned him loose. My traces were worn out: on every good tough climb a trace or two would break. I'd lose my best dog's strength just when it counted most. But it was pleasant traveling. And at just about the time when, normally, we'd have been getting up for breakfast we were racing downhill toward the northern fiord; racing despite each driver's dragging hard with heels dug in to slow the breakneck pace. Uphill is hard, but there you stop and breathe a bit when it becomes too much. Downhill you hardly can—and don't. Mile after mile we drove downhill; and we had just come off the snow slopes on to the glare ice of the stream when I collapsed in the ludicrous agony of a thigh cramp. They almost pulled the leg off curing it. The stream ice wasn't fun. No one got hurt, but Niels capsized and soaked himself from head to foot. He changed to dry clothes at the fiord.

The fiord ice lay under three inches of water and the trotting dogs sent a continuous fine shower over us. But it was easy sledging now: a water-covered level plain of smooth glare ice. I had no need to watch my dogs, they trailed the leading team. I dozed and Frances slept. But the sledge ran upon a lump of glacier ice that suddenly canted it and rolled Frances off into the water. We had neared Ikerasak when that occurred; she drove in wide awake.

In this story of the hardships and perils of life in the Arctic it is a little disconcerting to record that when we reached Ikerasak we had as though emerged from winter time. My boat lay floating in a summer sea five miles away; we motored home. At three o'clock in the morning of May 4 we landed in bright sunshine on the ice eight miles from Igdlorssuit—we and the passengers and crew we'd brought, eleven people, seventeen dogs—hitched up, piled all we could on board two sledges, raced for home. We drove up through the sleeping settlement straight to my door. There! Walk in, Frances; here is home.

III. IM WUNDERSCHÖNEN MONAT MAI

IGDLORSSUIT in Greenland: it is so remote a place, so far out of the paths of travel, an environment so utterly different from what most people have ever seen, that all the details of its social life may be of interest. Of many common happenings I therefore write about, their wonder lying in their likeness to such happenings at home. The wonder of it all is *that:* that Greenland people—how they act and think and work and play and *are*—are wonderfully like ourselves.

Within ten minutes of our arrival, although that had been at four o'clock, people in every house were up and all soon flocking to our place to welcome us, and *drink our health*, and *see the bride.* So that while our particular social set and we sat drinking coffee in the house, a great crowd hung around outside for any glimpse of things that opening doors might yield. From coffee we passed on to schnapps and beer. More people came. The music started up. From maybe seven until noon we danced. We got an hour's sleep that afternoon. That night a dinner party and a dance; the dance broke up at four. That day we rested.

May in North Greenland is such a month in such a place that if Greenland were thrown wide open to the world—which for this very reason God forbid!—the free, rich, pleasure-seeking people of the world would swarm there. "The thrills of winter with the warmth of spring," the travel posters would proclaim. Fair days, the sunset all night long, and all that virgin world of land and sea to travel on at will. All May, some years all June, the sea ice stays.

Seals are abundant then and hunters stay abroad for days, to come home laden to their sledge's limit with the kill.

Seal-hunting on the frozen sea is a comparatively simple matter, requiring in one method, netting, almost no skill whatever and in the others no more than any active enterprising white man might acquire with a season's practice. The setting of seal nets takes place as soon as the sea ice becomes sufficiently consolidated to remove the financial risk of putting out the nets. A diagram will best explain the game. After the holes have been made—and this is done with the invaluable pike—the pike with a cord attached to it is pushed with careful aim from hole to hole, being given such impetus as to cause its unweighted end to rise up through the next succeeding hole. This takes perhaps a little skill, not much. The nets for obvious reason are set in the close vicinity of a promontory or an iceberg, or out from where new ice joins old and thicker ice. For all other hunting methods the ice may be

considered as an adjunct of a trap: the breathing-hole or open lead. The spring jaws of that trap are the armed and watchful hunter. Seals must come up to breathe; that breath of life may be their last. The finding of breathing-holes may be difficult, for they are often marked by no more than a low and almost indistinguishable dome of snow. The seal breathes underneath that dome. The hunter, having found the breathing-hole, waits there with gun or lance or pike. He waits immovable in utter silence, for the least concussion or scraping on the ice is conducted through the medium of the water to the ears of the approaching seal. But if the unsuspecting seal comes snorting up, a shot, a swift sure thrust of lance, and it's all over.

In stalking seals the hunter, keeping to leeward, may approach to within two or three hundred yards of his game without any dissimulation beyond silence; from that distance on he stalks. The seal is, strangely, one of the best imitations of man in nature. Man is, we may presume, a splendid imitation seal. At least with practice in wriggling on his belly, and spitting and snorting, and raising his head to look around, he looks like seal to seal. He looks at least more like a seal than anything not seal that seals encounter. That, to the undiscriminating seal, is quite enough. The method of approaching the seal most in use today employs the shelter of a muslin screen borne on a tiny sledge on muffled runners. Crouching or creeping behind this, the hunter makes an easy near approach. Then pushing his gun through a slit in the muslin and resting it on props arranged for that he aims and fires. Both of these methods of stalking are commonly used when the seals, lured out of water by the warm spring sun, lie dozing at their breathing-holes. Less from the seal's intention, we may assume, than from the incidental erosion of his repeated egress from the breathing-hole, the ice inclines toward the hole; and the seal lying at its very brink slips swiftly in by the slightest movement of his body. Unless the shot brings instant death the seal glides under and is lost. In the early winter season and in late spring, when there are leads of open water, the hunter takes his kayak on his sledge and, leaving his team, either paddles about in search of seal or waits patiently at the ice edge for an appearance within range. Having shot the seal, he embarks to recover it. The hunter in the springtime, off for days, sleeps only when he's tired. He lies down on his sledge, generally without a sleeping-bag or any covering besides the reindeer skin he lies on—if he has one—pulled up around his legs. A prudent thrifty man like Abraham takes a primus stove along; he has hot coffee and boiled meat. A better hunter and a shiftless man, my David, lives on seal meat—raw. Raw meat is palatable; seal liver, raw and chilled, is a real delicacy. Of work in general the world around one can't say that men like it; they like to hunt in spring in Greenland.

Five sledges of us—we were but part of all that went—set out together to attend the birthday party of Nugatsiak's catechist. There were Rudolf and Marghreta, Abraham, Louisa and the children, Martin and Salamina, Niels Nielsen, and we two. The track was good; the snow on either side of it was deep and soft. So that with Rudolf leading in a race we merely strung along in line with little chance to pass each other. I made some desperate attempts and failed, and they all laughed. Then, near Nugatsiak, all the sledges stopped. "Come," said Rudolf, "you drive ahead, we'll follow"—as much as to say: You set a value upon being first; accept the honor with our compliments. I didn't value it enough for that.

Igdlorssuit has a church, in one end of which they hold school; Nugatsiak has a schoolhouse where on Sunday they hold services. It was no sacrilege to use the school as dance house. All the youth and beauty of Nugatsiak came, many came who were neither, and enough who were plain vagabonds. It was a well-spiced, mixed affair. Benjamin, the birthday child, a foolish fellow always, now became a fool. He hopped and skipped about as erratically as a grasshopper, performing convolutions that gratified himself and upset all the rest. "See, Kinte!" he would shout, "this is the way." And whirling madly upstream he'd annihilate the dance. Olabi—a lot of gay *Igdlorssuamiut* were there—with an air of "she deserves and will appreciate a good dancer," with a pompous dignity that was no doubt intended to rebuke that silly Benjamin, gave almost his entire attention to Frances. He danced holding himself proudly erect, whirling a great deal—and skillfully, and looking the personification of conceit. His partner found his excellence a bore. The disreputable Morton was the smoothest dancer of the lot. Big Pavia was there, of course, and shone at dancing with a luster no one envied him.

The race back home next day was an event. Six sledges had an hour's start of us; our group of five set out to overtake them. We had eight dogs apiece. I had two passengers, and Rudolf led. At fifteen miles we passed a laggard; we had the bunch in sight. We caught up, trailed them for a while—it was bad going there; then Rudolf started a hard sprint. Sledge after sledge he passed with Martin following, me third, then Niels and Abraham. Drivers were shouting, whipping up their dogs; eleven racing teams were pandemonium. Five teams I passed; the sixth was close ahead. I turned out, drew abreast of it—almost—when suddenly, just crazily, that team spread out. One dog got square in front of mine; my traces caught him, threw him down. And the next instant we were halted, with the dogs and harness of both teams snarled to a knot. And while we drivers labored to undo it, Niels, Abraham, and all the line I'd passed, swept by. They had a half-mile lead when I got clear.

Again I overtook the line, passed sledges, passed the whole slow lot, got clear of them, gained on the leading four, drew close. The track near home was broad, a traveled highway; here was my chance at last. Martin and Niels drove neck and neck; I drew abreast of them. That was a race!—we three. If one would forge ahead he couldn't hold it. On my sledge was half a sack of dried capelin, dog food. Urging my dogs into a sprint, I got a moment's lead; then, standing up, I hurled the fish right at the noses of the others' dogs. That settled things. I gained on Abraham; five hundred yards from shore I drew up even with him, couldn't pass. Dead heat, we two. Rudolf was standing smoking by his house. "Good work," said he as I drove by.

One day, my sledge laden with canvases and some days' food for man and dog, I drove to Kangerdlvgsuak to camp and paint. It was bad traveling in the fiord: the melting snows were streaming from the mountain sides and inundating the surface of the ice. The way grew worse as I advanced, and I had begun to feel some concern about finding in that sheer-walled canyon a piece of dry land to halt upon—for camping on the flooded ice was not my hope—when just the site I sought appeared: a bit of gravelly foreland facing south. I got to shore, unhitched and chained my dogs, and pitched my tent.

I suppose that every man would rather be an *inventor* than anything else. One gets such a thrill from having devised the simplest original thing. I suppose that every man *is* an inventor: how, otherwise, could everything that one invents have been already patented? My sledge tent is, so far as I know, original. I take pleasure in giving to the world, unpatented and free, the best sledge tent there is. The tent, which is shown in the chapter-head drawing, is permanently attached to the sledge by the lacing of the ground cloth to the sledge floor. When not in use it is folded in upon the sledge and serves there as a covering to sit on. It consists, besides its canvas, of two slender poles—equipped with lightweight metal straps which hook over the sides of the sledge to hold the poles in place—and a slender stick for the ridge. This is attached to the canvas. Arriving at a camp site one has but to throw the load off the sledge, pull the toe of the tent forward and hook its corners to the prows of the sledge, stick up the two poles, lift up the ridge and hook it on to the poles, draw the rear eaves back tight by two ropes secured at the corners, and make fast to the stanchions. It is all done in less than a minute. Now set your primus up and light it. In three minutes more your closed tent is too hot for comfort. The tent is big enough for two; four men have spent two nights in it.

It was a fine spot where I camped. A roaring torrent filled the air with sound of spring and furnished drinking water at my doorstep. But hardly had I gotten established than there came to my ears a startling distant roar as of prolonged thunder. Aghast at it,

I stared around. Across from camp the mountain wall rose sheer to fifteen hundred feet to lose itself in cloud-veiled pinnacles. From the base of this rock wall a cloud was rising up—steam, smoke, what could it be? And as, incredulous, I stared, a mass of snow came shooting from the heights: an avalanche. The thunder followed. I looked behind me quick. No, I was safe enough from such a burial: the land receded in a gorge. It was a gloomy evening of a clouded day. I fed my dogs, cooked dinner, dined, turned in.

I woke up early by my watch. I lay and listened. There were the roar of the torrent, the sough of the wind against the tent, the gentle pattering of snowflakes on the canvas walls. I opened up the flap, peered out: the world was virgin white again; it stormed. I tied the flap, lay down again, slept on. Most of the day it stormed. My tent was rigid, tight, and warm. What could we do on such a day but sleep—I and my dogs?

Toward evening it began to clear. The snowing stopped, the wind died down, the low clouds lifted and dispersed. That feathery darling of artistic souls, the fog, drove off; stark beauty, lurid, hard, immense, high snow-topped mountain pinnacles in evening light blazed down on me. *Too* much, perhaps; but that's our littleness. I tried to paint: what foolishness!

My dogs were a confounded nuisance with their noise. There were eight of them and, hoping to keep them at peace in their confinement, I had divided them into two groups, the five Lange dogs in one, three strangers in the other. But "Niakornet," the beauty from Nugatsiak, freed from the domination of the leader's clan displayed his mettle; and there was hardly an hour of the day or night that was not made hideous by the servile yapping of the other two. Several times I was driven to turn out to beat them into quiet; and I finally provided myself with a pile of stones just within reach outside the tent. I'm now world's horizontal-stone-shot champion: that's something.

I painted in the fiord for two days more; then packed, and drove away.

There is a rare satisfaction in traveling about as I did, house, stove, food, work materials on board, all set to be at home most anywhere. A nomad's life must have great charm. And though we rate the nomad low in the scale of social progress, his life, for all we know, may be the richest in contentment. His moving is at once the reflex and the cure of discontent. Home being always where he has chosen it to be, he'll always love his home. We are all such victims of the propaganda of civilization that we unreflectingly apply its standards in the measuring of human achievement, not realizing that their validity in the only matter of real concern to man—man's happiness—is not established. I had ill-advisedly chosen to bring to Greenland with me, to be the companion of my idle hours, a four-tome work on civilization by the learned Dr. Pangloss, of Yale. The Doctor, surveying from his armchair this best of all possible world's (Capitalism!), judges civilization by standard of living, and defines that, properly, in terms of *things*. Throughout the pages of his dreary work—prepared, one thinks, to fit young bankers' sons to oppose the French Revolution—we are allowed no thought that spiritual values count, no thought that anything may count but property; except —I quote a line of it in gratitude—one definition (by Petrie; Smithson. Rep. 1895, 591): "Civilization really means simply the art of living in a community." That does imply in peace and happiness.

But by no accepted definition could I, out camping on the ice alone, be classed as civilized. So for the information of the future student of the *true* problem let me record that I was extremely comfortable and contented for days; and that if there had been all of me along we'd have stayed on until the end of May; and then, just as it happened when we did, have barely gotten out alive.

That *was* almost a bad experience, the last trip that we took, the coming home. We had been spending some days in Nugatsiak, living in that chapel-dance-hall-schoolhouse, working, strolling about in the warm, fair out-of-doors, the outdoor universe, the *sila* of the Greenlanders. Summer was making, fast; the sea ice was a shallow pond, and all along the shore a river. We'd watch the dog teams swim across; it was a small adventure getting on and off the ice. Then one day people said to us, "If you don't go home now you won't get out of here until next summer." "All right," I said, "we'll start tonight."

If they had only not, in the meantime, told Frances a lot of tales about how bad it was—the ice and everything! I guessed that it was bad, but there is nothing gained by telling all you know. We'd lingered in the hope of colder nights and days. They just got worse. The day we started was, till noon, the hottest of the year; then it got raw and cold. Not cold enough to freeze, just clouded, mean, uncomfortable; a southwest wind came up. We packed and loaded down the sledge; we had a lot of gear, of canvases and camping stuff. "I hope you won't mind," said Frances, "if I'm a little frightened on this trip."

The track to Igdlorssuit was well marked by the ridge its hard-packed surface made above the melting plain; it was well buoyed by bergs, familiar landmarks after many trips. "Don't go that way," the wise men said. "Head out to sea an hour or more, then bear left for Igdlorssuit." We did as we were told. At six o'clock we harnessed up, said good-by to our friends, and drove away. The ice, surprisingly, was firm and dry. "Why, this is fine," cried Frances, nestling back. There was a bank of fog ahead. My back, I thought, won't give my fears away.

An hour passed; the fog rolled up, dense, black. I took last bearings of the sun and wind and land, and entered it.

If the ice had continued to be firm, if, as people had predicted, it had improved as we went seaward, I'd have had no worry. The fog was thick; it shut out all the land and swallowed everything beyond a hundred yards; we couldn't see the sun nor, most times, any sign of western brightness; but the wind blew steadily. The hitch was that the ice from good got bad, from bad got worse. It was a sea, at last, and only islanded with slush; I had to pick our route where ice allowed. Thus, deviating continually from a true course, leaving no tracks behind us in the wetness, I could only guess at the resultant, realizing that in such blind dead reckoning error will compound as fast as fact. The wind blew strong enough to raise a chop; the wavelets splashed against the sledge. "Rough night at sea," I said by way of cheer to Frances.

Driving on in the increasing gloom, picking my way through the morass of slush, driving in water that all but submerged the sledge, avoiding, dreading, deeper holes that showed up all around, suddenly without a warning to my eyes the dogs plunged in. They swam. I dug my heel in, jumped and gripped the stanchions, straining back. Right at the brink the sledge fetched up. "Oh, my God!" said Frances fervently. It was the only time through all that happened on that night that Frances prayed aloud.

Meanwhile the dogs were swimming, all eight dogs abreast. They climbed out on a reef of ice ten feet away. I called a halt. We had turned the sledge; with Frances guarding that, I pulled the dogs back one by one. We drove away from that, and quick.

We had gone but a little way when we came into the very midst of what I'd striven hardest to avoid: a nest of icebergs. The ice near bergs in thawing weather is always bad and often dangerous. The breaking up, the calving of the larger bergs, litters the ice with fragments that depress the surface and invite the surrounding meltage to its pools. In spring the water pours off bergs in rivulets. Dogs like the bergs. Even with the best of sledging conditions, when the surface of the snow is hard and dry, dogs, as though aggravated by the monotony of the level sea plain will make for near-by bergs, if given half a chance, as thirsty desert travelers, we read, stampede for an oasis. My dogs that day after hours of wallowing and swimming were desperate to "land." I'd given all the bergs a good wide berth, and used the whip to do it. And now we'd driven in the twilight murk of fog right into them. They broke. Plunging through water, reckless of everything and us, they rushed that berg, and made it. So there we were, all safely islanded. The thought of staying there did come to me. We had the tent and food and fuel; we could have camped. But we were soaking wet and cold, the wind was bitter. Besides, who knew what change for worse the hours might bring? No, we'd go on. But how?

I went exploring with the pike. The ice at best, I found, was but a sodden shell over fresh-water depths that at their worst would drown a man, and easily might drown the sledge and load. I sounded some holes with my pike and found no bottom. There was no good way off the berg; the choice lay between bad and worse. I chose. I whipped the dogs, reluctant now to move, and drove out into it. We hadn't gone a hundred yards before the dogs broke through to swim again. So much for judgment: now to hell with it! Drive on. We plunged, broke through, dragged out again, wallowed and splashed; drove on. We *did* get through. That murky plain, a sea with archipelagos of slush, became—we hardly realized the change at first—a continent of slush with lakes and ponds. And presently the dull-gray slush grew pale, then white; we rode upon firm snow. The dogs for joy of it lit out.

We had been driving some points off the wind; I wanted to keep off, for the drainage of the melting snow of our island would affect the ice for perhaps a mile or more from land. Most dogs will stubbornly keep off, even when headed home. They hate to face the wind. My dogs kept working into it. "*Eu, eu! Eu, eu!*" (keep left): that was my conversation as we drove. I had noticed soon after the fog had inclosed us that several of the dogs were from time to time looking back and upward over their right shoulders. They'd look, then settle down to work again. It was a definite, repeated, noticeable act: the quarter of the sky they looked at held the sun. It was some time before I realized that the windward course that they perversely sought was the direct course for Igdlorssuit. I believe that left to their own guidance they would have carried us straight there. I must add that the dogs, strangers until that winter to Igdlorssuit, had never before traveled within many miles of the route we that day followed. I spoke of it to Rudolf the next day. "Yes," said Rudolf, "good dogs know."

At the rate we were now going we should in half an hour bear southwesterly and head straight for the settlement. A sledge track crossed our course. The dogs, usually eager to follow any track, raced over it without a look. I had no doubt that they now knew the ice they traveled on, though, except the sledge track, I had seen no mark that might distinguish it. They raced; they'd slow up wallowing through puddles; then race on. They scented home, perhaps; we almost did. A black line showed across the snow ahead of us, across our path: a lead; a narrow one, not more than five feet wide it proved—thank God! You take a small lead on the run; dogs brought up slowly to it balk. I tapped my boot for speed and moved up forward on the sledge. The dogs all leaped, and made it, all but one; the sledge with undiminished headway followed them. The bows shot out across, dropped down and bridged the gap. The dogs, recovered from the spring, bent to the traces; the sledge moved on; the stern slipped off—and sank. Of course it sank with two-thirds of the load stowed aft. The rearing sledge bows stopped the dogs.

Things happen quickly at a time like that, things happen without thought. Frances was suddenly on the ice beside me pulling with all her strength. We pulled, I urged the dogs ahead. Between us all we drew the dripping sledge across. "Bad place," I said as we drove on. Frances said nothing.

A mile, as it turned out, from home we came upon an old sledge track that now stood up high and dry like a Roman road across the slushy plain. That led, all knew it now, to home. Soon land appeared; we passed out from behind some bergs and saw the settlement; the settlement saw us. And people thronged the shore, for it was Sunday night. Sit back, Americans, look nonchalant. I tapped my boot; the dogs lit out. We crashed across the shore ice, and were home.

Not midnight yet? Come in, dear friends, come in. We made a night of it till four.

IV. A BIRTHDAY

WE NEAR the end of May: the end of ice, the end of winter, and—a birthday. The Greenland custom of celebrating one's own birthday can only have been engendered by the prevailing unconcern about each other. Each has one day a year to make his neighbors notice him; each is a nobleman one day. Noblesse oblige: the measure of his obligation is his means.

The birthday party of Frances—and *she* was only giving it to the extent of slaving side by side with Salamina at the stove—was to be a tremendous affair; that was expected. Coffee and cake for all the settlement, and beer; a dinner party at the house; a public dance. A dance in that vile pesthole of a cooperage? No. Wait.

We stumble now upon a matter that, born of goodness as a happy thought, was to grow and grow to be at last an *issue* that involved the public, trader, Manager, and Chief Magistrate, that was to be laid before the Director in Copenhagen, and on which documents should be at last prepared, transmitted, and reported on, and filed in triplicate, and be the great concluding act of the small drama of our Greenland stay. It brings in, I am sorry, Trolleman.

For in the moment that I had the thought, far back in March, I waited on his Majesty and broached it. "It is too bad," said I, approaching the subject as tactfully as possible, "that the fine, good people of Igdlorssuit, who love to have good times and dance, have no *big* place to dance in. Don't you think so?"

"I do," said Trolleman. "Yes, Mr. Kent, I do. It *is* a shame, Mr. Kent, it is."

"Now then," said I, "it has occurred to me that we might give them one, we two. Let's build a dance house for the people."

Trolleman beamed. "The very idea, Mr. Kent," said he, "that I've had right along. I'll build these people here a house, I've said, *give* them a house. They want a place to dance. I'll give them one, I said. You see, Mr. Kent, when I was in East Greenland—now that was in, let's see . . ."

"Well, how about it?" I asked gently as, half an hour later, he concluded. "Will you chip in? Pay part with me?"

He looked surprised, a little shocked. "Now, Mr. Kent, now wait," said he, "now wait. You see now, Mr. Kent, not now. You see, I'll maybe go to Denmark in the summer or next year. No, Mr. Kent, I wouldn't do it now. You see . . ."

"I think I will," said I.

And so it happened that, beginning back in March, the people got to talking more and more about the dance house that they were to have, and even in their thoughts to see it standing on the spot they'd picked for it. It was a perfect spot: central, and as a former house site, occupied until two years before by Johan Lange, graded and dry and furnished ready-made for us with a concrete foundation. And if title to the old site had been needed its former owner made it ours by gift. On the auspicious morning of Decoration Day we laid the sills; the whole crowd helped. The floor, the dancing floor, was done, complete, that night. We put up posts and roped it like a prize ring. Now for tomorrow's bout!

The birthday was as beautiful as one could pray for, cloudless and mild. The sun that hadn't set moved round as though to bless all sides of everything. If we had had a house above that floor we should have wanted for that day to take it down. Need is an element of happiness, or premise to it; and Paradise should be just cold enough to make the Blessed need the sun. Just—cold—enough; like Greenland on that thirty-first of May.

The Blessed should be poor enough to need its fruits, to need the fruits of Paradise as all the people needed cake and coffee that May afternoon. And starved enough for sport to find the meadows of asphodel as good to dance on as pine boards. Yes, take it all in all, God might do worse for us than patterning the Promised Land on *lat.* 71° 15′ *N.*, *lon.* 53° 20′ *W.*, as it was on the thirty-first of May in 1932. All that bright night the thunder of the dancers' feet went on; in that, at least, the festival was heavenly.

Trolleman came out of his way to speak to me next day. "That dance house," said he, "can't be there. It is against the law."

"What law?" I asked.

"The administration's law that no private building can be put up within twenty paces of an administration building."

"What building is this near?" I asked, surprised.

"That storehouse," and he pointed. "You can't put up that dance house where it is."

Where Trolleman had pointed sprawled an ancient, largely ruined, sort of cave man's edifice—if that could be; a crumbling, gloomy, swamp-floored artificial cavern; a remnant, travelers might guess, of eighteenth-century whaling days. Low, sunken, tottering ramped walls of turf inclosed a piece of ground. Rough boards lay sagging over it to form a roof. A picturesque old pile, or eyesore to the place, as one might please. They used it still to store the barreled fat in; it matched the cooperage. Near it, well within the twenty paces of the law, stood the houses of Rudolf and Jonas. For ten years Johan Lange's house had stood where we had now begun to build. No one, it seemed, had ever thought before that that old store shed was a building; no one, till Trolleman. Well, people talked and, in their gentle manner, damned his eyes. We'll wait, I thought, and see the Magistrate.

But May—let's finish that. It isn't midnight yet, and its dramatic happening was then.

Old Emanuel, the proud and lusty grandson of an angakok, was far from finished with his hunting days; in springtime he grew young again and hunted with the best. When men *could* travel on the ice, Emanuel did, the first to start, the last to leave it in the spring. So, at about the time of our adventure in the fog, Emanuel set out with sledge and dogs, and a similarly equipped young companion, to hunt the seal off Svartenhuk. He had been away but a day or two when there came a big blow from the eastward: the rotten ice broke off for miles and sailed away to sea. With little hope of finding any trace of Emanuel and the boy, men searched the ice edge and the shore of Svartenhuk. Their fruitless search confirmed all fears: the fine old man, the boy, were gone.

There was at this time a distinguished visitor at Igdlorssuit, the fair painter, the gifted carver of ivory, the well-read, cultivated, charming pastor of Umanak, the Greenlander Otto Rosing. So to this priest I went, spoke of the lamented loss of Emanuel, and asked if it would be permitted me to erect a cross in the graveyard to his memory. It would; he thanked me for the thought. I made a study of the cross on paper.

"Eight days ago he left," said someone at our birthday feast. We raised our glasses, drank "Emanuel!" It was just midnight then. Tobias, our small chore boy, here came in. "Emanuel," he said, "is back."

When Emanuel came in—we sent for him, of course—the old pagan was grinning all over. "Here, Emanuel," I said, "pour out your own," and I set a bottle of rum before him. He was all right next day. I showed him the design I'd made; he liked it.

Whether for that cross in the graveyard or a drink of rum, he hitched his dogs again and drove away to hunt. He stayed three days, but nothing happened. I poured his rum myself—one jigger full. We're just as stingy with our earthly joy as they with theirs in Heaven.

V. CHARLOTTA DIES

THERE had been but one death on the island during the past fall and winter, that of a middle-aged woman long a sufferer from tuberculosis. That her death was imminent, all knew; yet when one bitter, gloomy January afternoon there appeared a huddled procession of dark figures crossing the snow field to the church, and I, going up to it, saw that they were carrying a bier, it was a shock. She had been alive an hour ago; one hour in that mortuary shed would freeze her stiff. Death is two-fisted in the North.

They're used to Death. They travel, hunt, and live with Death familiarly at hand. Death knocking at the door? He's in the bed with them. They know that presence, and are used to it. In 1860 (they are the only figures that I have at hand) 42 per cent of the inhabitants of Greenland were under fifteen years of age; 55 per cent were between fifteen and sixty; 2 per cent were over sixty; and 1 per cent unknown. If grief at death endured they'd all have died of it.

Old Charlotta, the mother of Olabi, had weathered one more period of darkness and come through into the light again, but she was weakening fast. One night in early June her old heart fluttered, stopped; and one more relic of the past was gone.

A funeral in Greenland is for everyone; the people fill the church. Across two trestles in the aisle is laid the bier; on it that hastily constructed box, the coffin. The coffin lid is off. Under a white cloth lies what is left of old Charlotta; it is huddled up, and very small. When the ceremony is over the bearers convey the bier out of doors, and set it on the ground; the people stand around, they are about to see Charlotta. The cloth is folded back. The people, children, all, crowd up to stare. It is a gruesome, grinning spectacle, Charlotta's face. There is silence: not even from Olabi who stands there head hung down, and weeping, comes a sound. They are waiting for him. Olabi steps up, and without flinching looks long and earnestly at the remains of the only woman who will ever have loved him in all his life. He stoops and lays on her breast a little bunch of paper flowers. As Olabi steps back they put the lid in place and nail it down. That has finality.

It is a long rough climb to the hilltop graveyard; not all go up. A few devoted friends, a few who like to sing, a few just curious, and Olabi—alone.

Charlotta is not to be interred this day; the frozen ground forbids the digging of a grave. For such a contingency—if that may be called a contingency which is the rule—there is a stone heap on a rocky knoll, a bed of stones left open by the last departed sleeper there. Here is Charlotta laid. They pile the stones upon her, carefully, the men and boys; they smother her with stones. Then, standing there, the people sing.

Chilled to the bone—the wind is blowing on the hilltop—the people hurry home. Dogs have been prowling round. When the last man has gone, the dogs come up and nose the stone heap.

The Christian burials are hardly different from the Greenland burials of pagan times. The reverent treatment of the dead, the handing on for nature to complete destroying that which it had made, the handing back to God, intact, of what God gave, is natural to man. The ground adjacent to the old Moravian stations in Greenland is honeycombed with rock-walled, rock-roofed graves through the interstices of which one peers at de-articulated human skeletons. These are all Christian graves. And they only differ from the pagan graves which are found all over Greenland in that they are of one chamber instead of two and, to judge from those that I have seen, less well constructed. In the antechamber of the pagan graves are found many little tributes to the spirit of the departed, which were often fashioned with care and skill, and which are of such substance—wood and ivory and bone—as time might not too easily destroy. Are Christian floral tributes evidence of frail belief in immortality?

All die, and all were born. And whatever, Christian or pagan, may have been the ceremonials adorning birth and death, the living flesh and blood was much the same.

The Greenlanders with "christenings" play safe. The little child that is put into the arms of the catechist or pastor to receive its Christian name has already had its pagan from the midwife. She is the pagan priest; and at the significant moment of the breaking off of the umbilical remnant she has named the child in Eskimo. "Karl Tobias Paulus," had murmured a solemn catechist over the mewling man child of Charlotta. But *she* had named him, as all people call him: Olabi.

nd here is Olabi, gamboling
s was his fancy.

VI. HIGH TIMES

Houses similar to this one on Schades Island are erected and maintained at public expense for the convenience of hunters

AND one day Jakob, the boy that Trolleman had picked on and got punished for, got into a boat and, with two little girls as companions, rowed down the shore to hunt for birds' eggs on the cliffs. They found a place, and came to land. There, leaving the girls to mind the boat, Jakob scrambled over the bowlders that lined the shore, and began to climb: the nesting ledges were far up. Jakob didn't get to them. He had climbed about forty feet when something happened: his foot slipped, or the piece of ledge that he stood on or that his hands gripped crumbled—these basalt rocks are bad—; something went wrong up there: he fell. It looked to the girls as though he fell very slowly; he turned, fell horizontally with arms spread out. He landed on the rocks, and lay draped over them.

I don't know how the little girls got Jakob to the boat. He was a heavy boy, and limp and cumbersome to drag. They did it somehow. They even got him into the boat, down in the bottom at the bow. They pushed the boat off—that was hard; and they rowed back to the settlement.

A great crowd of people stood around us as we worked on Jakob. No one seemed so much concerned as curious, and none of Jakob's family was in evidence to help. The boy was alive, but unconscious. We couldn't tell just what had not been broken. We bound him to a plank; that kept him rigid. Meanwhile the crew had gone aboard my boat; the torch was roaring. We carried Jakob out, sending for covers, and a feather bed to lay the plank on. I had to *order* Jakob's family to produce the bed. No member of his family embarked with him. In just eight hours he was at the hospital in Umanak. Within a month he died.

Picking birds' eggs on the cliffs is an established industry in season. All sea birds' eggs are food for man; all good eggs that I've eaten taste good. Cliff-climbing is but another of the many hazards in a Greenland hunter's life. We gathered eggs—but not on cliffs.

North of Ubekjendt Ejland is a little group of low, grass-covered islands to which in laying-time each year the people of Igdlorssuit, or such as had the means to travel there, would go egg-gathering. We planned to take a boatful of our friends, and spend two days. So when the Chief Magistrate . . . *What! Can't you even pick up birds' eggs in Greenland without* . . . *Yes, certainly you can. But wait a minute. This is about our dear friend Rudolf whom we wanted to take with us.* . . . So when the Chief Magistrate came to Igdlorssuit we asked him if Rudolf Quist, the cooper, who was always weeks ahead with his work, and who hadn't had a weekday off in two years, could take two days and go with us. For Trolleman, we told him, had said no. And the Magistrate was fine about it. He said he would make inquiries, and take the matter under consideration, and see what could be done, and that I would hear about it. And sure enough the matter was looked into and reported upon favorably; so that in the course of time the Manager in Umanak received a communication from the capital that caused him to communicate with Trolleman, that brought him to give Rudolf two days off. It may be said that not a sparrow falls in Greenland but foolscap, triplicate, records it.

And the Chief Magistrate was fine about the dance house; fine to me, and fine to Trolleman. He told us he'd look into the matter, give it thought, and see what could be done; and I guess he told Trolleman the same thing. And he told him last. We could see them from our window, the Magistrate sedate, the trader wild-eyed, frantic, pacing off the meters with his bandy legs. We thought he scared the Magistrate a bit. Anyhow, the Magistrate came back to the house and tried to sell me the idea of a piece of distant side-hill bog for the building. It wasn't good. "Well," said the Magistrate, "I'll give it thought." He piped his crew, stepped into the stern sheets of his pinnace, and, erect as an admiral, the sun sparkling from the gold and crimson epaulets, the gilt and pearl and nickel sword, the brass buttons, the breeze waving the skirts of the policeman's frock, and everyone merely smiling just a little bit, was rowed aboard.

The day, soon after Rudolf's permit came, that we set sail for eggs was made for prettier work than robbing nests. It was quite unimaginably lovely; and the low islands were as though set in its very midst, so open to the eye was the whole hemisphere of the heavens. There was just breeze enough to add a briskness to the air and wave the island meadows.

With twelve on board we almost swamped the skiff in scrambling to be first ashore. It might have been a gold rush by the wild excitement of our search for nuggets in the grass; and many must have been the eggs we missed before our eyes had grown accustomed to their near-invisibility in their environment. The air was filled with screaming birds by whose telltale distress we merely profited. A heartless business, robbing nests; but fun.

We combed the smaller islands first, and then, near evening, came to anchor in a sheltered cove of the largest island and went ashore to camp and spend the night. It was a perfect camping site: fresh water for our needs, luxuriant meadow grass to lie on; and, for those who wanted the luxuries of civilization—and several of the people did—a turf house with its sleeping-platform. We pitched a tent; and while the women built and tended a sweet-smelling fire of scrub brush, and prepared the feast, the men lay back and, tipping bottles up against the sky, prepared their spirits for the festival. The fragrance of the evergreen, the taste of beer, the goodness of good women who indulge men's idleness! It was a happy feast: we stuffed on scrambled eggs, drank beer, then danced. Elisabeth, the slightly aged wife of dapper Jonas, clucked.

One must have heard Elisabeth to know that one can dance to

clucking, that one can cluck in time, and loud, and keep it up; a sweet accomplishment. And Jonas jigged. They got us laughing so that, finally, *that* got Elisabeth. The orchestra collapsed from laughter, not fatigue. The new day had begun before we sought our lairs. The tent, a big one, was the women's choice. I found a nest of long rank grass the softest bed I'd slept upon for months.

That day we gathered eggs again, broke camp, and sailed for home. Such are high times in Greenland.

VII. HIGH LATITUDES

OUT of nothing at all, are good times had in Greenland life; that may be typical of happy living everywhere. In this story, which aims to be no more than a record of everyday life in Greenland, we can't drag in adventure by the heels. Adventures happen, sometimes; it is their rarity that gives this life its character. Despite the hazards of the hunter's work, the rule is uneventfulness; and people thrive in it. They live in peace, and peace, I think, means happiness. A bitter thought to us Americans! And an unacceptable thought to the spirit of our time. Yet we must realize that by our principles, our standards and ideals, by that we *call* our symptoms that, we only display ourselves as victims, playthings, of an evolutionary law termed Progress. Our masses lack—all masses must—the power of abstract thought. Our leaders lack it, all men do: there's no such thing. Uncage imagination, set it free, and it can soar no higher than the topmost twig of its familiar shade tree. Environment: its forces are as insidiously penetrating as the pressure of the atmosphere. Progress: its weight is 14.7 lbs. per inch.

Progress is premised upon discontent. What that drives man to do makes history; its high awards, with us, are love and honor. Our title to the prize we prove by discontent with it. Progress: we know that game; on Happiness we're not authorities.

Neither, for that matter, are the Greenlanders; they're not, today, the nature children that they were two centuries ago. They have unrest, they *want*. And of so glittering an aspect is even the first tentative advance of Progress that it casts into gloom all that which had been light before. The best men, strangely, fall for it, the men of energy. And by abandoning contentment to the weak and spiritless they cast discredit on the past where it survives today. Where Progress is, there lack of it is vile. It is, then, but the contentment of the least contented that I envy, the relative peace of those potentially equipped for Progress but living, by the grace of chance, away from most of it.

Illusive, indefinable, as happiness may be, it must submit to a pragmatic estimate. We should observe its tongue and pulse, test man for what it does to him. And if, as we may hope, it is the cause or symptom of a better manhood, we may on that criterion relate it to degrees of Progress as these are displayed from south to north in Greenland. Progress began at Godthaab in 1721. Thirty-seven years later it came to Umanak, and thirteen years after that to Upernivik. It is said in Greenland that the farther you go from the colonies, the better you will find the people; and it is said that the more northerly people are the best.

I may not, however, claim that it was with any thought of investigation along this line that we made excursions from Igdlorssuit north. We went to see the country; I, to paint. Summer travel in Greenland, merely sailing along the coast or climbing hills to look abroad, is, like egg-picking, one of those essentially uneventful pleasures which, in the degree of their uneventfulness, are both more memorable and least to be described. Yet having come so far together, we and you, let's see our Greenland.

Icebergs: the mouth of Karrat Fiord was filled with them—huge, floating, cliff-bounded tablelands, triumphal arches that small fleets could sail through, incredible top-heavy shafts, and Gothic pinnacles, a visual fantasia in ice. Ice forms are unimaginably varied, so many forces are at work on them: the sea—its waves and tides—the sun, the force of gravity. I've studied them to find a structural principle: they have no principle. Paint what you please, let your imagination play: the thing itself surpasses you. Their structural limit is their breaking-point. My, it was beautiful that day we started north! There was a northeast wind, a good fresh breeze; the sea was indigo, and flecked with white-caps: blue sea, and ice. Don't say that ice resembles jade or crystal quartz; say, if you like, in reckless praise of *these* that they're like ice—so beautiful. Ice is the absolute. We sailed through ice till in the lee of Svartenhuk.

We saw a walrus there; fooled round a while to get in range of him, but couldn't manage it. Sailed on.

Northwards from Svartenhuk's south shore for fifty miles or so the country changes character. Above low bluffs that line the shore are rolling moors; the bluffs, as one goes north, decline and yield to broad low-lying flats of shale or meadow land. The distances are great, the scale is large; large and monotonous. Such was the setting of the port we made that night at one, the trading-post, Söndre Upernivik.

All world's-end settlements attract adventurers; they offer one more chance, the last. To the fantastic stories about Kleeman I, unfortunately, listened with but half an ear. His name—I think the German government established that—was taken, with credentials, from the pockets of a German slain in the Schleswig or the Franco-Prussian war. He claimed high lineage. "That man," he said once, pointing at a picture of Pasteur, "is my uncle." (Or his grandfather or his mother's uncle, I don't recall.) Anyhow, Kleeman got to Greenland, got a post there, married there, begat at least one son; there died. And of our port that night, Kleeman, the son, was king. He rowed out to the boat to welcome us.

He was a gentle little man, kindly, and a bit forlorn. Seeing him later at his house playing the fiddle to his little son's accordion, we got to think of him as like an old Italian organ-grinder down at heel. The little child that played was blue-eyed and ash-blond, a small child for his years, and pale. He sat with dangling legs, the big accordion strapped over him, and played with the assurance and the skill of an accomplished adult. I think that we shall never forget the loveliness of that child's face as he sat playing there, nor his smile when now and then he'd look and meet our eyes. It was almost a tearful scene, that sad old half-breed fiddler and his blue-eyed son. The family was sad, the house; futile, it seemed, dispirited, the lot of them. And very kind to us.

The whole place was forlorn: we wondered how the people kept alive. They barely did. Most of them dressed in almost rags, and lived in squalid, dirt-walled huts. We met the only beggars that I've seen in Greenland. The settlement is not well spoken of. The people lock their doors. One wonders what a thief could steal. And yet despite its reputation and its dirt, we liked the place for Kleeman's sake. We promised to come back. Next day we sailed on, north.

From there on, northwards, the character of the whole coast changed. Low bluffs became huge cliffs, hills became mountains. "Beautiful!" said our crew, staring at it. "Beautiful!" said we. "Beautiful!" would have cried the traveler from the steppes of Russia or the pampas of the Argentine, or the Tyrolean or Tibetan mountaineer. Mountains have power absolute to thrill. The vertical: *that* is significant to man.

For we are, generically, not only the products of environment in its more palpable manifestations—earth, water, air, the climate, food, the general and particular exigencies of life—but, in a more subtle sense, of cosmic principle as it prevails about us and in all of these. We *are:* in flesh and blood what mundane life has made us; in our senses what the esthetics of our world have made them; and in our brains—rationalizers. "Great things are done when men and mountains meet." I'd like to make that rational, know *why*. (*Good Lord, what now! Why this? Why that? Why is the ocean wet—or flat? Why . . .*) The ocean is flat because water seeks its own level, and, being fluid, gets there. All things inert or live incline that way. "The lone and level plain" of Ozymandias is—death, oblivion, the end and norm of everything. And such a factor upon earth is the relentless urgence of gravity toward *that* that one might define the evolution of organic life as an age-long striving to attain the vertical. Sit up, we tell our young; stand up, stand straight; be upright all your life. How from the vertical, from up and down, we take our terms of praise: a *lofty* mind, *deep* thoughts, *high* purposes. How, in return for these, we praise the mountains as we praise our kings: grand, noble, splendid, and magnificent. God we have put on high. Our spires and pinnacles reach up. God's mountains have moved *us;* may ours, we pray, move God.

God's mountains of the region of Umanak, the cliffs and mountains north, from 72° 10′ to the inmost corner of northern Nugsuak's northern shore at 74° 20′, or thereabouts—I've been no farther north—are worth a pilgrimage. Why don't men in a godless age go worship mountains? We did, the lot of us, those days up north.

A virtue consequent to mountain awfulness is the rare affection that one feels among them for the occasional small human settlement. If these but come a little way to meet our thoughts, just *look* the promise of security and warmth and homely comfort, our grateful thoughts endow them with all lowly comfortable virtues. And what *we* look for, those who built their homes there sought: a sheltered spot, a sheltered anchorage, a shelter, maybe, from immensity.

As we neared Tasiussak it was blowing hard. We'd had a long day's run, and it was evening; and the wind was cold. We sailed in through a narrow, steep-walled gateway in the land, and came to anchor in a pond as calm, as utterly removed from wind and sea, as any hidden forest pool. We needed shelter, and we found it there. We stayed some days at Tasiussak, for it stormed. And liking so its very aspect of security, camped insecurely high upon a windy spot to look at it.

There was one other lovely place like that: our farthest north. We put in to visit the advance party of an American expedition that was to winter there; dropped in to call on strangers, and found an old friend Schmeling, from Ann Arbor. Their camp was in a pass between the heads of two fiords, a valley hardly more than one mile long. One saw both waters from its crest. Straight in the view across the southern fiord lay a broad glacier, its ice cliffs and serrated plain a dazzling spectacle that sunlit day. A lovely place: God spare me its November gales!

Two storm-bound days at Kraushavn, five hours homeward from our "farthest north." We *tried* to sail, but had hardly left the harbor when a snow squall hit us. With tail between our legs we scurried back. The next day's clear-up proved worth waiting for.

The Northern scene, besides being illuminated at so low an angle that long shadows cast its forms into singular prominence, besides the stark intrinsic grandeur of those forms, besides the contrast that is present between level ocean plain and towering mountains, has one unique attribute that makes it stirring as no Temperate scene can be: that is its ice. Picture a Temperate sea and mountain view: Clear day, late afternoon in fall; blue sea, and golden-purple shadowed land, and pale-blond lower sky; purple to gold, pale light to deep-toned madder. Now, into that, like a shaft of sunlight into a lamplit room, like violins and flutes above the bass, high-pitched, ethereally pure, so clean, sharp, dazzling that it almost hurts, see ice appear. The pale-gold sky is somber now; sea, sky, and land are of one low tonality against which *sings* that poignant whiteness.

On the southwest of Kugdlerkorsuit Island, a short day's run south of Kraushavn, is a mountain peak that has achieved that basic structural form, the pyramid, which mountains, one believes, aspire to. Across a little bay from that fine peak lies a low point of land, and there we camped. We took a tent and sleeping-bags ashore, a little cooking-gear, some food, my paints and canvases; and having, fortunately, neglected to take on petroleum at Kraushavn, sent the boat back north. An hour later, tent up, new wash strung on a line, all things in order at the camp, Frances sitting in the sun, I painting on the shore, one would have thought we'd been established there all summer. The tent site was a level, mossy piece of fill among the ledges; a rain pool was at hand to wash in, a cold clear rill to drink; the mountain peak to look at, and the sun for warmth. The sun? While we rejoiced in it the shadow of a mountain at our backs stole over us, a chill wind blew. The shelter of the tent, the primus warmth, hot food, were good. The sky that evening became veiled with cloud.

Next day was ominous of storm: the hills were dark against a livid lemon-colored lower sky; above the band of light dark clouds hung low. I had hardly begun to work when rain squalls came; by afternoon the rain was falling steadily. It was blowing hard. By night it had become a gale.

Tent pegs are of little use in Greenland; the ledges and the stony soil prohibit them. But rocks are plentiful: they serve as anchors for the guys and to weight down the ground flap with which the Greenland tent must be provided. A storm in prospect, we must by night have piled a half a ton on ours. My canvases I stacked outdoors, face up to shed the downpour from their painted mountain sides; stacked them and weighted them. If pictures can't stand rain and sun we'd better find it out. All things secured, we sat with the primus roaring out its warmth, and waited. Whew, but it blew! The light-weight canvas flapped as though each moment it would go to shreds. The weight of wind —southeast—against that gable end surpassed belief. The tent pole bent, bent like a long bow drawn to the shoulder, snapped. Down came the tent, the whole of it. I barely saved it from the burning primus. I propped the canvas up somehow, and with a spare stick spliced the broken pole; we raised the tent and made it fast. We lugged more stones. That done, we turned in dressed; we feared the worst; it came.

It must have been about one o'clock when, without diminishing velocity, the wind veered to the southwest. Well, let it blow, I thought, it can't get worse. The noise was deafening: behind the turmoil of the canvas was the roar of breakers. We dozed from weariness in spite of it.

Then something happened. I emerged into consciousness to find Frances holding up the dripping canvas which had fallen on us. The other pole had broken. The storm was at its worst now, wind and sheets of rain. No matter, up and into it. I spliced that pole, rigged center guys to stiffen it, lugged half a ton more rock;

repaired the wreck; stripped off my saturated clothes, and found the still warm reindeer bag like Heaven. That day, by ten, the storm was past.

When at seven that night the boat returned for us a heavy surf was running on the shore. The boat stood off while Peter in the little dinghy tried to land: impossible. We finally conveyed our gear out on to a projecting ledge that stood up sheer three feet above the surf; and from there, when an inrushing sea swept the dinghy within reach, threw in some things. Thus, little at a time, we moved aboard. We had one minor mishap: it required a moment's time to stow the canvases athwart the dinghy's bows; that was too much. And the next instant the dinghy was whirling in a maelstrom of white water, and the canvases were swimming. We saved the canvases and Peter saved the boat. It is good manners, and perhaps good art, that when a painter's works at last make their début they should display no sign upon their well-groomed countenances of what their trials have been.

And there are
lots like her!

VIII. DECLINE AND FALL

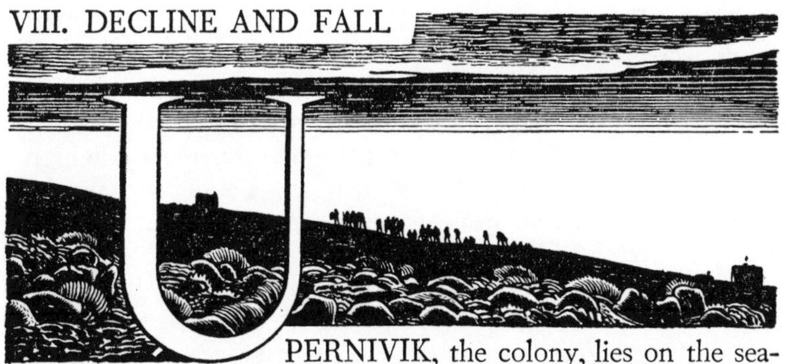

UPERNIVIK, the colony, lies on the seaward extremity of a small, outlying island. Beginning at the ship's harbor on one side of a rocky promontory, it straggles across for half a mile or so to the store and the administration's residences on the other. The settlement is dominated by the church, which, standing like a robed and mitered bishop on the hillside, looks down upon its squalid, lowly pauper flock. Next in splendor to the church is the doctor's residence, a large, ornate pseudo-Norwegian jigsawed edifice. Then comes the fine old mansion of the Manager, then the substantial houses of the assistant and the priest; and last the hospital. It is a flimsy, portable affair, bought from a coal mine second-hand. Big doctor's houses, little hospitals. The doctors, I must add, are not to blame.

On a little point of rock in the ship's harbor stand today two monuments: they commemorate the "farthest north" of Denmark's Prime Minister, Stauning, and of America's Minister to Denmark, Mrs. Owen. There is a granite monument to Peary in the Far North, and a monument near Söndre Upernivik to Denmark's king—commemorating the royal rescue there of shipwrecked passengers and crew. There are in Greenland monuments to many men, commemorating noble lives or deeds or deaths. And there is at Upernivik a memorial of the unique affection of a colony Manager for his people. It is a dance house.

Lembcke-Otto, the beloved long-time Manager of Upernivik, was through. Half of a lifetime spent in Greenland; it was enough. Half lay before him still, and Denmark, home, held out its arms.

"Yes," he said to me a little sadly, "it will be good to go." His goods were being packed, his wife was on the round of all the settlements to say good-by. His daughter was at home, a pretty fair-haired girl just out from Denmark; amusing, in that Greenland scene, in fashionable Danish clothes and white suède high-heeled shoes. But we should meet them all again on board the ship for home. Good host, good, kindly man; we said good-by as though for always.

Over in the harbor lay the Upernivik schooner that should take the Lembcke-Ottos south to meet the ship, and stop for us. That was arranged that day. I found the skipper on board and took him to my boat to fix up something or other that had gone wrong with the motor. He was a young, good-looking, blue-eyed Dane, but somewhat strange and hypersensitive. He nursed a grudge that I had cut him once. "I'd made up my mind," he said, straight as George Washington, "that I would never speak to you again." I was, fortunately, so innocent in the matter that we quickly fixed it up, and drank a pint of schnapps to celebrate. Good thing, I've thought since then, we got that straightened out.

There was a dance that night; I sauntered up. The door was crowded and the place was jammed. I sat down on the grass, took out a package of cigarettes, passed some around, lit one, and put the package back into my pocket. A young man left the dance-house door and strode over to me. "Give me a cigarette," he demanded, "come!" His tone of sharp command was peculiarly offensive; I said no. He blustered threateningly for a minute or so, then left me and rejoined the crowd. I smoked my cigarette. Now, I thought, throwing the butt away, I'll dance.

The crowd at the doorway parted to admit me, I walked in. My friend, I noticed, followed at my back. At dances all the girls stand backed against the wall; you take your pick. I did; reached out to take her arm, when—bang! a shoulder hit me, knocked me to one side; and the young fellow grabbed the girl. I should have quit. I didn't. I was mad. As he led out the girl I backed against him and relieved him of her. I thought it rather neatly done. I got away with it, with her; we started dancing. Up rushed the fool again, belligerent; not letting go of the girl, I caught him with my shoulder just off balance. He went spinning back two yards or more and hit the wall. Now he came on again, he grabbed the girl and pulled. I let him have her, and walked out.

My crew stood at the door: Hendrik, Peter, Knud. "If more had happened we'd have all come into it," said Knud. I wonder. "*Imaka,*" they say in Greenlandish; "Perhaps." But, I have thought, what if they had? I've seen Knud take on one after another of the best men of a settlement in their lifting and finger-pulling trials of strength, and beat them all. Hendrik concededly was stronger. I'd put my money on my three Igdlorssuit musketeers against that rabble of Upernivik. But gentlemen don't fight in Greenland.

The harbor of Pröven, a fair day's run to the southward of Upernivik, is a narrow passage between two islands. Into that passage every fall white whales in hundreds come; few whales get out. It is North Greenland's whale trap. The fishing master there, the man who nets the whales, is Drosvej, one of Denmark's poets. The trader there, in '32, was Nikolaiessen, a patron of American art, his wife's. An arctic Athens, Pröven.

Some few years ago I met on shipboard a Danish-American gentleman who said to me: "My daughter, sir, has done a dreadful thing. She has married, and gone to live in Greenland." Now, here at Pröven was that perverse girl; she lived there and she liked it. And who should be there too but my old friend, her agitated sire—come there, no doubt, to plead with them. "I've offered that young man," he told me at that earlier time, "a good position, twice the pay he gets. And they won't come."

"Now will they come?" I asked of him at Pröven.

"Who come? Come where?" he answered me, amazed. "Why, I'd never leave here myself if I could stay. It is the greatest place, the grandest place, the only place to live."

So we got to planning how we both could manage to stay on, support ourselves in Greenland. "Milk is the thing," said he (milk products was his line), "whale milk." And before we got through we had all but sold stock in one of the most plausible gigantic enterprises of our century: "*Whale Milk to Feed the World*," "*Beluga Babies*." They killed the fatted whale calf in our honor; and when we'd eaten it, we sailed away.

We leave the mountains now, and in that drearier region in the south drop anchor in a vale of tears. Something was wrong at Söndre Upernivik; we felt pervading sadness as we came to land. We walked with Kleeman to his house; he told us on the way: a little child, his daughter's child, was dying.

The house of Willum Kleeman's daughter was not to be entered but stooping very low, or on all fours; inside, one couldn't stand. The floor and walls were turf, the roof was turf supported on a basketwork of sticks. The place was filled with people, and the air was foul. On the platform lay a little child, a baby of eight months. It was moaning piteously. A woman was moving its legs up and down. The child's whole head was enormously swollen and misshapen; from one eye oozed pus. I looked, and then crawled out again; the parents followed me. The mother was hardly more than a girl; she was white-skinned, blue-eyed, blonde. She looked sickly, and she was quite distraught with care and sorrow. Her husband was a stolid, handsome little man, dark-skinned, black-haired, true Greenlander in type. I told them that the child must be taken immediately to the hospital in Upernivik. They started to protest; the midwife backed me and they yielded.

A great procession attended the departure. In front walked Rasmus, Willum's strapping son. He bore the child, all swathed in white and laid upon a pillow; he bore it tenderly, and walked with care. Beside him walked the midwife, dressed in her uniform of white, and Willum. Slowly they came; one heard no sound as they drew near but shuffling feet. Rasmus, still bearing the child, descended the almost upright ladder to the awaiting boat; men held his shoulders that he might not fall. The parents, Willum, and the midwife followed and were rowed on board; only Willum returned. All stood and watched until the streaming stars and stripes at the boat's stern had turned the land.

When Frances and I, who were to tent on shore, had established ourselves, we left a watchman in charge—not against men, but dogs—and went to Willum's house. He then unburdened his poor mind of all that troubled him; it was enough. Willum had lost his job. The Kleeman clan was slipping.

That the fatal order had not yet been signed was immaterial. They had the goods on Willum, or, rather, had the gaps in his accounts and stores where goods should be. Willum was doomed, and knew it. And his pathetic rattle-brained attempts, to me, at explanation only betrayed his own bewilderment and, proving his unfitness, proved the case. The dismissal was the culmination of years of mismanagement, of authority in management so weak that it could not control the almost wholesale pilfering of stores by his own children. He begged a word from me, in writing, to the Magistrate. What use? Trade isn't run on sentiment. I wrote.

It was near midnight when we left the poor old couple for our tent, and bed. How very still the evening had become! No breath of wind, no sound. Sometimes in utter stillness one can hear, one thinks, the cosmic pulse. Listening, we heard it then. "Hear it?" we whispered. "That far-off throbbing sound?" We climbed the hill near by that looked out seawards; before we'd reached the top we knew the sound: a motor. We saw it then, our boat; not five hours gone, now back again. Where the stars and stripes had been was now the cross of Dannebroge. It was at half-mast.

From all the houses came the people; they stood in a crowd about the wharf and in silence watched the motorboat steam in and come to anchor. A boat put out from land to bring the passengers ashore. And into it stepped all those who five hours earlier had departed: the young parents, the midwife dressed in white, and Rasmus bearing in his arms with the same tender care the pillow and the bundled child. Rasmus, held to the ladder of the wharf, came up. Standing there, he uncovered the child's face that Willum might see it. Then Willum took the bundled body in his arms and carried it. Almost as it had come, the long procession made its slow way back.

It seemed but a few minutes until people again streamed out of the turf house and followed Willum, still bearing the child in his arms, into his own house. Rasmus came out for us.

The people stood in a circle about the room, and in their midst, upon a pillow laid across two chairs, was the dead child. She had been beautifully dressed. She wore a trouser suit of unbleached muslin, fastened with a bright red bow about the throat. Her tiny feet were dressed in kamiks. She lay there as though sleeping, eyes closed, the long dark lashes flat against her cheeks: dear little infinitely lovely child. "How beautiful she is!" I murmured. "Yes," whispered those about.

Now someone brought a piece of muslin. We lifted the child and slipped the muslin under. They folded it—up over the feet, over the body, over the lovely, sleeping face. A woman stitched it deftly. When that had been done, Rasmus took up the bundle and, followed silently by all of us, walked to the rude stone mortuary on the hill. Side by side on this long walk went the child's parents. Both were calm, the mother as though broken by her grief, the father nonchalant, his hands in pockets.

The mortuary was built of rough stones, laid without cement; it was a damp, dark hole. The floor was littered with chips from the making of the last coffin. There were two rough table shelves; men cleared one off, and Rasmus laid the bundle there. When all filed out one stayed to close the door and put a crowbar as a brace to hold it shut.

We sailed that day at nine. Six hours after us the Chief Magistrate arrived, and thereby ended Willum's life as trader.

IX. WAR

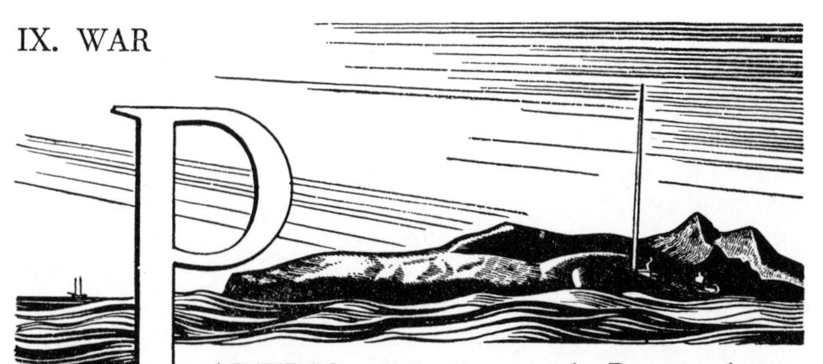

PAINTING; painting incessantly. Pursuing beauty in bewilderment at its profusion, greedy to get in one short year the whole of what might thrill a man a lifetime. As well might one by spinning a kaleidoscope hope to exhaust its permutations in a day. I mention art to tell how time was filled, not to enlarge on it. Art talk: *that's* true perversion of our faculties. We traveled the fiords, camped where it pleased us most, and worked.

We went to find new scenes, prospecting, I may say; and to get away from a preposterous moving-picture outfit that with tents, airplanes and motorboats, and ping-pong tables on the beach had settled on the district like a locust blight. "Your being here," I said to some of them one day, "affects my work about as my running in on all your shots would affect yours." It was the senseless populousness of the enterprise, its countless useless members idling round, the turning of night time into day, the sleeping all day long, the drunkenness, the brawls, the sickening spectacle of wasted food, drink, money, time, that gave the whole performance the complexion of prolonged debauch.

The natives saw it, got it all. They saw their trader crawling in a ditch and all but barking. They saw white men get drunk and stagger to their feet to crash their fists into each other's faces. They listened to white women scream and curse. Their kids peeked under tents to watch white people do it. They got it all: *adliskutak*, "the mattress," so they christened one.

Respect for law? People to whom the mere possession of petroleum within the sacred precincts of a settlement is forbidden saw gasoline rolled in and stored right in their midst; saw their crusading trader and their Chief Magistrate *not* see high-candle-powered gasoline lamps and primus stoves that lit and warmed them as they drank Kirschwasser in that movie domicile, the church loft. *That* got me, I must say: those lamps to drink by, when I must struggle through the long dark winter days and nights to draw by blubber light in my own house. The people grasped all that; they got it all. Demoralizing? No. You can't change people's ways like that. Old ways are in the blood; old ways of doing things, of thinking; their age-old moral values: these endure. But what they *think* of *us:* that's different.

The matter of the dance house—now we have touched on fire risks—the decision as to whether two candles burning in a crowded dance house endangered an old turf ruin standing fifteen paces off, when gasoline and petroleum burning for a drunken party in a littered church loft were of no risk to the church, was, apparently, one for such deep and delicate consideration that, having been passed for decision from the trader to the Chief Magistrate, it had now been appealed to the Director of Greenland, in Copenhagen. Law, we have seen, was abrogated; plain common sense, I hoped, might now prevail. But August passed and no decision came. Meanwhile—we hadn't thought of quitting yet—we'd ordered lumber for the house, from Umanak. September 6 it came. The schooner came, brought that, brought store supplies, brought mail; brought not a word about the house. September! In three weeks we leave.

The skipper of the schooner was, I trust, my friend. At any rate, visiting back and forth between the rival strongholds, whatever he bore Trolleman he brought this news to me: that Trolleman had told him he'd prevent the dance house from going up. "Put it up on the hill," said Olsen laughing. "It's the only place they'll let you put it. Mind me; I *know*." I knew it too. The schooner stayed two days; then in the afternoon, at four, set sail for Nugsuak—for Nugsuak, for Umanak, then, some days off, for Igdlorssuit again. And on the schooner went the Trollemans.

"Here, Hendrik, Peter, Knud, get things on board in shape, fill up the tanks. We sail for Umanak tomorrow."

It was a miserable day; we sailed. Two hours out we met strong wind and heavy seas; worse threatened us. We cravenly turned back. Three hours later, against all warnings from the wiseheads, we put to sea again, and at ten that night we were at Umanak. I went straight to the Manager.

"Yes," said the Manager, "I've heard. I didn't think to write. No, the Director says you can't. The law, you know, not twenty paces off." He laughed a merry laugh—that was his way. "No, no, not there." He laughed again. I blew up.

"Let me get it straight," I said. "I'm a stranger here, and I want to understand how things are done in Greenland. You call that tumble-down affair of turf a building? Then why two private houses close to it? You let a private house go up and stand right there for years—there where we're putting ours. But our *community* affair can't go there. Why? Just tell me why. What *is* the law? You've hogged the choicest building-ground in the whole settlement, sprawled senselessly all over it. Who built the settlement? Whose is it anyhow? Why can't the people have a decent place to put their house? Ah! Fire risks! You make me laugh. You let a drunken outfit play with high explosives in the church, live, cook, and burn petroleum in storage lofts.—Ah! Germans! Now I get it. The rest, the people here, are *only* Greenlanders. Just tell me: is that true?"

"Yes, yes, quite true." The Manager laughed merrily.

"And you realize, don't you," I raved on (I think he hardly understood a word of it), "that the whole administration is just playing into the hands of that half-mad Trolleman? That far from helping in a decent public project you, the lot of you, are blocking it in every way you can? Is that so, too?"

"Yes, yes, that's so." He laughed in uncontrollable delight.

"Well, then, where *may* we build this house?"

"Anywhere, Mr. Kent, that is twenty meters away from our buildings."

"If I move it to *exactly* twenty meters, may we build it there?"

"Yes, certainly."

"Good, then, that's where it goes."

I asked him for a carpenter. The Manager at once agreed to lend me one. "And I will only charge you," he said, "what we have to pay him."

For that, God bless the Manager. At last someone had helped.

X. DRAWN SHADES

The house of Rudolf and Marghreta, God bless them!

WE'D BEATEN Trolleman to Umanak; we still had work to do before he got back home. That he would try to stop us, no one doubted. We had the law at last; he still had his authority. We sailed next morning and were home that night. And there—we've left her long enough—was Salamina waiting for us, for the Kents and—no one knew it then—their carpenter.

Love, as *we* understand it, as we, fabricators throughout the centuries of the now top-heavy structure of romantic love, have made ourselves believe it to be, is all but unknown in Greenland. It is as though the interdependence of the sexes both for the satisfaction of their sexual appetites and for the performance of the routine of living had left no need for the romantic stimulant. They fornicate: they like to. They mate: they have to. And mutual possessiveness with its attendant jealousy, which is virulent in Greenland, only appears as a safeguard of the economic partnership and of its biological result, the family. In studying a transitional civilization like that of Greenland one must be careful to distinguish between indigenous traits and those which show imported influence. Between the highly Europeanized family of a Greenland pastor and the family of an outpost hunter there is the blending of the two in all degrees. It is, however, with the immediate transitional moment that we are concerned; our subject is the hybrid people, hybrid culture, of today. Two hundred years of missionary work and trade prosecuted with energy, and backed by the prestige of economic, social, and cultural superiority: they worship the Holy Trinity and accept the precepts of Christ; they read and write; they deal in money and exchange; they have their legislators and their written laws. Two hundred years: and they're not moral yet. I think that few of them have ever felt for anything they've done the torturings of conscience. They function, and don't agonize. If one steals it is but one's appropriation to his own use of another's property—his meat, his chunk of coal, his wife—that then and there is wanted. It is done secretly through fear. They fear—both punishment and ridicule. And the ridiculous calisthenics of love are practiced secretly. The *fact* is not ridiculous: they tell about it—afterwards. It is possible that if the promiscuity of the unmarried were more fruitful there would long ago have been developed a taboo against it. It is far from fruitful. And to forestall some ponderous explanation of so strange a fact let me here hazard that girls' breeches are its cause. Let speculation start with that.

Jealousy, the fear of losing to another what is ours, is so closely woven into the fabric of romantic love that only those of us who don't much care, or who are preternaturally wise and self-controlled, are free of it. In Greenland life its sordid nature stands exposed, and none are free. Its object is the establishment, of which the man and woman are to each other the personification. With allowance for temperament, it is proportioned to what is risked. And whether in the establishment, native or foreign, the woman be the mistress, wife, or servant, it is a direct expression not of her status, not of love, but of the privileges, authority, and *prestige* with which she is invested.

Salamina, until the coming of my wife, enjoyed unbounded privilege, assumed unlimited authority, and basked in a prestige that she supported well. And if I view her attachment to me, and her fantastic jealousy, as consequence, I must yet find it too instinctive and uncalculated to be classed as mercenary. She was touched by kindness, generosity, and thoughtfulness, by such human virtues as might show themselves in me *for her;* their evidences were the material and worldly advantages which I bestowed. We may not, even among our romantic selves, distinguish harshly between bought and given love. One *wins* love: How?

Enjoying as she did, until May 4, that almost unlimited authority at home which is the prerogative of Greenland women, one might have looked for some show of resentment at the prospect of being superseded by a lawful and desired housewife. She showed none. And she was too emotionally uncontrolled to have concealed the slightest shade of jealousy. I believe that her own pride in those virtues of household management which had made her so indispensable to me led her to be confident without a passing fear that she would be as indispensable to both of us. That in good-fellowship we'd be alike, she had no doubt; she judged my unknown wife by me. She'd be *our* friend. But there was more than that. The indefatigable vigilance, that *damned* vigilance and energy with which she'd dogged my steps, I had not valued: Frances would. "Here," was her attitude, resigning me, "here, take him now. He has given me a lot of trouble but I've done my best. We'll see now what we two can do." And, sure enough, up she'd come running with what tales she could: "Kinte is talking to Amalia on the beach"—and such.

Salamina was a woman of character and of virtue. For what I gave her, for, and in, the position in which I had established her, she held herself to be mine. And she was not without bitterness that I failed in my appreciation of her whole-souled gift. May, spring in Greenland, set her free.

Salamina, an attractive widow in her late twenties, was not one to sit her life out on the sidelines. And although her principles, her taste, perhaps her common sense, forbade a second marriage, neither her conscience nor her sense denied her love.

Among the careers that the Danish administration has opened to Greenlanders, one of the most honorable is that of carpenter, one of the most honorable, useful and, possibly, ennobling careers in the world. A man's work makes him, in the end; and carpentry was starting well with young Jens Lange. *Life* started well with him: gave him good looks, good brain, gave him a lot of charm. Gave him, I'll say, good taste. He picked out Salamina.

And certainly in part of Salamina's holiday—we gave her three weeks off at home and Umanak—she was beguiled by Jens. How must she have been thrilled when we sailed off to fetch a carpenter! There was but one. So Salamina stood there on the shore to welcome us—and Jens. From that time on—almost until we sailed for home—Marghreta's house where she now lived was Jens's too. It was the only native house with windowshades. They drew them: let them be.

XI. THE DANCE HOUSE

BRIGHT and early next morning, Sunday, a crowd assembled at the dance-house floor. They'd brought what spades and shovels could be found, a crowbar, hammers, saws. They'd come to work.

First day: We measured twenty paces from the sacred relic, added five more to show goodwill, drove in a stake. From that as a corner we laid out and staked a rectangle, 21′ x 28′, drove stakes, stretched lines. Now, diggers, get to work! They sailed in with a will. Some dug, some carried stones, some knocked together concrete forms. That night we had the forms in place.

Second day: A crowd showed up to work. Some carried stones and sand, some mixed, some poured. By night the forms were full.

Third day and Fourth: The crowd again; no use today for most of them. We're getting out the frame, sawing the posts to length, sawing the rafters, splicing and mortising the plate. That took two easy days.

Fifth day: Early, the crowd again, but not enough. Get more, get everyone, get out the women. Meanwhile we'd knocked the forms off the foundation; the cement had set. Now man the platform! We had enough to crowd all sides; we needed all we had; that floor was heavy. Now ready: up with it! And like an enormous centipeded crab the platform ambled to its final place. We raised it shoulder-high, and gently—not to jar the bolts—lowered it over them. And at that everyone went into such a fit of coughing as might be their last. Beer cured it, beer all round. By six that night the frame was up, two sides were boarded, and a stage was in place for the rafters. Any sign of the returning schooner? Of returning Trolleman? Not yet.

SIXTH DAY: By night we'd boarded all four sides, set the rafters, and mostly boarded up the roof. No Trolleman.

SEVENTH DAY: It threatened rain. We worked like mad till eight at night, glazed window sash, put paper on the roof, made doors and hung them; we worked like mad, and—*finished it!* Yes, that evening Trolleman came back. He landed, went straight to his house, and stayed there. They told us later, in Umanak, that when on arriving there he'd learned what was afoot he'd acted like a madman, paced like a captive animal, and raved. He'd stop that house, he screamed. He'd wanted them to rush him back; but no one heeded him.

I've said we'd finished it. The *structure* was complete; it still lacked paint and *architecture*. The architecture consisted of a flagpole at the peak, and a rather elaborate, very elegant sort of carved scroll applied in relief over the doorway in the gable end. But why describe it? See the chapter head. The scroll was of white and silver, and the lettering was red and black. The house we painted blue, light blue; it was the people's choice. The trim we painted cream, the double doors dark blue. We made accessories: an elevated corner shelf for the accordion player to sit on, two long benches for the guests, and a broad concrete doorstep. We did landscape architecture: dug a deep ditch to conduct the surface drainage away from the house, and bridged it handsomely. Then we stood back and looked.

It was a pretty house. Like Justina in her Christmas clothes, the settlement was proud.

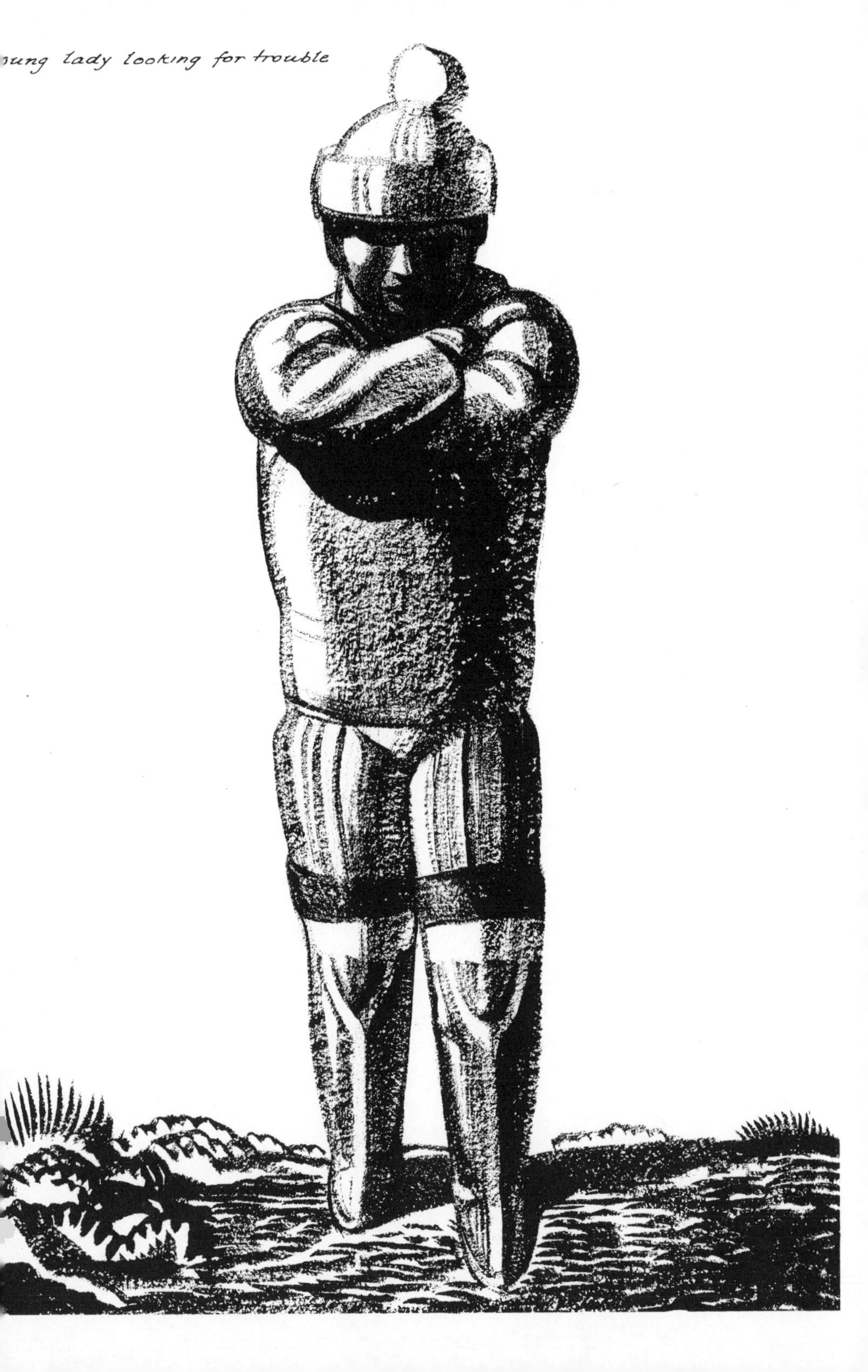
oung lady looking for trouble

XII. THE ANIMALS

INVITED to go south on one of the comfortable and stanch motorboats of the Danish Geodetic Institute! We canceled our passage on the Upernivik schooner: it would spare that craft the inside detour to Igdlorssuit, give us the company to Godhavn of an old friend, Janus Sörensen; and anyhow, we'd see the Lembcke-Ottos on the homeward voyage. We were to sail from Umanak October 1. So few days left, so much to think about, so much to do! For all we had to do, thank God!

The thought of home *was* good. Good Lord! sometimes it seems to me that all my wandering is contrived to no end but to make America, *its* mountains, its rocks and rills—all that, in spite of much of it—more dear. We loved America no less, I think, that we loved Greenland so.

But does belief in Heaven make believers cling less fiercely to their life on earth? And, if they could, would friends at death not promise to be back? "We'll meet again": believers have that faith. "We'll meet again," we said in Greenland to our friends. "We're coming back." But people doubted it; so much could happen in two years, so far away. Then Salamina wept. "Maybe we'd better kill ourselves," said Martin mournfully. "You, since Isaak died, are as my father," said Abraham. "You two are as the father and the mother of us all," said Rudolf, Jonas, Peter, Knud. Such things did not make parting light. You know it *is* a tragic thing to leave dear friends—and feel it at the time—forever. *We* never know such partings short of death. Europe, America, our world, is small, the continents flow back and forth. We'll meet again, we *can:* that robs all parting of its agony. Greenland is different. It is the world, to Greenlanders. We come there as might visitors from Mars, come there, and stay a while, get loved, get needed there, and go—as though to Mars again—forever.

Not even we could know that we'd come back. It's not that Greenland is so far away that one *can't* come again. Greenland is closed: one *may* not. Just to a crack they'll open up the gate: you show your pass that states how long, what for. Good: for that purpose and that time you enter. And to revisit there for love of friends?—love is no purpose in the mind of government. Yet I don't know, I'm back, I write this now in Greenland. "I wrote to the Director," said Abraham, "and told him that we wanted you."

It is so easy, and so virtuous, to sentimentalize about the poor and, in Greenland, warmed by the gratitude that one can there so easily evoke, blushing happily under the tributes that emotional warm natures will bestow, and puffed up, of course, in that "little fatherhood" which with your little pittances you've lightly earned, to adulate the commonplace. Exalting them, you buttress up your pride. I know all that, am victim of it, like it. Let this admission clear the boards of sentiment, and permit a dispassionate appraisal of those human-creature products of a rude, cold, comfortless environment, hard life, and still quite simple culture.

It would be, today, sheer foolishness to reassert the laughed-down dogma of our Declaration: "that all men are created equal." They're not, and we all know it. Yet on the heels of that disgraced grand gesture of Democracy appears today the same thought in another form: All *races* are created equal. Confirming this, let me add to the growing voice of intelligent opinion in America that Negroes are no better men than we, the voice of at least considered opinion in Igdlorssuit: that we—they spoke in praise of us—were like themselves. Let us, too, add our voices—we two whites agree: By every sign that we could judge by, by their laughter and their tears, by what they laughed and wept about, by what they cared for, how they cared, by every quality their minds in intimate association showed, those people were equivalent to us.

Yet in this considered estimate I must make it clear that it was of hardly more than quality that we with our slight knowledge of their speech could judge. Our conversation when not limited to the commonplace was constrained to childishly inadequate simplicity of expression that barred the spoken interchange of every subtlety of thought. I cannot therefore *know* that they had intellectual subtlety, nor that familiarity with their tongue would have disclosed realms of common interest as material for that most social pastime, conversation. I speak of them as friends, yet we were mutually deprived of friendship's bread and butter: talk.

Talk *is* in large degree its staff of life, sustaining it; by the community of interests that it reveals, enlarging it. But friendship isn't *born* of that. Talk is, rather, but one of the lesser channels through which sensibility and character, which are the foundation of friendship, are brought to light. By the rare sensibility of the Greenlanders we were affected, and by the characters of many of our friends, impressed.

It is my belief that advances in the study of evolution will eventually demand that, for the proper explanation of the many coexistent differences and likenesses between isolated races of mankind, environment must be distinguished as a trinity, and we may as follows name its parts, and qualify them: the Local—climate, resources, and manner of life—by which man's physical attributes are affected; the Incidental—the exigencies of daily life under the limitations of the various cultures and their resources—by which character is formed; and the Cosmic—the esthetic aspects of physical law—by which man's sensory organism is determined. Take this hypothesis, or leave it; facts are our concern. To the recorded evidence of Salamina's sensibilities, and Martin's, let me add that the Greenland people's taste in the combining of colors, their feeling for harmony in music (they use our scale today), their sense of flavor in foods (disregarding prejudice as to its form and nature), their sense of what smells good and what feels nice, are like our own. Their quiet voices, their gentle, noiseless ways, their abstinence from quarreling: these are degrees of sensibility that we may envy them. Environment so peaceful *should* breed quietness; environment so beautiful *must* tune man's nature toward itself. Outdoors—I've told of that—is more to them in Greenland than to us. They nearly are—we've coined the term ourselves—a nature folk.

Character is another matter. It is largely the antithesis of sensibility; it disciplines it, keeps its carefree self-indulgence within bounds: a kill-joy rôle. I have hoped, in this story of Greenland, to avoid overstressing the hardships of the life of the Greenland hunter. His land—the frozen North; his element—the sea; its risks—storm, ice, the hazards of the hunt: these are enough to send a shiver through the spine. To play them up would be to melodramatize the North, and to falsify completely the truth that they are undramatic everyday to Greenlanders. The hunter takes his risks, endures his hardships, easily. That's character.

To have to get up out of a warm bed—he likes warm beds and has one—and, breakfastless, in the darkness and the bitter cold of a January morning lift his kayak upon his head, carry it across a mile or two of rough ice to the open water, launch it there, and paddle out to where at the first streak of the day's twilight seals may come; to stay there hours on end, be cold, get frozen cheeks and wrists; no factory whistle, time clock, boss: to *will* that of yourself and do it, day succeeding day—makes character. They're men, strong men, inured to hardship and hard times, to working on their own, to shifting for themselves. They've needed no Lycurgus for their laws; necessity imposes them. They are heroic men, and I'll venture that there are more Danish Royal Diplomas for exceptional bravery framed on the walls of the turf houses of the peaceful fifteen thousand Greenlanders than we can show of Congressional Medals among millions.

But now that we have set the Greenlanders upon a pinnacle let us climb up there ourselves and, finding it perhaps crowded, push a few of them off. The Greenlanders are good men: they endure

nd though she has had to
ait till winter time, she
s found it.

hardships uncomplainingly, stand exposure, hard work, hunger, cold, mosquitoes. And so can we. In the high temperature of the foundry of the Ford works at Detroit they employ mostly Negroes: it has been found that they endure the heat better than white men. That may be race, or Southern cotton fields. A Negro stood with Peary at the Pole. It used to be said that Eskimos could not long survive a temperate climate. That is sheer nonsense; plenty live in Denmark. It is popularly thought that Eskimos don't *feel* the cold as we do: that too is probably a myth. At any rate, their fat cheeks aren't an asset; they freeze while our lean jowls stay warm. And almost pure white Greenlanders work side by side with those almost pure Eskimo. They're no bit better, but they're just as good. A white man if he *will* can stand most anything. And like it. Doubt it? My son, of whom I have spoken, aged fourteen (I am now writing of 1935), accompanied the post to Umanak in February. They attempted one route and, encountering thin ice, were compelled to take another, the land passage at the head of Kangerdlugsuak. Conditions were bad: on the sea ice they broke through the covering of snow into water; on the land they found deep snow and heavy drifts. The passage overland that takes normally from two to three hours occupied them most of two days. It took them four days to reach Umanak; and two nights were spent in the open. The days and nights were the coldest of the winter, the temperature falling to between −35° and −40°. Two of the Greenlanders—there were, all told, four in the party—wore reindeer garments. The boy wouldn't take his with him: "too hot," he said. All four slept sitting up in the boy's 3′ x 6′ sledge tent. The boy got his nose frost-bitten, the Greenlanders all froze their cheeks and noses, and one went lame from strain ("water on the knee"). The boy arrived home in perfect shape and fine spirits. "It was fun."

These Greenlanders whom I have praised so much are not, remember, moral or romantic; and the affecting friendship and gratitude of a few friends may not be taken as characteristic of the people. For what one does for them the masses are not grateful.

To begin with, they don't understand why Europeans should be rich while they are poor; why *anyone* should have a lot of property when others haven't. (I tried explaining it, but got mixed up.) In times of scarcity, when one is fortunate he shares his meat around the settlement. All share in it by ancient communistic right; and no one thanks the giver. When I hand around a hundred dollars' worth of stuff at Christmas, few say thank you; and most of those don't mean it. They know it flatters us: they're skillful flatterers.

It is hard to tell just what they think of us; they are secretive with the European. They respect ability as it is shown in work; they don't call adding figures work. And they don't appreciate that the fatiguing nature of "brain work" entitles men to an enormous wage and the privilege of lying in bed. (I didn't try explaining that.) They've mostly never seen a white man lift his hand. They don't respect us and, I think, don't like us.

When you buy from a Greenlander he won't mention the price. "These simple, trusting, childlike people!" says the tourist. Simple as Satan; trusting as a banker; childlike as Henry Ford. Try bidding low: they'll catch you up on that. They want the limit that your ignorance will yield. The Danes, we learn, encourage them in that. And let the visitor be Santa Claus himself—most visitors play Santa—on high advice they'll soak him in a trade. "The Director has told us," say the Greenlanders, "that we should charge outsiders thirty kroner for a dog, but not the Danes." Ten kroner is the price. Sweet business principles! They'll flatter to an end, they'll cheat on price; they lie.

In the fall of '34 Peter, of my Three Musketeers, was lost at sea. They found his kayak later, torn to shreds. Only a walrus, it is thought, could have done it. At Christmas time Amalia, Peter's sister, comes with a present: it is an anorak, a second-hand one neatly pressed. "It was Peter's," says Amalia almost tearfully. "We've kept it for you." It was a pleated anorak such as the dainty Olabi makes for himself. She had bought it of him for a pittance only the day before. They think *we're* children.

They steal. Through the generosity of an American woman I

came in '34 with fifty pounds of coffee, to be given to the people of Igdlorssuit. At the general kaffemik in the dance house at which the coffee was distributed I left my cup, for just a moment, standing on the table. It was stolen. A young woman whom I had brought in my boat from Söndre Upernivik to visit relatives at Igdlorssuit, and fed and treated well en route, next night was reaching through my cellar window stealing canned goods. My friend Boye, the young hunter, while a guest at dinner at my house loaded his pockets with my cigars. I saw the bulging pockets, guessed the fact. "Come out with me," I said to Boye. We stood outside together in the dark. "Let's have them, the cigars," I said. There was a moment's pause. Then Boye brought them out and gave them to me. "Thank you," I said. "No, wait," said Boye, "there are more." He gave me more. "Still more," he said. "And cigarettes." I put the lot into my pockets; that was ended. "Now, Boye," I said, "would you like some cigars? Here are cigars, take them, they're for you. I give them to you." Boye was hit. "No, no," he said, "I can't. I am bad. Yes, I am bad. It was Sahra who told me to take them." (I didn't doubt it in the least.) "No, I can't take them." I forced them on him. As Boye left for home that night he drew me to one side outdoors. He said, "Here, take these. I can't keep them. I am bad." "No, you are good," I said. "Good night." Two or three times coal was stolen from my bin; it stood outdoors. Someone entered my meat shed once and took a small piece of white-whale meat. One tent pole (it would make a good pike handle) was taken from a pile of such things. That, in more than two years' time, is all.

Greenlanders' guile is artless, unprofessional; a class to prey upon is new to them. But we have come, we whites; and to a lot of them we're only prey. Pot-bellied clerks, or measuring-worms that crawl about their hills, or putterers with paint: how can we qualify as much to them? Why should they in their hearts feel more respect for us than self-respecting workmen feel for nitwit bankers' sons? They have their pride.

The *primitive* that still endures in us may envy them. Theirs is a life that we at times, in thought, revert to. They *fit* that life; we don't. I envy them.

I think I could turn and live with animals, they are so placid and self-contained;
I stand and look at them long and long.

They do not sweat and whine about their condition;
They do not lie awake in the dark and weep for their sins;
They do not make me sick discussing their duty to God;
Not one is dissatisfied—not one is demented with the mania of owning things;
Not one kneels to another, nor to his kind that lived thousands of years ago;
Not one is respectable or industrious over the whole earth.

I think that I could turn and live with animals: I couldn't.

XIII. GOOD-BY, IGDLORSSUIT

VERY GOOD, Mr. Trolleman," said I; and glancing at the total of his bills, I paid it. "And now, Mr. Trolleman"—oh it was honey sweet, that farewell interview; there'd never been an open row—"Now, Mr. Trolleman," I said, "this dance house. I had hoped to build it by subscription from the friends of the people. No one has helped. Won't you? Won't you contribute to the house?" I've never seen such sudden fury in a man. He leaped up like a dog gone mad; he screamed at me; he shook his fist. "I'll tear that dance house down, I will. You'll see, you'll see." It was a little funny how he screamed.

I went to Abraham and reported the threat. He summoned the community council and the catechist; they drafted a complaint to the Chief Magistrate. I carried that away with me; delivered it. And at the Chief Magistrate's they filed it, unanswered, in the archives. Besides that, there is now in the archives our deed of gift: the people of Igdlorssuit, free of all control by whites, hold title to the house.

That evening the community council held the formal opening of the house: a kaffemik for us. The building that had seemed so large was filled to overflow. The crowd, that parted for us at our entrance, had left a clear space in the center; here stood two chairs and a small table laid with a white cloth and two cups and saucers. When the coffee-drinking was over the people arranged themselves in an even circle about us; there was a moment's hush. Then, led by Samuel, the catechist, they sang. It wasn't easy not to cry. At the conclusion of the singing, Samuel addressed us. "Tonight," said Samuel, "we welcome Kent and his wife, and thank them for the great gift they have given us; but we regret having had no time for preparations. It is clear that we cannot thank them enough for this costly gift; not in the whole of North Greenland is there a better house, not even in places where people are more advanced than we are. The house belongs to ourselves. This night we *feel* that this pretty, expensive house belongs to us, for which we are very thankful. We can do nothing but say thanks. We shall remember Kent and his wife as long as this house lasts, with thankfulness for the wonderful gift. The sight of it will show people from other settlements, who don't know Kent, his affection for Igdlorssuit. We are very thankful to Kent for all his other gifts and for the feasts he has given us, and for what he has given to the poor people. There are many people who are thankful to Kent for his stay here. Now when they are leaving for their own country we wish them a good and blessed voyage. The people of Igdlorssuit will remember Kent very long; and his gift here in the midst of our settlement shall be his memorial."

When Samuel had ended, the people sang another psalm. I rose and thanked them in a speech, a speech in that pigeon dialect which Salamina had come to understand. Phrase at a time she rendered it in proper Eskimo; her version of my words was brief and to the point. "We," I would say, "having lived among you for so long a time, want now at parting to tell you of the deep affection that we have come to feel for you, and how our hearts are wrung at leaving you." Which Salamina would translate as follows: "He says they like you."

My speech, I'd thought, would end the ceremonies, and so, apparently, did everyone. And they had just broken into a buzz of general chatter when, charging through them like a young bull, came Boye. Boye planted himself square in the middle of the circle, and the crowd fell silent. Boye spoke. He spoke with energy and fire; no pulpit voice and parson gestures his. God, he looked beautiful! his fine young face alight with purpose. Boye said:

"There have come many travelers from foreign countries, and some have in the past come here. Yet never have we met such foreigners as are here now. They do all the good they can and, what is not the least, they give us presents with which we are delighted. But while we thank them all, we especially thank Kinte and his wife, for by them came the goodness of the foreigners. So that in comparing them with those who have come before we may say that they equal the goodness of Hans Egede and his wife in olden times. Our thanks to *them* are great, and likewise to the Kintes. We shall never forget either the material or the spiritual good that you have done us." (And the transcript of this speech which Boye gave me he signed as follows: "A hunter in the country of the Greenlanders, Boye Malakiesen, at Igdlorssuit, wrote this.")

And now again the people sang:
Glory be to God in Heaven, peace on earth!

It was raining in the morning, drizzling from a gloomy sky. We sipped our coffee with a little group of friends while people moved our goods down to the shore. I think that everyone was there to help. The doors stood open; people came trooping in to carry down what we would indicate. At last, when everything that was to go had been removed, we lingered on forlornly in the littered house. Come! it is time to go. It was high time when Knud, the tallest man of the settlement, bearded like General Grant, was weeping on the shoulder of Frances and calling her his mother; when Martin and Jonas were talking of killing themselves; when Rudolf, Abraham, and I were holding hands. You'd think the parting was forever. Come! let's go.

Down on the shore stood all the people. I know that we shook hands with everyone, even the babes in arms. Rudolf and Abraham rowed out with us. Just as we came on board the people began to sing. It was at last too much for all of us: we wept.

The people followed on the shore as we sailed off; they climbed the harbor hill. We'll always see that hilltop in our memories, see the crowd of little figures there, their waving handkerchiefs, see puffs of smoke and hear the detonation of the guns. Good-by, Igdlorssuit!

The two boats of the Geodetic Survey, on one of which we were passengers, came into Godhavn on the eve of one of the worst storms on record on that coast. The schooner from Upernivik did not come in. No one will ever know just what happened. The bit of hatch, or whatever it was, that was picked up a year later doesn't tell much.

THE END

ABOUT THE AUTHOR

Rockwell Kent (1882–1971) was one of America's most famous graphic artists, particularly well known for his illustrated travel books. Kent attended Columbia University.

ABOUT THE EDITOR

Scott R. Ferris is an art historian, former director of the Rockwell Kent Legacies, and co-author of *Rockwell Kent's Forgotten Landscapes* (1998) and *The View from Asgaard: Rockwell Kent's Adirondack Legacy* (2000). He is the editor of *CRSA Forum*—the newsletter of the Catalogue Raisonné Scholars Association—and is himself compiling the catalogue raisonné of Kent's paintings.